✓ W9-ACD-784

Their Place
on the
Stage

Recent Titles in
Contributions in Afro-American and African Studies
Series Advisers: John W. Blassingame and Henry Louis Gates, Jr.

THEIR PLACE ON THE STAGE
Black Women Playwrights in America

ELIZABETH BROWN-GUILLORY
Foreword by MARGARET WALKER ALEXANDER
Afterword by GLORIA T. HULL

CONTRIBUTIONS IN AFRO-AMERICAN AND AFRICAN STUDIES,
NUMBER 117

Greenwood Press
NEW YORK • WESTPORT, CONNECTICUT • LONDON

Library of Congress Cataloging-in-Publication Data

Brown-Guillory, Elizabeth.
  Their place on the stage : Black women playwrights in America /
Elizabeth Brown-Guillory.
      p.   cm. — (Contributions in Afro-American and African
studies, ISSN 0069--9624 ; no. 117)
  Bibliography: p.
  Includes index.
  ISBN 0-313-25985-2 (lib. bdg. : alk. paper)
  1. American drama—Afro-American authors—History and criticism.
2. American drama—Women authors—History and criticism.
3. American drama—20th century—History and criticism.   4. Afro-
Americans in literature.   5. Women and literature—United States—
History—20th century.   6. Afro-American theater—History.
I. Title. II. Series.
PS338.N4B76   1988
812'.52'099287—dc19   88-10237

British Library Cataloguing in Publication Data is available.

A paperback edition of *Their Place on the Stage* is available
from Praeger Publishers (ISBN 0-275-93566-3).

Library of Congress Catalog Card Number: 88-10237
ISBN: 0-313-25985-2
ISSN: 0069-9624

First published in 1988

Greenwood Press, 88 Post Road West, Westport, CT 06881
An imprint of Greenwood Publishing Group, Inc.

Printed in the United States of America

The paper used in this book complies with the
Permanent Paper Standard issued by the National
Information Standards Organization (Z39.48-1984).

10 9 8 7 6 5 4 3 2

To

Lucius

and

Lucia

and all the other roots, branches and
twigs of the Brown and Guillory trees

Contents

Acknowledgments

Just as our ancestors have paid debts with their sorrows and sweat so that we may live and prosper, so too have many people metaphorically bought this book.

I am particularly appreciative of the support given me by my husband, Lucius M. Guillory, who is a brilliant thinker and who challenged me to go beyond the obvious, the mundane. He never allowed me to become complacent or to think that I had explored deeply enough. Many were the nights when he stayed awake with me when I wanted to go to bed or, better yet, run away to the land of the Lotus Eaters.

I cannot forget the encouragement given me by my parents, Marjorie and Leo Brown, particularly by my mother who every week asked me, "How is the book coming? How many chapters to go?" Bless her heart. I am grateful for the support given me by my 7 brothers and sisters.

I am especially thankful to the United Negro College Fund for the grant that allowed me a year's leave from Dillard University to work on this manuscript. I must not forget that it was the president and vice president for academic affairs at Dillard University, Dr. Samuel Dubois Cook and Dr. Elton C. Harrison, respectively, who recommended me for the grant and who over the years have enthusiastically supported my research, creative writing, and play productions.

Dr. Harrison's incisive thinking and perseverance served as an inspiration to me as I wrote this manuscript. The man is a genius-general.

There are many people who lovingly edited and offered suggestions about the manuscript at various stages, including Yvonne Ochillo, Violet Harrington Bryan, Monte Piliawsky, Winona Somervill and Fabian Worsham. My dear friend Fabian is to be commended for her meticulous editing of all but one chapter. I am indebted to Miss Venola Jones, a Dillard librarian, who lovingly went many extra miles for me during my research. She was a real gem.

I am deeply appreciative of the support and encouragement given me by Florida State University professors Fred Standley and Anne Rowe. Anne, my major professor and dear friend, encouraged me to continue to work in the area of black women playwriting, a field that begs for scholarship.

Finally, I thank Susan Carter and Vivian McAskill who nurtured both me and my infant daughter, Lucia, while I worked on the initial drafts of the manuscript.

Foreword

Margaret Walker Alexander

Elizabeth Brown–Guillory has accomplished three major tasks in this very important and absorbing book. She has first of all given an historical overview of black women playwrights in this twentieth century; second, she has analyzed and assessed the works of three major examples: Alice Childress, Lorraine Hansberry, and Ntozake Shange; and third, she has given some objective thought to the general structure and criticism of drama as a whole, with particular emphasis on black drama.

It is good to remember that American drama has really come of age in the twentieth century, that plays on the American stage in the eighteenth and nineteenth centuries were really little more than glorified minstrels, farces, and melodramas. Eugene O'Neill is the first great name in the Hall of American Playwrights and following him there may be about a half dozen great names: Maxwell Anderson, Robert Sherwood, Edward Albee, Tennessee Williams, Arthur Miller, and Lillian Hellman. So it is not surprising that black theater in America had its real beginnings with the Harlem Renaissance, and in that famous group at least four women wrote plays. They were May Miller, Georgia Douglas Johnson, Alice Dunbar-Nelson, and Angelina Weld Grimke. Since Johnson was the most successful of these four, with her *Plumes* (1927) appearing off-Broadway, Brown-Guillory chooses her as her first example, showing the tradition out of which subsequent black women playwrights have come.

Between the Harlem Renaissance and the Black Arts Movement of the 1960s are three decades, the thirties, forties, and the fifties. While the Chicago Renaissance of the thirties and forties produced few playwrights, mostly men, hardly any women appear until the decade of the fifties, when three important examples emerge. They are Beah Richards (1950), Alice Childress (1955), and Lorraine Hansberry (1959). Brown–Guillory deals with two of these in detail.

The Civil Rights Movement and the Women's Movement exploded in every direction, and the three decades following the fifties have been replete with black women playwrights. Sonia Sanchez is an early example of Revolutionary Black drama, combining the two revolutions, the Negro Revolution led by Martin Luther King, Jr., and the Black Revolution led by Malcolm X. During the past twenty years (1968–1988), Sanchez has written eight plays that have been published and produced. The most famous of these are *The Bronx is Next* (1968) and *Sister Sonji* (1969), both of which appeared off-Broadway and on college campuses.

At the end of the sixties and the beginning of the decade of the seventies, the works of black women playwrights exploded all over the country. J. E. Franklin's *Black Girls* (1971) led the group. Adrienne Kennedy's *Funnyhouse of a Negro* (1962) was a good example of the new theater of the absurd. The most explosive of these new women playwrights, however, was Ntozake Shange at the end of the seventies with her choreopoem, *For Colored Girls Who Have Considered Suicide/When the Rainbow Is Enuf* (1976) and *Spell # 7* (1979). Brown–Guillory chooses her as the third major woman playwright.

Two other women working in the same vein are Alexis DeVeaux with her *Tapestry* (1976), and Aishah Rahman with her play *Unfinished Women Cry in No Man's Land While a Bird Dies in a Guilded Cage* (1977).

The decade of the eighties is truly the decade of the black woman in American literature, whether in fiction, poetry, drama, or nonfiction. Three black women are examples of this luxuriant flowering in drama. They are Kathleen Collins with *The Brothers* (1982), Elaine Jackson with *Paper Dolls* (1983), and P. J. Gibson with *Brown Silk and Magenta Sunsets* (1985). It is this decade to which Brown–Guillory belongs, with two plays produced and published, *Bayou Relics* (1983) and *Snapshots of Broken Dolls* (1987). Shirley Hardy is an upcoming playwright in Chicago.

With these successful black women playwrights we have run the gamut of the century. These are serious craftswomen. They understand the form and structure of drama. Frequently, the major conflict centers on race or family. They understand the social implications in black drama, and they are aware of our African heritage of myth and ritual. Brown–Guillory further explains these as they apply to Afro-American drama, and precisely to these women exponents of this particular form of literature.

Black women have undergone an age-old struggle to find their place on the American stage, and these examples indicate that their heroic struggle has not been in vain. When the twentieth century is written in history, these names shall shine in the heavens and maybe they shall lead all the rest.

Their Place
on the
Stage

1

Black Theater Tradition and Women Playwrights of the Harlem Renaissance

Alice Childress, Lorraine Hansberry, and Ntozake Shange, three of America's most outstanding playwrights, are crucial links in the development of playwriting in America, particularly black playwriting. An assessment, however, cannot be made about their contributions to American theater without first examining the long and vibrant tradition out of which they have emerged.

Black playwriting in America is directly linked to African theatrics. Genevieve Fabre, in *Drumbeats, Masks, and Metaphor,* traces the development of black playwriting from its earliest roots: Africa. Fabre suggests that many Africans expressed grievances against family members or the tribal leaders while avoiding confrontation via satire. Explosive situations were diffused and resolved by criticism cast in the form of public entertainment.[1] Fabre argues that these African dramatic renderings that were comprised primarily of dance and mime took on the appearance of a show.[2] It is believed that these African ceremonies served to preserve certain customs and a cultural heritage. James Hatch and Ted Shine, in *Black Theater U.S.A.: Forty-Five Plays by Black Americans, 1847–1974,* argue that Africans have traditionally celebrated life and death in theater rituals.[3]

This tradition of oral drama was transferred to American soil by enslaved Africans. Fabre contends that even aboard ships coming to America, Africans provided shows for the entertainment of whites. According to Fabre, "On plantations, masters continued to request these performances. The slave was cast in the double role as laborer and entertainer."[4] Paul Carter Harrison, in *Kuntu Drama,* explains that these African shows were comprised of song, dance, and drums and that these three modes continue to characterize contemporary black theater.[5] From these slave theatricals sprang the minstrel show, which remained popular for decades. William Couch, in *New Black Playwrights,* has observed that "as early as the mid-eighteenth century, Negro minstrels like the Congo Melodists, the Ethiopian Serenaders, and the Georgia Minstrels were delighting American audiences."[6] Stereotypes, as promoted by these groups, once given birth did not die easily.

The movement from the oral tradition to the written play form was a very gradual one. The first African American playwright of record is William Wells Brown, whose play *The Escape; or a Leap for Freedom,* written in 1858, marks the beginning of the impetus from dramatic oral tradition to formal playwriting.[7] *The Escape,* like much of the writing of the mid-nineteenth century, is a melodramatic, closet drama. This play levels an indictment against slavery and reveals the South as a corrupt society. *The Escape,* which was not produced until 1972, was read to white abolitionists of the North. It is the first in a long line of protest plays that would dominate early black plays and that made an appeal for justice for African Americans.

Two occurrences marked a revolution in black theater in America and ushered in the Harlem Renaissance. First, in 1910, the National Association for the Advancement of Colored People (NAACP) was newly formed, and in that year the first issue of *Crisis* magazine was published. Black artists could now publish their works, and even win literary contests. *Crisis,* edited by W.E.B. Dubois, who insisted that there should be a theater by, for, about, and near Negro people, sponsored annual playwriting contests.[8] This maiden magazine served to create a networking of black authors across the country, particularly in New York City, Cleveland, Chicago, and Washington D.C., many of whom were playwrights desperately in need of an audience. *Crisis* served as a laboratory for novice playwrights. Soon the NAACP's Drama Committee of Washington D.C. was established to encourage black playwrights to develop their craft by writing and producing their plays.[9] As a result of support from the NAACP, between 1910 and 1930 blacks owned and operated approximately 157 theaters.[10]

The second occurrence that some critics say sparked the Harlem Renaissance was Ridgely Torrence's New York production in 1917 of *Three Plays for a Negro Theatre,* including *Granny Maumee, The Rider of Dreams,* and *Simon the Cyrenian.* This white playwright's interest in blacks as subject matter on the American stage opened the floodgates, and the Negro became popular material for such writers as Eugene O'Neill, William Vaughn Moody, Marc Connelly, and Paul Green. Responsible for the popularization of the primitivistic motif, these playwrights served as an impetus to African American playwrights who began creating their own images of black men and women in an attempt to eradicate stereotypes of well-meaning white playwrights.[11] This emphasis on primitivism and exoticism resulted in the relegation of blacks to the musical rather than to the serious dramatic stage. Both black and white playwrights selected musicals as a medium. Between 1910 and 1940 over eight hundred musicals featuring blacks were produced.[12]

Sterling Brown contends that during the Harlem Renaissance, black playwrights were in the learning stage of their craft.[13] However, playwrights like Wallace Thurman (*Harlem,* 1929), Hall Johnson (*Run Little Chillun,* 1932), and Langston Hughes (*Mulatto,* 1935) made great strides in their craft and had their plays produced for large audiences on Broadway. Too often, however, this burst of dramatic creativity is associated solely with black male playwrights of the period.

The Harlem Renaissance, or as Alain Locke termed it the "New Negro Renaissance," must be reexamined and redefined to include the heart of this movement: its women, particularly its black women playwrights.[14] Plays by early twentieth-century black women are rarely anthologized and are infrequently the subject of critical interpretation. Burns Mantle's *American Playwrights of Today* (1929), which includes brief discussions of some fifty-odd women dramatists, does not mention any black women playwrights.[15]

It is time that scholars reclaim the sensitive, compassionate, and insightful works of these mother playwrights. These plays are vital because they supply a unique view of the black experience during the period between 1910 and 1940, dates that Arthur P. Davis and Michael W. Peplow, in *The New Negro Renaissance,* set as the time span for this sunburst of writing by and about blacks.[16] Early black women playwrights offer much to American theater in the way of content, form, characterization, dialogue, and heart. These women mavericks who have come from a long and efflorescent tradition were instrumental in paving a way for black playwrights between the 1950s and 1980s.

Before 1940, the suggested cut-off date of the Harlem Renaissance, marked by the publication of Richard Wright's *Native Son,* there was a host of black women playwrights who felt compelled to speak their minds and to express their hearts.[17] Like white women playwrights of the period, including Rachel Crothers, Neith Boyce, Susan Glaspell, Zona Gale, Zoe Atkins, Edna St. Vincent Millay, Sophie Treadwell, and Ann Seymour, black women turned to writing about women whose lives had been blighted by society.[18] Unlike many white women dramatists, however, "who wrote, like the [white] men with whom they competed, those serviceable melodramas, farces, mysteries, and [romantic] comedies that made up the season during the teens and expansive twenties," black women playwrights were writing serious drama, characterized most frequently by racial and social protest.[19]

In fact, during the years between 1916 and 1935, [a period that also gave birth to such significant black women writers as Regina Andrews, Helen Webb Harris, Ottie Graham, Alvira Hazzard, and Thelma Duncan], nine black women playwrights captured the lives of black people as no white or black male playwright could. Angelina Weld Grimke, Alice Dunbar-Nelson, Georgia Douglas Johnson, May Miller, Mary Burrill, Myrtle Smith Livingston, Ruth Gaines-Shelton, Eulalie Spence, and Marita Bonner were all original voices that were unwelcome in the commercial theater of the period. These authors are crucial to any discussion of the development of black playwriting in America because they provide the feminine perspective, and their voices give credence to the notion that there was a "New Negro" in America.

Nearly all of the early black women playwrights are connected with the Washington D.C. area, a fact that is not surprising since the NAACP's Drama Committee operated out of Washington D.C. With the exception of Eulalie Spence, they did not write about Harlem, as did many of the black male playwrights of the period from New York City. Though most of these women grew up in various sections of the United States, they attended college at Howard University, a seminal college for training black teachers and artists. Several were acquaintances, and some even close friends.[20] It may be argued that these dramatists document black life more accurately and with greater variety than did the Harlemite playwrights because their works portray blacks from various regions of the United States in a myriad of roles.

The nine black women playwrights previously mentioned are, indeed, the heart of the Harlem Renaissance. They wrote mainly one-act plays about middle class and common folk, about passion and apathy, love and hate, life and death, hope and despair, self-effacement and race pride, oppression and equality of the races and sexes. Most importantly, they wrote with intensity to reach the hearts of black people across the nation. They did not write for a Broadway audience that brought with it monetary remuneration. Eulalie Spence, a daring and vociferous woman playwright who might one day be credited with initiating feminism in plays by black women, after accepting an option given her by Paramount Productions for her full-length play *The Whipping,* commented that the pittance received was the only money that she had ever made by writing plays.[21]

These pioneering spirits seriously impacted black community theater. Many of these women were acquaintances of W.E.B. Dubois who, in a 1926 *Crisis* essay, strongly advocated community theater by saying, "If it is a Negro play that will interest us and depict our life, experience, and humor, it cannot be sold to the ordinary [commercial] theatrical producer, but can be produced by our churches, lodges, and halls."[22] With this admonition in mind, these early dramatists conscienciously wrote for the black community where their plays were produced in black-owned and operated community theaters, churches, schools, social club halls, and homes. Turning to a black audience that desperately needed theater that would teach them how to live better, these mother playwrights developed their craft while supplying their audiences with compassionately drawn, multidimensional characters.

These sages wrote for the sheer joy of capturing and preserving the essence of black life for future generations. They were able to turn theaters into nurseries where the black race is given roots, nurtured, tested, healed, and provided with the spirit to survive. They are, indeed, the missing pieces to a multifaceted puzzle of black life during those decades when blacks were becoming aware, and awakening to their own self-worth, and struggling for an identity robbed from them as a result of mutilated African roots.

A close study of these plays reveals seven forms: (1) protest, (2) genteel school, (3) folk, (4) historical (interchangeable with race pride and black nationalism), (5) religious, (6) fantasy, and (7) feminist. One of the limitations of attempting to assign labels is that there are no clear-cut delineations. It is difficult to designate form because many of these early plays contain a balanced blend of protest, folk, and historical elements. Generally speaking, however, the plays contain recognizable, dominant features of one or more of the above mentioned forms.

Following the tradition of William Wells Brown, black women playwrights wrote protest plays. Margaret Wilkerson, in *9 Plays by Black Women*, contends that "the early works of black women were strong protests against these conditions [racism, sexism, and capitalism] and were produced largely within the fold—in churches, lodges, and social halls of the sympathetic few."[23] Mance Williams, in *Black Theater of the 1960s and 1970s*, comments that protest is what characterized the bulk of black drama prior to the 1960s.[24]

Early black women playwrights protested four inconsistencies in American society. First, they were appalled by the dichotomy of Christian doctrine and the actions of white American Christians toward African Americans. In this category, lynching was the principal impetus for protest. Second, they were outraged at the fact that black soldiers fought abroad to keep America safe and free only to return to a land in which their basic constitutional rights were deprived. Third, these women were indignant about the economic disparity between black and white Americans; they felt that poverty was threatening to break the spirit of rural as well as urban blacks. Fourth, miscegenation was a source of fury and was condemned. Several early plays with a dominant element of protest or propaganda are *Rachel* (1916) by Angelina Weld Grimke; *Mine Eyes Have Seen* (1918) by Alice Dunbar-Nelson; *They That Sit in Darkness* (1919) and *Aftermath* (1919) by Mary Burrill; *A Sunday Morning in the South* (1925) by Georgia Douglas Johnson; and *For Unborn Children* (1926), by Myrtle Smith Livingston.

Angelina Grimke (1880–1958), born to the biracial Grimke family and educated in Boston, spent the bulk of her life writing poetry and teaching English in Washington D.C., a cultural mecca to DuBois' talented tenth. Grimke's *Rachel* is said to be the first play of record by a black, excluding musicals, to be produced and publicly performed by black actors.[25] Alain Locke and Montgomery Gregory, in *Plays of Negro Life* (1927), acknowledge Grimke's contribution to black playwriting when they observe that Grimke's play is "apparently the first successful drama written by a Negro."[26]

Rachel centers around the Lovings, a proud middle-class family that has suffered the lynching of the husband and the eldest son.[27] Mr. Loving was lynched for verbally attacking in a "Colored" newspaper the lynching of another man, and his teenage son was lynched for trying to save his father. The heroine, Rachel, vows never to have any babies after her mother tells her of the lynching and after she learns that her adopted son has been pelted with stones and called nigger.

Grimke protests against the lynching of innocent black people by white Christians. Rachel, when she speaks of the dark mothers who live in terrible, suffocating fear that their husbands and sons might be murdered concludes, "And so this nation—this white Christian nation has deliberately set its curse upon the most beautiful—the most holy thing in life—motherhood!" (p. 149). It is not surprising that lynching should be a subject treated by Grimke and many other writers of the Harlem Renaissance. Davis and Peplow, in *The New Negro Renaissance*, contend that between 1885 and 1919, there were 3,052 lynchings in the United States, methods of torture involving hanging, shooting, burning, drowning, beating, and cutting.[28]

Grimke's lyrical, almost sermonizing language makes a strong appeal when Tom, Mrs. Loving's son, passionately comments on the condition of blacks because of the moral degeneracy of whites. Seething with anger, Tom says, "Their children shall grow up in hope; ours in despair. Our hands are clean;—theirs are red with blood—red with the blood of a noble man—and a boy. They're nothing but low, cowardly, bestial murderers" (p. 153).

A contemporary audience might find the sentimentality in *Rachel* objectionable, but one must bear in mind that Grimke was born in 1880 and grew up with Victorian influences. Michael Greene asserts that "the play's intensity and Grimke's ability to make Rachel's vulnerability matter force the reader to become involved in her own disillusioning recognition that the world does not love as she is capable of loving."[29] Grimke, a gifted poet, uses language eloquently, sensitively, and powerfully to draw the reader into a world that made some black women of the period reluctant to give birth to little black and brown babies. Grimke's protestations do not end with a call for the reciprocity of violence. In fact, there is no call for action; she merely mirrors life for blacks in American society at the turn of the century.

Georgia Douglas Johnson (1886–1966), best known for her several volumes of poetry, including *The Heart of a Woman and Other Poems* (1918), *Bronze* (1922), *An Autumn Love Cycle* (1928), and *Share My World* (1960), wrote approximately twenty plays, making her the most prolific of the black women dramatists of the Harlem Renaissance. She spent the bulk of her life in Washington D.C., where her home was christened "Halfway House" and was for four decades a mecca for such intellectual and artistic giants as Langston Hughes, May Miller, Owen Dodson, Sterling Brown, Alain Locke, Angelina Grimke, Zora Neale Hurston, James Weldon Johnson, Claude McKay, and others. As a result of her associations with these leading racially conscious authors, Johnson's later work, which is different from the earlier romantic, raceless pieces, reflects her feelings of protest against injustice and racism.[30]

Johnson's play *A Sunday Morning in the South,* like *Rachel,* levels an indictment against lynching. The play opens with the grandmother, Sue Jones, discussing the recklessness with which whites have been lynching blacks in their town.[31] Johnson makes an appeal for justice when the grandmother says, "I believes in meeting out punishment to the guilty but they fust ought to fine out who done it though and then let the law hanel 'em" (p. 214). The grandson, Tom Griggs, chimes in with, "They lynch you bout anything too, not jest women. They say Zeb Brooks was strung up because he and his boss had er argiment. . . . I sometimes get right upset and wonder whut would I do if they ever tried to put something on me" (p. 214). Tom's expressed indignation at the lynchings foreshadows his own victimization. That same day, he is accused of raping a white woman, a crime that supposedly took place two hours after he had been asleep as attested to by his brother and grandmother.

When it is discovered that the weak and confused Southern belle, at the insistence of the mob, participates in the ruination of a young black life, the victim becomes a symbol of black oppression. Though the young white woman can only vaguely recollect what her assailant looks like, Tom is arrested because he comes close to the stated description, "age around twenty, five feet or six, brown skin" (p. 215). Johnson's point here is that a white mob cannot be contained or pacified until black blood is spilled, in spite of the fact that a description of that type fits probably half the black population in America.

Georgia Douglas Johnson's play touches the heart and both angers and pains modern readers. Hatch and Shine argue that *A Sunday Morning in the South* is a protest play by a woman who has difficult time believing in the judicial system when unjust or unenforced laws provide little or no protection for African Americans.[32] Wilkerson makes an insightful evaluation of Georgia Douglas Johnson's plays when she says, "Lynching informed most of her works—one-act plays that are spare in dialogue and action based on the very real drama of terrorist acts directed at the Southern black community. . . . The subject matter left no room for humor."[33] Wilkerson, in demonstrating common threads in Johnson's plays, links *A Sunday Morning in the South* to *Safe* (1935–1939), in which a mother strangles her newborn baby [to keep him safe] when she hears the pathetic cries of a black man being dragged away by a lynch mob.[34] Johnson's play starts out like a low murmur and then blossoms into a deafening plea for whites to treat blacks like human beings who possess hearts and souls.

Alice Dunbar-Nelson (1875–1935), born in New Orleans, Louisiana and a graduate of Straight University (now Dillard University), taught school in West Medford, Massachusetts before marrying Paul Laurence Dunbar and moving to Washington D.C. She spent her last years in Delaware. *Give Us Each Day: The Diary of Alice Dunbar-Nelson,* edited by Gloria T. Hull, chronicles Dunbar-Nelson's extensive travel across the country as poet, journalist, lecturer, and organizer, a factor that provided her with the substance of her writing. In her later years she traveled widely, delivering militant political speeches.[35] Dunbar-Nelson's later writing, like Johnson's, reflects the voice of social protest that was probably shaped by three major factors: a severed attachment to the New Orleans creoles of color, World War I, and the developing Harlem Renaissance.

Dunbar-Nelson's *Mine Eyes Have Seen* (1918)[36] grew out of her work as a member of the Women's Committee on the Council of Defense where she helped organize Southern black women in nine states for the war effort.[37] It is a protest play that centers around a young man, Chris, who has been drafted to fight in World War I, but who debates whether he should honor the draft. Dunbar-Nelson suggests that black men who gladly fight for their country should not have to face degradation when they return to find that the freedom they fought to maintain for America is for white Americans only. Dunbar-Nelson's voice is piercing when Chris comments on blacks and war: "Haven't you had your soul shrivelled with fear since we were driven like dogs from our home? And for what? Because we were living like Christians. Must I go and fight for a nation that let my father's murder go unpunished?" (p.175)

Not only does this passage indicate Dunbar-Nelson's indignation about soldiers who are forbidden to bask in glory, but it alludes to her disdain for the American lynch mob and, particularly, for the Southern tradition that includes active and overt racism. Chris's reference to his father is poignant because his father was shot in the South while trying to save his home, which was being burned down by a mob.

Mine Eyes Have Seen contains sympathetically drawn characters. Perhaps Dunbar-Nelson's experimenting with protest as a literary form accounts for the fact that *Mine Eyes Have Seen* did not win for her as much popularity as her early works, such as *Violets and Other Tales* (1895) and *The Goodness of St. Rocque and Other Stories* (1899).[38] Pauline Young, Dunbar-Nelson's niece, recalls that her aunt, who taught English in the high school where she attended, produced her play. Young notes that though the audience was very enthusiastic about the play, her aunt was unsuccessful in securing a publisher.[39]

Dunbar-Nelson will gain stature in years to come because of her depth of perception and her skill at mirroring universal concerns. Ora Williams says that "in all her writings . . . Dunbar-Nelson is always direct. . . . Her concerns about racism, the roles of men and women in society, and the importance of love, war, death, and nature appear as recurring themes. . . . Hers was one of the most consistent, secure, and independent voices of the black community."[40]

Mary Burrill (1879–1946), like Grimke and Dunbar-Nelson, taught English in Washington D.C.[41] Burrill's *Aftermath* (1919), like Dunbar-Nelson's *Mine Eyes Have Seen*, levels an indictment against an American society that forces blacks to fight in foreign wars to protect white Americans while African Americans go unprotected from terrorists who lynch and burn.[42] Set in South Carolina, the play centers around the homecoming of John, a black soldier who earned a medal, the French War Cross, for single-handedly fighting off twenty Germans and thereby saving the lives of his entire company.

Additionally, Burrill protests against lynching. John's glory is short-lived when he returns to discover that his father, who had argued with a white man over the price of cotton, had been burnt to death. Burrill, unlike Grimke, calls for retaliation with violence as John goes out gun in hand to collect retribution. Bitter and vengeful, John says, "You mean to tell me I mus' let them w'ite devuls send me miles erway to suffer an' be shot up fu' the freedom of people I ain't nevah seen, while they're burnin' an' killin' my folks here at home!" (p. 61). Rachel France, in *A Century of Plays by American Women,* says that "*Aftermath* echoes an editorial by DuBois in which he called for returning Negro soldiers to marshal their wartime courage to fight 'the forces of hell' at home."[43] Burrill's *Aftermath* initiates a host of plays that would advocate Hammurabi's code of an eye for an eye.

Burrill's *They That Sit in Darkness* (1919), which is as equally explosive as *Aftermath,* protests against poverty.[44] Burrill very sensitively treats the issue of the poor who, often because of a lack of education and income, bring babies into the world that they can neither feed nor clothe. Additionally, Burrill makes a plea for the government to assist the poor by instructing them in the methods of birth control. The central character is a black woman, Malinda Jasper, who has had ten children, leaving her with a debilitating heart condition. Though she and her husband work to make ends meet, there is still rarely a crust of bread for the entire family. A washerwoman by trade, Mrs. Jasper drags herself out of bed to complete a job only a couple of days after giving birth to her tenth child, with which she had suffered complications. The result is that she dies of a massive heart attack.

One strong point that Burrill makes is that poverty strips many black parents of the ability to nurture their children, especially spiritually. In very precise and colorful language, Burrill quietly but powerfully levels an indictment against poverty in American society when Mrs. Jasper comments, "We has to wuk so hard to give 'em de lil de gits we ain't got no time tuh look at'er dey sperrits" (p. 182). Mrs. Jasper tells that her husband is unable to guide his children because when he leaves for work and returns, the children are sleeping. She laments that when she gets through with doing laundry for whites all day, "Ah doan wants tuh see no chillern!" (p. 182). Additionally, Burrill calls attention to the inhumanity of the American government, which at that time enforced laws forbidding the distribution of birth control information. The white relief nurse, Miss Shaw, says "When I took my oath as nurse, I swore to abide by the laws of the State, and the law forbids my telling you what you have a right to know" (p. 182).

Another early twentieth-century black woman playwright who provides modern readers with a special window on the black experience in America is Myrtle Smith Livingston (1901–1973), also a graduate of Howard University in Washington D.C. Livingston's subject of protest in For Unborn Children (1926) is miscegenation.[45] According to Hatch and Shine, miscegenation is the one racial theme that both black and white playwrights invariably agree upon: mixing is untolerable and degenerative.[46]

For Unborn Children is a taut play that deals with a young black lawyer and a young white woman who plan to circumvent state laws forbidding interracial marriage by fleeing to the North. Parallels can be drawn between Eugene O'Neill and Livingston. O'Neill's All God's Chillun Got Wings, written in 1933, just three years before For Unborn Children, has as its subject a love relationship between a black law student and a white girl. Just as Jim in O'Neill's play is selfless and risks his life to protect the white woman he loves, so does LeRoy Carlson in For Unborn Children.

One twist that does not occur in O'Neill's play is the notion that love between the races must be sacrificed to prevent children from coming into a world that will be hostile, at best. Livingston further complicates the plot by having Grandma Carlson tell LeRoy that he is half white, a product of a marriage that failed desperately because of miscegenation. She tells LeRoy that his white mother could not love him, a black baby, and therefore abandoned him. Grandma Carlson becomes the catalyst for LeRoy's reconsidering his plan to escape to the North when she says, "Think of the unborn children that you sin against by marrying her, baby! Oh, you can't know the misery that awaits them. . . . Every child has a right to a mother who will love it better than life itself; and a white mother cannot mother a Negro baby." (p. 187)

At the end of the play, when the mob reaches the Carlson home, LeRoy triumphantly and defiantly goes to his death. Unlike anything to appear in any play during these decades, LeRoy offers himself up to the mob with great restraint and dignity. Livingston shapes LeRoy into a Christ figure as he goes to the mob, arms outstretched, with these final words: "Don't grieve so; just think of it as a sacrifice for unborn children" (p. 187).

In addition to the preponderance of protest plays written by early black women playwrights, plays of the genteel school of writers managed to appear on the African American stage. Some young writers of the early years of the Harlem Renaissance shied away from the black nationalist approach to literature and were preoccupied with proving to white America that they were just like them, except for the superfluous matter of color. Two types of genteel literature produced by early black women playwrights are "raceless" and "best-foot-forward." These two types, according to Davis and Peplow, were written by black writers who felt that literature by and about blacks and in the black dialect might be perceived as limiting, and not good literature.[47]

"Raceless" literature deemphasizes recognizable aspects of black culture. Much of this nonracial, "universal" writing is insipid because it is stripped of the very particulars necessary to constitute universality in any work. Some of the early works of Countee Cullen, James Weldon Johnson, and Claude McKay may be considered raceless literature. In early plays by some black women, race is apparent as an issue, but it is secondary to the issue of humanity and universal good, honor, and decency. This universal literature, which silences the voices and the hearts of blacks, implies that the black experience is not an integral part of the American and human experience.

The "best-foot-forward" approach to black writing includes only the best and the positive about blacks, generally middle-class blacks. Grass-roots blacks and their sometimes seamy existence are ignored as subjects. The aim of these writers was to demonstrate that blacks were no different than whites, and thus when whites read about these characters, who are only painted black, they would be receptive to such writing.

The genteel school of writers wanted an audience, and they wanted to get published. Willis Richardson, in *Plays and Pageants From the Life of the Negro,* sheds light on the triple difficulty he and other black writers encountered when they sought to publish an anthology of black plays:

> The plays must be written by Negro authors, must be for the most part not in dialect, and must have subject matter suitable for young people of school age. The difficulties were increased by the fact that most Negro plays are not written by Negro authors and that most plays written by Negro authors are written in dialect.[48]

Many black playwrights who wanted to reach a broad market compromised, perhaps sacrificing the flavor of their works.

Alice Dunbar-Nelson's play *Mine Eyes Have Seen* is one such play that contains both genteel and protest elements. The imagined, stilted, vacuous language, the middle-class, black characters who are only superficially black, and the "best-foot-forward" philosophy are evident in the passage spoken by Dan, the older brother of the young man who has been drafted into World War I but who doubts his loyalty: "It is not for us to visit retribution. Nor to wish hatred on others. Let us remember the good that has come. Love of humanity is above the small considerations of time and place or race or sect. Can't you be big enough to feel pity for the little crucified French children?" (p. 177) Dan feels that he has to prove to the world that black people are worthy people. It is this character that highlights Dunbar-Nelson's leanings toward the genteel tradition. Nonetheless, the play has significance because of its central message: black soldiers are willing to fight for their country but will demand full citizenship when they return.

May Miller (1889-), born in Washington D.C., is a graduate of Howard University, where her father was an eminent professor and scholar. Once a student of Grimke and Burrill, May Miller was influenced by her mentors to write. A teacher of speech and drama and a poet, Miller coedited along with Willis Richardson two volumes of Negro plays for school children.[49] Goldfarb and Wilson maintain that Miller, along with Willis Richardson and Randolph Edmonds, "decided that black children needed plays and skits about their own history and heroes . . . and wrote a total of 100 plays and published six books."[50] One of the most prolific of the early black women playwrights, Miller experiments with several different forms, including genteel, folk, historical, and feminist.

Three of May Miller's historical plays contain strong elements associated with the genteel tradition: *Graven Images* (1929),[51] *Samory* (1935), and *Christophe's Daughters* (1935) are set in pre-Christian Ethiopia, the African Sudan, and Haiti, respectively.[52] *Graven Images* is a play in which the black son of Moses suffers abuse because he is different. As the play concludes, he puts his best foot forward and persuades his young enemies that he is very much like them, only tanned. *Samory* presents a culturally sophisticated African general of the same name who fights off French colonizers to protect his family and home. *Christophe's Daughters* shows the courage and strength exhibited by two princesses as their father's throne is being usurped. The language in all three of these plays is artificial, vapid, and saturated with euphemisms, such as when Marion in *Graven Images* politely tells Eliezer, Moses's son, that he is a disgrace to his father. Marion says, "Black one, you had best hide your shame from the followers of your father and not place your complexion where all may see" (p. 127).

In spite of the fact that the voices of black characters in these plays are imagined, at best, and the characters are one-dimensional, positive images of noble or royal blacks, the plays merit serious critical treatment because of their thematic and historical value. Miller comments on sexism, racism, miscegenation, political backstabbing, reconciliation, gossip, provincialism, illegitimacy, and family loyalty. Pinkie Gordon Lane contends that Miller is a writer "of deep personal insight, of unquestioning moral courage and one who has suffered imbalances of our society yet retained a grace and wholeness of spirit."[53] Miller's works suggest that she is perceptive and compassionate.

Another form popularized by early black women playwrights is the historical drama written to teach blacks, especially the children, about the heroes and heroines of their race. According to Hatch and Shine, black playwrights write historical dramas "to liberate the black audience from an oppressive past, to present a history that provides continuity, hope, and glory. Such feelings and knowledge have positive survival value for the race."[54] This emphasis on the black folk hero represents a new pride in the black person's past, particularly the militant past.

May Miller and Georgia Douglas Johnson are leading figures in the area of historical drama during the Harlem Renaissance. Miller, who devoted much time to anthologizing historical dramas, gives depth and breadth to such major African American heroines as Harriet Tubman and Sojourner Truth in plays of the same titles.[55] *Harriet Tubman* (1935), set in Maryland, gives an account of one incident when Tubman helps slaves escape in spite of blockages on land and water. Miller juxtaposes Tubman's heroism against the disloyalty of the mulatto house servant, a theme that continues to dominate black literature. Tubman's indomitable will is apparent when she says, "Trouble or no trouble—thar's two things Ah got de right to, an' they is death an' liberty. One or de other, Ah mean to have. No one will take me back into slavery alive" (p. 277). Miller insightfully comments on slavery as a corrupt institution, on its engendering mistrust and deception among an enslaved people, and on the existence of strong black male and female relationships that have endured in spite of the shackles of slavery. Miller's Harriet Tubman has a heart that compels her to reach out to free those in bondage.

Sojourner Truth (1935), set in Northampton, Massachusetts, dramatizes an incident in which the legendary heroine persuades a group of white teenage boys that to burn down tents at a camp meeting means possibly killing the children of their neighbors. In a compassionate sermon, Sojourner Truth mesmerizes these young pranksters with her history and that of her people:

I could tell you 'bout when I was a little girl an' how my master once whipped me 'til the blood streamed down my body and dyed the floor beneath me. But whipping like that is common. . . . Their children are snatched 'way an' sold where they never see nor hear o' 'em again; still they toil on an' pray. . . . (p. 329)

Miller, with quiet anger, mirrors the plight Sojourner Truth and thousands of slaves endured, many of them heroically willing to fight, escape, and die for freedom.

Georgia Douglas Johnson's *William and Ellen Craft* (1935) and *Frederick Douglass* (1935) are historical dramas that are enhanced by the feminine perspective.[56] In *William and Ellen Craft,* Johnson writes of a black couple who escape when the woman, who is the mulatto daughter of the master, dresses as a white man and her husband pretends that he is the servant. Johnson comments sensitively on the power of strong black male and female relationships, on religion as a coping mechanism, and on the importance of dark-skinned blacks loving themselves.

Frederick Douglass (1935), set in Baltimore, centers on Frederick Douglass' love for his girlfriend, Ann. This focus on Douglass' personal life, as opposed to his political life, is not captured in history books. Johnson shows blacks expressing love and tenderness, something that is quickly disappearing in contemporary black literature. When Ann chides Frederick Douglass about not wanting her once he is free, Douglass tenderly answers, "Oh my little honey, I'm goin' to love you all my life. We goin to work together, you an'me, in that great big free country up North" (p. 147). When Douglass escapes dressed as a sailor, Johnson shows the spirit of survival of blacks. Throughout the play, Johnson emphasizes the need for blacks to educate themselves and to give back to the community education and service. Another strong element in this historical drama is the extended black family and its importance to blacks not only surviving but succeeding in America. Miller and Johnson have created folk heroes and heroines who possess great strength, wisdom, and courage. Yet they have added the element of compassion and dedication to one's spouse and immediate community. Of particular interest are the genuine, supportive, loving black female-male relationships. These plays still hold value for readers today.

Another identifiable form in the plays of early black women playwrights is the folk tradition, which stresses the lives of common black people. Some of the historical plays contain folk characters, distinguishable by language, customs, and beliefs, but they are not legendary heroes. Writers of folk plays take great pains to capture the customs, dialect, myths, earthiness and very essence of the down-home black person. Davis and Peplow cogently articulate the basic tenets of the folk tradition:

> Writers like Georgia Douglas Johnson, Arna Bontemps, Jean Toomer, and Sterling Brown invested the ordinary black man with epic dignity and courage. They showed his ability to endure in spite of all the hardships that American race prejudice could rain down upon his head."[57]

Playwrights before the Harlem Renaissance, such as Ridgely Torrence, Paul Green, Charles W. Chestnutt, and Paul Laurence Dunbar, experimented with folk characters. It was during the Harlem Renaissance, however, that black playwrights, with any degree of frequency, began to take a serious look at and to treat with understanding grass-roots blacks.[58] Langston Hughes' folk play, *Little Ham* (1935), is fairly well known. Few folk plays by black women, however, are a part of the established canon.

May Miller's *Riding the Goat* (1929), perhaps her most skillfully crafted play, is a powerful comedy about a young black physician who feels it demeaning to have to take part in community rituals and festivals dominated by plain folk.[59] As grand marshal in the United Order of Moabites, he must lead the parade by riding a goat. His ambivalence lies in the fact that his marching is directly connected with his success in the black community. He is all too painfully aware that if he refuses to participate in this community ritual, he will lose patients and will face being ostracized.

Riding the Goat, set in South Baltimore, is a fast-paced, witty, suspenseful play in which Miller captures the spirit, idioms, dialect, aspirations, and foibles of the people. Miller depicts the colorfulness of the folk of the area when Aunt Hetty, the sage of the community, comments, "I 'clare ev'ry time that nigger gets tir'd of workin' he gits 'nother spell of rheumatics" (p. 147). Miller's central message in this play is that blacks must depend upon each other for survival and strength. She stresses that a person outside of the community must not expect to be supported by it. In one instance when Ruth, the sweetheart of the physician, covers for him, a delightfully folksy young man from the community quips, "Ruth, you oughta be shamed of yourself agoin back on your own folks fo' some outside nigger" (p. 173).

Georgia Douglas Johnson's *A Sunday Morning in the South,* in addition to its protest strands, is a folk play. One of the strengths of this play is the manner in which the poor, rural folks band together in a crisis. Several members of the community come to aid Grandma Sue when her grandson is about to be lynched. When someone is needed to get help, Matilda, the consummate example of the folksy character, pleads "Lemme go; I kin move in a hurry, lemme go!" (p. 216). The speech of these uneducated, humble characters is unpretentious, earthy, and alive.

Johnson's *Plumes* (1927)[60], produced by the Harlem Experimental Theatre in New York City, is a folk drama that centers around superstitious and uneducated blacks who are poor but honest.[61] The nobility of the characters is revealed by the fact that they can laugh at their own abject poverty while continuing to strive for a better future. *Plumes* treats the dilemma of its heroine, Charity, who has to choose whether she will allow a money-hungry doctor to attempt to save her fading daughter, or whether she will hold on to the last fifty dollars she owns to pay for a grand funeral—plumes, hacks, and all the flamboyant trimmings—for the child. Closely resembling *Silver Nails* (1945), by the Irish playwright Nicholas Bella, *Plumes* is saturated with light and sardonic humor as the heroine explicitly shares with her confidante, Tildy, her dream of an exquisite funeral, if not for herself then for the daughter to whom she was never able to give much in life. Tildy reads the coffee grounds in Charity's cup and foretells a big funeral, a fact that almost convinces the folksy Charity who gives credence to fortune telling. Charity's daughter dies before a choice has to be made.

Eulalie Spence (1894–1981), a West Indian who came to New York City via Ellis Island when she was eight, earned a B.B. from Teacher's College in 1937 and an M.A. in speech from Columbia University in 1939.[62] *Undertow* (1929), Spence's gripping and realistic play about folk life in Harlem, was first published in *Carolina Magazine* in 1929 and has over the years been produced on black college campuses.[63] This jewel of a play focuses on a man and woman who live through a loveless twenty years together after the husband is caught having an affair. The wife, Hattie, spends her whole life nagging and degrading him because of internalized hurt. When Clem, the other woman, returns to rekindle the fire, Hattie and Dan struggle, leaving Hattie dead. This play is saturated with folksy dialect that practically dances across the page. Hattie snaps at Dan, "You ain't gonna tro no dust in mah eyes no second time—not ef Ah know it" (p. 195). Hattie's boldness and streetwiseness, characteristic of folk drama, is evident when she levels verbal blows at her husband's mistress:

But long's Ah got breaf tuh breathe, Ah ain't gwine say Yes! 'bout no divo'ce. Ef he kin git one 'thout me, let him git it! Yuh hear me? Now ef yuh's tru, yuh better get outa here. Ah ain't sponsible fer what Ah says from now on! (p. 197)

Another element of the folk tradition in *Undertow* is the constant stream of people flowing in and out of Hattie's boarding house. Spence dramatizes tenderly the day-to-day lives of these Harlemites of the twenties.

Religious plays, like the folk dramas by early black women playwrights, often center around the Southern, rural poor. Like the Medieval mystery plays that presented the whole scheme of salvation, nearly all of the plays of these mother playwrights contain some reference to God, Christianity, or religion in general. Using religion as a coping mechanism, the characters in many of the plays call on God to help them survive in an oppressive world. Grandma Sue, in Georgia Douglas Johnson's *A Sunday Morning in the South,* turns to God when her grandson is about to be lynched: "Sweet Jesus, do come down and hep us this mornin. Yo knows our hearts and you knows this po boy ain't done nothin wrong. You said you would hep the fatherless and the motherless; do Jesus bring this po orphan back to his ole cripple grannie safe and sound, do Jesus" (p. 215). This gripping plea is characteristic of the bulk of these early religious plays.

A different kind of religious play is one by a woman who chose to experiment with religious allegory. Ruth Gaines-Shelton's (1873–?) play, *The Church Fight* (1925), distinguishes itself on three levels.[64] First, it is a comedy, a rarity during the Harlem Renaissance because of racial unrest, World War I, and an approaching depression. These early black women playwrights, as a rule, did not use humor to effect social change. Second, the play is a religious allegory, wherein the characters in *The Church Fight* are personifications of abstract qualities. Third, the play does not deal with the issue of race. *The Church Fight,* not written in dialect, is a play by, about, and for blacks. Oscar Brockett, in *The Theatre,* says of black theater of the 1960s, "In recent years, black playwrights seem to have been moving away from defining black experience through negative pictures of whites and toward depicting blacks in relation to each other."[65] Brockett's generalization holds true for Ruth Gaines-Shelton, a writer of the 1920s, who emphatically portrayed blacks solely in relation to each other.

The Church Fight, a play for which Gaines-Shelton won second prize in a *Crisis* contest in 1925, examines church politics.[66] A humorous group of religious leaders, including Investigator, Judas, Instigator, Experience, Take-It-Back, and Two-Face, band together to oust Parson Procrastinator. The problem, however, is that no one can come up with a decent charge against him. Sister Instigator says with enthusiasm, "Well Brother Investigator, we ain't got no charge agin him, only he's been here thirteen years and we are tired of looking at him" (p. 189). When the parson confronts his accusers, they deny that they are plotting to eject him. They each flatter the parson in his presence and can hardly wait for him to adjourn the meeting. Brother Investigator in his prayers, after Parson leaves, mouths the sentiments of the religious leaders: "Lord, smile down in tender mercies upon those who have lied, and those who have not lied, close their lips with the seal of forgiveness, stiffen their tongues with the rod of obedience, fill their ears with the gospel of truth, and direct Parson Procrastinator's feet toward the railroad track" (p. 191).

Gaines-Shelton pokes fun at the fickleness and pettiness of some elders of the church. She seems to be suggesting that it is a waste of time and energy to get involved in church politics because there usually are no resolutions, only a limitless stream of questions and complaints. On another level, Gaines-Shelton demonstrates the power wielded by black religious leaders who are, generally, a driving and persuasive force behind the congregation and the community. *The Church Fight* also illustrates that the black church is a viable gathering place, serving as a social club for the community.

Like Ruth Gaines-Shelton, Marita Bonner experimented with form in the theater. Bonner (1905–1971) was born and educated in Massachusetts. After graduating from Radcliff College, she went on to teach English in Washington D.C.[67] Bonner's *The Purple Flower,* which first appeared in *Crisis* in 1928, is a fantasy that takes place in a nonexistent world, concerns incredible and unreal characters, and serves as a vehicle for her to make a serious comment on reality in America.[68] Bonner's play, devoid of humor, is a biting, militant fantasy that is every bit as powerful as the radical plays of three decades later.

The Purple Flower is set on a hill called Somewhere inhabited by White

Devils (whites) and in the valley called Nowhere peopled by the Us's (blacks). Bonner creatively describes these otherworldly Sundry White Devils as, "artful little things with soft wide eyes such as you would expect to find in an angel. Soft hair that flops around their horns. Their horns glow red all the time—now with blood—now with eternal fire—now with unholy desire" (p. 202). On the other hand, Bonner says of the the Us's, "They can be as white as the White Devils, as brown as the earth, as black as the center of a poppy. They may look as if they were something or nothing" (p. 202).

In this fantasy land, the White Devils scheme to keep the Us's off the hill and away from the Purple Flower, which represents the good and the best in life. Several Us's offer suggestions about how to get up the hill: Booker T. Washington's philosophy of hard work and indispensability; W.E.B. DuBois' notion of books and education; or the religion/God, or money philosophies. When all these offerings fail, an old man takes charge and initiates a symbolic destruction of those things that hold the Us's from rebelling against the White Devils. The old man insists that only when the Us's are willing to shed and draw blood will they defeat the White Devils. Bonner's play addresses the issue of revolution. She insists that there will be a bloody revolution. *The Purple Flower,* written three decades before the volatile 1960s, signals change in America. Bonner sets the stage for militant writers like Amiri Baraka, Sonia Sanchez, and Ed Bullins.

Bonner's essays, short stories, and plays, which appeared in Crisis between 1925 and 1928, provide insight into her life. Bonner's anger is evident in her December 1925 *Crisis* essay "On Being Young—A Woman—And Colored":

> You long to explode and hurt everything white; friendly; unfriendly. But you know that you cannot live with a chip on your shoulder . . . For chips make you bend your body to balance them. And once you bend, you lose your poise, your balance, and the chips get into you. The real you. You get hard.[69]

Instead of exploding, Bonner channeled her energies into a dynamic work of art. Containing drumbeats, chants, and dancing, *The Purple Flower* is highly imaginative and structurally new and different in black women's playwriting.

Just as many of the early plays by black women are dominated by elements of racial protest, so do a number of them focus on women's rights. These women refuse to be shuffled into a corner and be told what is appropriate for them. They are articulate, outspoken heroines who demonstrate that they are as competent and confident as their male counterparts and will not be pampered or coerced into silence.

Rachel by Grimke, *Riding the Goat* by Miller, and *Undertow* by Spence are three plays with strong feminist strands. *Rachel,* as early as 1916, centers around an independent and challenging heroine. Rachel holds her own with John Strong, a man who inadvertently oversteps his boundaries. When John asserts that Rachel needs more fun in her life, and that he will arrange to take her to the theater, Rachel snaps: "I wonder if you know how—how— maddening you are. Why, you talk as though my will counts for nothing. It's as if you're trying to master me. I think a domineering man is detestable" (p. 157). Rachel eventually breaks her engagement with John, in part because he is a bit overbearing and, in part, because she chooses not to be a wife and mother who will bear little black babies who may some day be lynched.

Riding the Goat, by May Miller, has even stronger seeds of feminism than *Rachel.* Of particular interest is Ruth's relationship to Carter, the physician. She pleads with him, as grand marshal of the lodge, to march in the town-folk's parade if he wants to keep his patients. Carter, however, refuses to ride a goat and snaps at Ruth, "Since you are crazy about parading, it's really a pity you can't march yourself" (p. 167). Ruth, disguising herself in Carter's hood and uniform, takes his place, and goes before the entire town on a goat. Her ride is particularly bold because women were not allowed to participate in lodges or parades. Ruth forgets her place and, in the end, wins Carter's respect.

Eulalie Spence's *Undertow* is decidedly a feminist play. Hattie, a wife whose husband is having an affair, refuses to sit idly by and allow him to take advantage of her. She challenges him when he comes in after having been with the other woman: "Whar yuh bin, dat you ain't had nuthin 'tuh eat? Yuh kain't say, kin yuh? . . . Keep outa mah kitchen! Ah kep yuh supper till eight o'clock. Yuh didn't come, and Ah's throwed it out" (p. 195). Later, in a heated argument over the mistress, Hattie very passionately lets Dan know that she does not intend to let him hurt her anymore. Seething with anger, she tells him, "G'wan, Is Ah keepin' yuh? Take yuh street walker back whar she come frum" (p. 198). Hattie is an indomitable, ex-plosive woman who stands up for her rights as wife. The only way a woman of this type can be silenced is by death. Spence's heroine dies when Dan pushes her, and she hits her head on the corner of a marble table.

Deeply feminine and deeply human, Grimke, Miller, and Spence depicted black women as loving and supportive of their men but also as strong, willful women demanding to be treated equitably. These early black women playwrights deal successfully with the issue of the emergence of woman as an individual who has her own tastes, aspirations, and uniqueness.

Lynching, poverty, disenfranchised war heroes, miscegenation, race pride, folk heroes and heroines, family loyalty, church politics, revolution, and women's rights are subjects frequently explored in early black plays by women who deserve a place among the best writers of the twentieth century. These same themes are echoed in the works of three of America's finest contemporary black women playwrights: Alice Childress, Lorraine Hans-berry, and Ntozake Shange. Because of the strides made in content, form, characterization, and dialogue by these mother playwrights, there could be Broadway and off-Broadway productions for these three powerhouses of the American stage.

These maverick black women playwrights, whose works have for several decades been overshadowed by masculine literature, looked at the world with their feminine hearts and saw much that disappointed and angered them in the American society. In fact, one might conclude that the black women dramatists of the Harlem Renaissance were as much tortured as talented. Each of these women speaks to and for African Americans then and now. Becoming increasingly socially aware of the problems facing African Americans, these women move from the concerns of women to the concerns of Colored women and their families. Sometimes plaintive but always passionate, optimistic, and committed they set out to illuminate the conditions of African Americans with the hopes of bringing about social change. With feeling hearts, they present a slice of United States history from the unique perspective of women who have been both midwives and pallbearers of African American dreamers.

NOTES

1. Genevieve Fabre, *Drumbeats, Masks, and Metaphor: Contemporary Afro-American Theatre* (Boston, Mass.: Harvard University Press, 1983), p. 4.

2. Fabre, p. 4.

3. James V. Hatch and Ted Shine, *Black Theater U.S.A.: Forty-Five Plays by Black Americans, 1847–1974* (New York: The Free Press, 1974), p. 353.

4. Fabre, p. 4.

5. Paul Carter Harrison, ed. *Kuntu Drama: Plays of the African Continuum* (New York: Grove Press, 1974), p. 22.

6. William Couch, *New Black Playwrights,* (Baton Rouge, La.: Louisiana State University Press, 1968), p. x.

7. Hatch and Shine, p. 34.

8. Alvin Golfarb and Edwin Wilson, *Living Theater: An Introduction to Theater History* (New York: McGraw-Hill Book Co., 1983), p. 422.

9. Mance Williams, *Black Theatre in the 1960s and 1970s: A Historical-Critical Analysis of the Movement* (Westport, Conn.: Greenwood Press, 1985), p. 107.

10. Goldfarb and Wilson, p. 422.

11. Sterling Brown, *Negro Poetry and Drama* (Washington DC: The Associates in Negro Folk Education, 1937), p. 115.

12. Goldfarb and Wilson, p. 425.

13. Brown, pp. 120–123.

14. Arthur P. Davis and Michael W. Peplow, eds. *The New Negro Renaissance* (New York: Holt, Rinehart and Winston, 1975), pp. xix-xx.

15. Joseph Mersand, "When Ladies Write Plays," in *The American Drama Since 1930* (New York: Kennikat Press, Inc., 1949), pp. 150–151.

16. Davis and Peplow, pp. xix-xx.

17. Ibid., p. xxi.

18. Rachel France, *A Century of Plays by American Women* (New York: Richards Rosen Press, Inc., 1979), pp. 18–22.

19. Helen Rich Chinoy and Linda Walsh Jenkins, *Women in American Theatre* (New York: Crown Publishers, Inc., 1981), p. 130.

20. For details about the friendships of Mary Burrill, Angelina Grimke, Georgia Douglas Johnson, May Miller, and Alice Dunbar-Nelson, see Gloria T. Hull, ed. *Give Us Each Day: The Diary of Alice Dunbar-Nelson* (New York: Norton, 1984).

21. Hatch and Shine, p. 192.

22. Aishah Rahman, "To Be Black, Female, and a Playwright," *Freedomways,* vol. 19 (Fourth Quarter, 1979), p. 256.

23. Margaret Wilkerson, *9 Plays by Black Women* (New York: A Mentor Book, 1986), p. xv.

24. Williams, p. 113.

25. Hatch and Shine, p. 137.

26. Michael Greene, "Angelina Weld Grimke," *DLB,* vol. 50, p. 152.

27. Angelina Weld Grimke, "Rachel," in *Black Theater U.S.A.: Forty-Five Plays by Black Americans, 1847–1974,* eds. James V. Hatch and Ted Shine (New York: The Free Press, 1974), pp. 139–171. All quotes and references to the play are based upon this source.

28. Davis and Peplow, p. 21.

29. Greene, p. 153.

30. Winona Fletcher, "Georgia Douglas Johnson," *DLB,* vol. 50, pp. 153–156.

31. Georgia Douglas Johnson, "A Sunday Morning in the South," in *Black Theater U.S.A.: Forty-Five Plays By Black Americans, 1847–1974,* eds. James V. Hatch and Ted Shine (New York: The Free Press, 1974), pp. 213–217. All quotes and references to the play are based upon this source.

32. Hatch and Shine, pp. 211–212.

33. Wilkerson, p. xviii.

34. Ibid.

35. Gloria T. Hull, ed. *Give Us Each Day: The Diary of Alice Dunbar-Nelson* (New York: Norton, 1984), pp. 13–35.

36. Alice Dunbar-Nelson, "Mine Eyes Have Seen," in *Black Theater U.S.A.: Forty-Five Plays by Black Americans, 1847–1974,* eds. James V. Hatch and Ted Shine (New York: The Free Press, 1974), pp. 174–177. All quotes and references to the play are based upon this source.

37. Hull, p. 231.

38. Ibid., p. 467.

39. Hatch and Shine, p. 173.

40. Ora Williams, "Alice Dunbar-Nelson," *DLB,* vol. 50, p. 227.

41. Hatch and Shine, p. 178.

42. Mary Burrill, "Aftermath," in *A Century of Plays by American Women,* ed. Rachel France (New York: Richards Rosen Press, Inc., 1979), pp. 55–61. All quotes and references to the play are based upon this source.

43. France, p. 50.

44. Mary Burrill, "They That Sit in Darkness," in *Black Theater U.S.A.: Forty-Five Plays by Black Americans, 1847–1974,* eds. James V. Hatch and Ted Shine (New York: The Free Press, 1974), pp. 179–183. All quotes and references to the play are based upon this source.

45. Myrtle Smith Livingston, "For Unborn Children," in *Black Theater U.S.A.: Forty-Five Plays by Black Americans, 1847–1974,* eds. James V. Hatch and Ted Shine (New York: The Free Press, 1974), pp. 184–187. All quotes and references to the play are based upon this source.

46. Hatch and Shine, p. 184.

47. Davis and Peplow, pp. 70–72.

48. Willis Richardson, ed. *Plays and Pageants From the Life of the Negro,* (Washington D.C.: The Associated Publishers, 1930), p. vii.

49. Winifred L. Stoeling, "May Miller," *DLB,* vol. 41, p. 242.

50. Goldfarb and Wilson, p. 431.

51. May Miller, "Graven Images," in *Plays and Pageants From the Life of the Negro,* ed. Willis Richardson (Washington D.C.: The Associated Publishers, 1930), pp. 109–137. All quotes and references to the play are based upon this source.

52. May Miller, "Samory" and "Christophe's Daughters," in *Negro History in Thirteen Plays,* eds. Willis Richardson and May Miller (Washington D.C.: The Associated Publishers, 1930), pp. 289–311 and 241–261 respectively. All quotes and references to these plays are based upon this source.

53. Stoeling, p. 247.

54. Hatch and Shine, p. 351.

55. May Miller, "Harriet Tubman" and "Sojourner Truth," in *Negro History in Thirteen Plays,* eds. Willis Richardson and May Miller (Washington D.C.: The Associated Publishers, 1935), pp. 265–288 and 313–333 respectively. All quotes and references to these plays are based upon this source.

56. Georgia Douglas Johnson, "William and Ellen Craft" and "Frederick Douglass," in *Negro History in Thirteen Plays,* eds. Willis Richardson and May Miller (Washington D.C.: The Associated Publishers, 1935), pp. 164–186 and 143–162 respectively. All quotes and references to these plays are based upon this source.

57. Davis and Peplow, p. 250.

58. Brown, pp. 115–123.

59. May Miller, "Riding the Goat," in *Plays and Pageants From the Life of the Negro,* ed. Willis Richardson (Washington D.C.: The Associated Publishers, 1930), pp. 141–176. All quotes and references to the play are based upon this source.

60. Georgia Douglas Johnson, "Plumes," in *A Century of Plays by American Women,* ed. Rachel France (New York: Richards Rosen Press, Inc., 1979), pp. 74–78. All quotes and references to the play are based upon this source.

61. France, p. 75.

62. In a phone conversation on April 25, 1988, Kathy Perkins, a researcher of plays by black women before 1950, confirmed that Eulalie Spence died in 1981.

63. Eulalie Spence, "Undertow," in *Black Theater U.S.A.: Forty-Five Plays by Black Americans, 1847–1974,* eds. James V. Hatch and Ted Shine (New York: The Free Press, 1974), pp. 192–200. All quotes and references to the play are based upon this source.

64. Ruth Gaines-Shelton, "The Church Fight," in *Black Theater U.S.A.: Forty-Five Plays by Black Americans, 1847–1974,* eds. James V. Hatch and Ted Shine (New York: The Free Press, 1974), pp. 189–191. All quotes and references to the play are based upon this source.

65. Oscar Brockett, *Historical Edition: The Theatre* (New York: Holt, Rinehart, and Winston, 1979), p. 382.

66. Hatch and Shine, p. 188.

67. Ibid., p. 201.

68. Marita Bonner, "The Purple Flower," in *Black Theater U.S.A.: Forty-Five Plays by Black Americans, 1847–1974,* eds. James V. Hatch and Ted Shine (New York: The Free Press, 1974), pp. 202–207. All quotes and references to the play are based upon this source.

69. Hatch and Shine, p. 201.

Lorraine Hansberry

Ntozake Shange

Alice Childress

2

Alice Childress, Lorraine Hansberry, Ntozake Shange: Carving a Place for Themselves on the American Stage

Early twentieth-century black women playwrights paved a way for the next generation of black women dramatists, as Margaret Wilkerson contends in *9 Plays by Black Women*:

> Women playwrights before 1950 were full partners in the theatre's protest against conditions for blacks, whether in the form of 'race propaganda,' folk plays, or historical dramas. They also made the unique perspective of black women's reality a part of that protest. Not until mid-century, however, would their voices reach beyond their communities into the highly competitive world of professional theatre.[1]

It is out of this long and groundbreaking tradition that three of America's most talented black women playwrights have emerged. Alice Childress, Lorraine Hansberry, and Ntozake Shange, the three principal authors to be discussed in remaining pages, have profited from the theatrical breakthroughs made by the women playwrights of the Harlem Renaissance, many of whom continued to write during the 1930s and 1940s.

The works of Childress, Hansberry, and Shange are crucial links in the development of black playwriting in America from the 1950s to 1980s. Traditionally, the American theater has excluded women, particularly black women. It is because of their dogged determination to have their voices heard that these black women dramatists have been able to carve an indelible place for themselves on the American stage. Each has made significant contributions to the development of theater in America, particularly black theater. An examination of their plays reveals that their works are both similar to and different from plays written by black males between the 1950s and 1980s.

Beginning in the 1950s, black women playwrights, like their male coun-terparts, made considerable efforts to create new images of blacks and to counteract stereotypes that had been presented in earlier decades by white dramatists and by some black playwrights who had conformed to standards that were acceptable on the American stage. Before 1950, with the exception of Harlem Renaissance efforts, black male and female playwrights had a difficult time securing professional productions because there was not a great demand for plays about black life, and the plays about black life that were being produced were authored by well-known white dramatists. The theater-going public was largely white [tickets were beyond the means of most blacks, who had not fully recovered from the Great Depression of a decade previously], and because white dramatists frequently presented fa-miliar stereotypes, black playwrights had a difficult time competing. Langs-ton Hughes once observed, "Sometimes I think whites are more appreciative of our uniqueness than we are ourselves. The white 'black' artists dealing in Negro material have certainly been financially more successful than any of us real Negroes have ever been."[2]

Genevieve Fabre, in *Afro-American Poetry and Drama, 1760–1975,* contends that the 1950s saw the definite emergence of black playwrights who could and did compete with highly crafted plays. Fabre points out that William Branch's *A Medal for Willie* (1951), Alice Childress' *Trouble in Mind* (1955), Lorraine Hansberry's *A Raisin in the Sun* (1959), and Loften Mitchell's *A Land Beyond the River* (1957), are among the best-known plays by black playwrights of the 1950s.[3] These and other writers of the period wrote on an array of subjects that were defined by such historical events as the Korean war, McCarthyism, the Supreme Court decision favoring school integra-tion, Martin Luther King, Jr. and the Civil Rights Movement. The deni-gration of black soldiers who returned triumphantly from World War II is a major theme in plays of the 1950s. One case in point is Branch's *A Medal for Willie,* which explores sensitively the invalidation of the contributions of African American soldiers who were often more mistreated by their own countrymen than by foreign enemies.

In the majority of these plays protest is voiced, but violence as a solution is dismissed. The message in several of these plays, however, is that violence may soon become the only possible course of action. Mance Williams, in *Black Theatre in the 1960s and 1970s,* argues that "plays during the 1950s expressed a new form of protest, one that not only exhorted Black people to stand up for their rights but warned Whites that Blacks would settle for nothing less than their full share of the American Dream."[4] These play-wrights indicate that the hope of blacks lies in the fortitude and strength of black people. Characters in these plays are often assertive and strong-willed; they hold firm to their right to speak freely and on their own terms. The old images and stereotypes of the servile blacks are almost nonexistent in nearly all of these plays.

The 1960s saw a more radical, militant theater with Amiri Baraka (LeRoi Jones) at its head. Williams has observed that "whether playwrights of the 1960s fell into the category of realism/naturalism, Marxism or structuralism, the prevailing mood of the period was that of revolt, outside and inside the theatre."[5] Writers of this revolutionary theater accuse whites of persecuting or victimizing blacks but chastise blacks for facilitating their own victimization. Plays of this militant theater generally center on violent verbal and/ or physical confrontation between blacks and whites. Baraka shows in *Dutchman* (1963) that blacks remain victims when they refuse to rid themselves of middle-class sensibilities forbidding the liberating act: violence. James Baldwin's *Blues for Mister Charlie* (1964) asserts that blacks will remain victims as long as they depend on white liberals to free them from racial injustices. Like Baraka and Baldwin, Hansberry, in *The Drinking Gourd* (1960) and Childress in *Wedding Band* (1966), express anger, disappointment, and a sense of helplessness during the 1960s. Though less overtly violent than Baraka's plays, the works of Childress and Hansberry are an outgrowth of the militant tradition in that their black characters are atypically assertive, brutally caustic, and unyielding to the demands of whites. Other playwrights of the revolutionary theater include Sonia Sanchez and Martie Charles, whose plays, generally speaking, advocate that blacks disassociate themselves from the decadent white society and its values.

Following the ritualistic dramas of the 1960s, black theater began devoting itself to the building of the black nation. A great deal of black drama since the 1960s deals with black awareness or black consciousness and incorporates black music, dance, language, and lifestyles as integral parts of form. This drama of self-celebration aims at capturing the flavor of the black experience and at uniting black people, such as Joseph Walker's *The River Niger* (1973) and Leslie Lee's *The First Breeze of Summer* (1975). Characters in these plays are not exotically caricatured; they are simple, down-to-earth, loving, suffering, laughing blacks preoccupied with living and surviving. Ed Bullins (*The Fabulous Miss Marie,* 1971 and *The Taking of Miss Janie,* 1975), Ron Milner (*What the Wine Sellers Buy,* 1973), and Lonne Elder III (*Ceremonies in Dark Old Men,* 1969), are generally regarded as the leading playwrights of this type of drama. With the steadily growing interest in the works of black women playwrights, however, the established canon is quickly broadening to include plays by Alice Childress, Martie Charles, and Ntozake Shange as poignant dramas of self-celebration.

A close examination of the plays of black women between the 1950s and 1980s reveals that, though they treat many of the same themes as black male dramatists, their vision is different. Unlike their male counterparts, Childress, Hansberry, and Shange have brought to the American stage a multiplicity of images of female heroines and have not confined themselves to such limiting images of black women as immoral, promiscuous, wanton, frigid, overbearing, or pathetically helpless.

Some of the major playwrights of the period have risen to prominence on the backs of narrow portrayals of black women. In Louis Peterson's *Take A Giant Step* (1953), the mother is self-effacing, the grandmother is conniving and domineering, and the three other females are manipulative prostitutes. Ed Bullins, in the naturalistic *Goin' A Buffalo* (1966), writes about the vile-mouthed Pandora and the pathetic prostitute, Mama Too Tight. In Lonne Elder's *Ceremonies in Dark Old Men* (1969), the daughter helplessly falls victim to disillusionment and bitterness. Ted Shine, in *Herbert III* (1974), portrays Margarette as a frigid woman who emotionally wounds the men of her family.

The portraits of black life simply are not complete without the unique perspectives of women. Peopling their plays with heroines who are challenging, innovative, and multidimensional, Childress, Hansberry, and Shange are frontrunners in the development of black playwriting and, thus, warrant serious critical study.

Alice Childress is the only black woman playwright in America whose plays have been written, produced, and published over a period of four decades. Like a giant in a straitjacket, Childress has remained faithful to the American theater even when it has looked upon her with blind eyes and turned to her with deaf ears. Having had plays produced in New York City, across the United States, and in Europe, Childress' legacy to the American theater is monumental. In her thirty-eight years of writing for the American stage, Childress admits that she has never compromised her vision. Her sagacity and total commitment became apparent when she, almost in a whisper commented, "I will not keep quiet, and I will not stop telling the truth."[6] Though she writes mainly about the genteel poor, a diverse audience looks to her for the truth that she gives to them in numerous small doses and without adulteration.

Alice Childress has written plays that incorporate the liturgy of the black church, traditional music, African mythology, folklore, and fantasy. She has experimented by writing sociopolitical, romantic, biographical, historical, and feminist plays. Striving to find new and dynamic ways of expressing old themes in an historically conservative theater, Childress has opened the door for other black playwrights, particularly Hansberry and Shange, to make dramaturgical advances. Her litany of "firsts" invariably paved the way for a line of black women playwrights to insist upon craft and integrity over commercialism. Doris Abramson writes, "Alice Childress has been, from the beginning, a crusader and a writer who refuses to compromise. . . . She refuses productions of her plays if the producer wants to change them in any way that distorts her intentions."[7]

Alice Childress writes about poor women for whom the act of living is sheer heroism. In fact, Childress' own background resembles that of the heroines in her plays. In a recent essay, "Knowing the Human Condition," Childress acknowledges that her grandmother was a slave. Claiming that she is neither proud nor ashamed of her past, Childress has observed:

> I was raised in Harlem by very poor people. My grandmother who went to fifth grade in the Jim Crow school system of South Carolina inspired me to observe what was around me and write about it without false pride or shame.[8]

Indeed, her poor, dejected heroines are depicted as morally strong, sometimes vulnerable, but resilient. She portrays these women honestly as they fight daily battles not just to survive but to survive whole.

Childress' contributions to the American theater have been varied and consistent.[9] In the early 1940s, Childress helped to found the American Negro Theater (ANT), a phenomenal organization that served as a beacon of hope for countless black playwrights, actors, and producers, such as Sidney Poitier, Ossie Davis, Ruby Dee, Frank Silvera, and others. ANT, like the African Grove Theatre that was founded in 1821–1822 and marks the beginning of "alternative theatre" for blacks, has been instrumental in institutionalizing black theater.[10] Another major achievement of Childress, a long time Broadway and off-Broadway actress and a member of the Author's League of the Dramatists' Guild, is that she was instrumental in the early 1950s in initiating advanced, guaranteed pay for union off-Broadway contracts in New York City.

Childress became one of the beneficiaries of her efforts to establish equity standards for off-Broadway productions. Her first two plays, *Just a Little Simple* (1950) and *Gold Through the Trees* (1952), were the first plays by a black woman to be professionally produced, i.e., performed by unionized actors. Three years later, Childress became the first black woman to win the Obie Award for the best original, off-Broadway play of the year with her production of *Trouble in Mind* (1955), which was subsequently produced by the BBC in London. Ten years later, Childress' *Wedding Band* (1966) was broadcast nationally on ABC television. *Wine in the Wilderness* (1969) was presented on National Educational Television (NET). With all of the kudos of a seasoned playwright, the author basked in the glory of the officially designated Alice Childress Week in Columbia and Charleston during the production of *Sea Island Song* (1979), commissioned by the South Carolina Arts Commission to capture the flavor of the Gullah-speaking people of the area.

As a result of Childress' innovative achievements and commitment to quality theater, she has been the recipient of a host of awards and honors, including writer-in-residence at the MacDowell Colony; featured author on a BBC panel discussion on "The Negro in the American Theater;" winner of a Rockefeller grant administered through The New Dramatists and a John Golden Fund for Playwrights; and a Harvard appointment to the

Radcliffe Institute for Independent Study (now Mary Ingraham Bunting Institute), from which she received a graduate medal for work completed during her tenure.

Serving as spokesperson for the masses of poor, Childress continues to write about "the complexity of relationships between blacks and whites and the various ways blacks survive in contemporary society."[11] Sharply observant and unsentimental, she is one of the most influential theater pioneers whose works serve as a precursor to the black naturalistic plays of the 1960s, and whose efforts substantially shaped the ethnic theater of black experience of the 1970s and 1980s.

Alice Childress, born on October 12, 1920, in Charleston South Carolina, is an actress, playwright, novelist, essayist, columnist, lecturer, and theater consultant. At the age of five, Childress boarded a train for New York where she grew up in Harlem. Childress attended Public School 81, The Julia Ward Howe Junior High School and, for three years, Wadleigh High School, at which time she had to drop out because both her grandmother and mother had died, leaving her to fend for herself. Forced to assume the responsibility of teaching herself, Childress discovered the public library and attempted to read two books a day.

Beginning in the early 1940s, Childress began establishing herself as an actress and writer, during which time she worked to support herself and her only child, Jean, in a number of odd jobs, including assistant machinist, photo retoucher, domestic worker, salesperson, and insurance agent. Harris believes that "the variety of experiences and the constant contact with working-class people undoubtedly influenced Childress' approach to the development of characters and her overall writing philosophy. Her characters in fiction and drama included domestic workers, washerwomen, seamstresses, and the unemployed, as well as dancers, artists, and teachers."[12]

Alice Childress has to her credit fourteen plays, six of which will be discussed in the remainder of this chapter and in succeeding ones: *Florence,* pr. 1949, pb. 1950; *Just a Little Simple,* pr. 1950; *Gold Through the Trees,* pr. 1952; *Trouble in Mind,* pr. 1955, pb. 1971; *Wedding Band: A Love/Hate Story in Black and White,* pr. 1966, pb. 1973; *The World on a Hill,* pb. 1968; *String,* pr. 1969, pb. 1971; *The Freedom Drum,* retitled *Young Martin Luther King,* pr. 1969; *Wine in the Wilderness,* pr. 1969, pb. 1974; *Mojo: A Black Love Story,* pr. 1970, pb. 1971; *When the Rattlesnake Sounds,* pb. 1975; *Let's Hear it for the Queen,* pb. 1976; *Sea Island Song,* pr. 1977, retitled *Gullah,* pr. 1984; *Moms,* pr. 1987. A versatile and prolific writer, Childress has published four novels, including *Like One of the Family: Conversations from a Domestic's Life* (1956), *A Hero Aint Nothin but a Sandwich* (1973), which was made into a movie, *A Short Walk* (1979), and *Rainbow Jordan* (1981). Additionally, she is editor of *Black Scenes: Collection of Scenes from Plays Written by Black People about Black Experience* (1971), and author of an impressive host of essays on black art and theater history. Though she demonstrates skill in a variety of literary forms, Childress considers herself principally a playwright.

Childress' first play, *Florence,* produced by the American Negro Theatre in 1949, levels an indictment against presumptuous whites who think they know more about blacks than blacks know about themselves. It is also a play about a need for blacks to reject stereotyped roles. On another level, *Florence* pays tribute to black parents who encourage their children to reach their fullest potential at all cost. It reveals Childress' superb skill at characterization, dialogue, and conflict.

Florence is set in a Jim Crow railway station where Mama discovers that Mrs. Carter, a white liberal, is irrepressibly racist. Mama, awaiting a train bound for Harlem, confides in Mrs. Carter that her daughter has been able to secure only minor and infrequent theater roles. Vehemently trying to persuade Mama to make Florence give up her dreams of becoming an actress before she becomes completely disillusioned, Mrs. Carter explains that Florence's efforts are futile, especially since she, a white woman, is an actress who cannot find work. Mama becomes outraged when, after asking her to help her daughter, Mrs. Carter speaks of getting Florence a job as a maid. Resolving not to go to New York, Mama sends her last money to Florence with a note attached saying "keep trying."

The theme of rejecting stereotypes and of not compromising one's integrity is further explored in Childress' *Trouble in Mind,* which was produced at the Greenwich Mews Theatre in New York in 1955. Running for ninety-one performances, *Trouble in Mind* won for Childress the Obie Award for the best original off-Broadway play of the 1955–1956 season and was subsequently produced twice in 1964 by the BBC in London.[13] When offered a Broadway option, Childress refused because the producer wanted her to make radical script changes. Alice Childress says of her rejection of the Broadway offer, "Most of our problems have not seen the light of day in our works, and much has been pruned from our manuscripts before the public has been allowed a glimpse of a finished work. It is ironical that those who oppose us are in a position to dictate the quality of our contributions."[14]

Childress' *Trouble in Mind* needed "pruning" because it is a satiric drama about white writers, producers, and directors who, because they are ignorant of blacks, support or defend inaccurate portraits. Childress insists in this drama that blacks must maintain their integrity and identity in the theater, refusing to accept roles that characterize them as exotic or half-human creatures, regardless of the monetary losses.

Making use of the play-within-a-play, *Trouble in Mind* is set on a Broadway stage where the characters rehearse *Chaos in Belleville,* a play written by a white about blacks. Wiletta Mayer, a veteran black actress, offends the sensibilities of the white director when she asserts that no black mother, as in *Chaos in Belleville,* would tell her son to give himself up to be lynched, regardless of his innocence or guilt. Appalled by other untruths, Wiletta announces that she will not perform unless some changes are made in the script. Because of her frankness, she is summarily dropped from the cast.

Trouble in Mind, Childress' first professionally produced play outside of Harlem, received glowing reviews. Loften Mitchell, in *Black Drama,* commented, "Now the professional theatre saw her outside of her native Harlem, writing with swift stabs of humor, her perception and her consummate dramatic gifts."[15] Equally laudatory is the assessment made by Arthur Gelb of the *New York Times,* who says that Childress has "some witty and penetrating things to say about the dearth of roles for Negro actors in contemporary theatre, the cut-throat competition for these parts and the fact that Negro actors often find themselves playing stereotyped roles in which they cannot bring themselves to believe."[16]

Like *Trouble in Mind, Wedding Band* (1966) was deemed controversial and missed Broadway because of Childress' refusal to make script changes that would alter her intent. Produced at the University of Michigan in 1969, and at the Public Theatre in New York during the 1972–1973 season, *Wedding Band* became the first play by Childress to be televised nationally on ABC in 1974.[17] *Wedding Band* centers around an interracial love affair that is destroyed by white and black bigotry. The theme that emerges is that blacks and whites must learn to judge each other on individual merit, instead of blaming an entire race each time a white-black relationship, intimate or casual, terminates.

Set in a small town in South Carolina in 1918, the plot revolves around Julia and Herman, who have been secretly meeting for ten years because of state laws forbidding interracial marriage. Giving Julia a wedding band on a chain that she can wear only around her neck until they leave the South, Herman encourages her to go to New York to prepare for his coming within a year, at which time he hopes to have settled a debt owed his mother. Calamity strikes when Herman falls sick with influenza at Julia's house in the heart of the black community, an occurrence that outrages both whites and blacks. The promised escape to the North never materializes, and Herman dies in Julia's arms.

Wedding Band, subtitled *A Love/Hate Story in Black and White,* received mixed reviews. Clive Barnes of the *New York Times* wrote, "Indeed its strength lies very much in the poignancy of its star-cross'd lovers, but whereas Shakespeare's lovers had a fighting chance, there is no way that Julia and Herman are going to beat the system. Niggers and crackers are more irreconcilable than any Montagues and Capulets."[18] In quite a different vein, Loften Mitchell commented, "Miss Childress writes with a sharp, satiric touch. . . . Characterizations are piercing, her observations devastating. . . . The play reaches a rousing climax when the Negro woman defines for a white woman exactly what the Negro has meant in terms of Southern lives.[19]

Following *Wedding Band,* Childress wrote *Wine in the Wilderness,* which was aired on National Educational Television (NET) in 1969. Set in Harlem in 1960 during a race riot, this play pokes fun at bourgeois affectation and is one of the first plays about middle-class Negro life by a black woman playwright. Childress levels an attack at blacks who scream blackness, brotherhood, and togetherness but who have no love or empathy for poor, uneducated, and unrefined blacks. Tomorrow Marie, the dynamic heroine, is dragged in from the violence of the riots only to experience the emotional violence inherent in the discovery that her new associates think that she is the dregs of society, a poor black woman who is crass. Serving as a catalyst for the growth of Bill Jameson, Cynthia, and Sonny-Man, Tomorrow Marie calls them phoney niggers and teaches them the ugliness of their own superciliousness.

Wine in the Wilderness is Childress at her best. Hatch and Shine note that, "The beauty of *Wine in the Wilderness* is in part due to the author's sensitive treatment of Tommy. . . . Alice Childress has created a powerful, new black heroine who emerges from the depths of the black community, offering a sharp contrast to the typically strong 'Mama' figure that dominates such plays as *Raisin in the Sun.*"[20]

Another play by Childress in which the heroine serves as a catalyst for growth is *Mojo: A Black Love Story,* produced at the New Harlem Theatre in 1970.[21] *Mojo* is a domestic drama dealing with the misfortunes and misunderstandings of a poverty-stricken black couple who, though they love each other, have spent the bulk of their lives apart and hurting. Teddy's ex-wife, Irene, returns unexpectedly for emotional support as she readies herself for cancer surgery. Each recalls the mistakes of earlier days and comes to realize the strength fostered by uncovering past anger, wounds, and fears. Childress' perceptions are devastatingly accurate in this complex drama where people are pressured into causing each other pain because of financial exigency. The author skillfully, but without condoning or relieving the black couple of their past indiscretions, depicts two people who have survived rats, garbage, and minimum wages earned for cleaning toilets.

Unlike Childress' other plays, her historical dramas have not met with a great deal of success. Barbara Molette argues, "It's not that black playwrights have not written historical plays; it's that we have a difficult time getting them produced."[22] Like the early black women playwrights of the Harlem Renaissance, such as May Miller and Georgia Douglas Johnson, Alice Childress' historical heroines have remained silent. One case in point is Childress' *When the Rattlesnake Sounds* (1975), which has no record of a professional production. This children's play illustrates Harriet Tubman's commitment, strength, and fear during the days of the Underground Railroad. Childress' talent in this play has not gone unrecognized as critic Zena Sutherland comments, "the play is moving because of its subject and impressive because of the deftness with which Childress develops characters and background in so brief and static a setting."[23]

Alice Childress writes because she is compelled to tell the truth about black life in America. According to C.W.E. Bigsby, in *A Critical Introduction to Twentieth-Century American Drama*, "Childress' humanism is evident, and her resistance to ruling political and cultural orthodoxies apparent."[24] She is a writer of great discipline, power, substance, wit, and integrity. A pioneer in the theater, Childress' steadfast efforts of forty years have substantially shaped black playwriting in America.

Signing L.H. in 1950 to the first review of an Alice Childress play, *Florence*, the critic touted the author as "our first" and "our best."[25] Alice Childress had left a mark on this young *Freedom* reviewer who eventually picked up a pen to tell her own truths in *A Raisin in the Sun* (1959). Lorraine Hansberry had seen productions of Childress' plays in Harlem and was impressed, as is evident by the striking linkages between their plays, particularly *Florence* and *A Raisin in the Sun*. Like Mama in *Florence*, Lena Younger in *A Raisin in the Sun* is portrayed as strong, unabashed, compassionate, reflective, and supportive. The children of these two women are their prime concerns, and they encourage them to fulfill dreams against all odds. Noteworthy is the fact that presumptuous whites attempt to place restrictions or harnesses on the families in both plays. Lorraine Hansberry apparently held Childress as a role model, a springboard from which to carve a new and broader place for black women on the American stage.

Lorraine Hansberry revolutionized black theater in America when her play *A Raisin in the Sun* became the first play on Broadway by an African American woman. This trailblazing play won for Hansberry the coveted New York Drama Critics Circle Award, making her the fifth woman, the youngest playwright, and the first black woman in America to be so honored.[26] Theophilus Lewis has written that the emotional impact of the play "among the lay audience as well as the critics was one of unrestrained enthusiasm. The play was an overnight hit."[27]

Several phenomenal occurrences are associated with this historical production. First, Lloyd Richards became the first black producer on Broadway of a play by and about blacks with essentially a black cast.[28] Second, this show was financially solvent. It was perhaps the most artistically and financially successful Broadway show by an African American. Loften Mitchell wrote, "*A Raisin in the Sun* not only won the Critics Circle Award; it made money. And it projected its cast members beautifully."[29] Third, never in theater history had such large numbers of blacks supported a Broadway show. James Baldwin noted, at the Philadelphia tryout, that he had never in his life seen so many black people in the theater. Additionally, he stated that never before in American theater history had so much of the truth of black people's lives been seen on stage.[30] It was, indeed, Hansberry's realistic portrayals that drew blacks to join the large number of whites going to see *A Raisin in the Sun*.

Opening on Broadway on March 11, 1959, *A Raisin in the Sun* successfully ran for 538 performances and has since become a classic.[31] Evidence of its greatness and popular appeal is that Hansberry's stageplay was made into a movie by Columbia Pictures in 1961, and produced on Broadway in 1975 as a musical, adapted by Judd Woldin and Robert Brittan, who won a Tony Award for this show.[32] Lorraine Hansberry's contribution to American theater is magnified by the fact that two of her other plays were produced on Broadway: *The Sign in Sidney Brustein's Window* (1964) and the post-humously produced *Les Blancs* (1970).

Hansberry's plays are basically sociopolitical. She recalls the incidents that shaped her vision, and thus her writing, in her autobiography *To Be Young, Gifted and Black*:

> I was born on the Southside of Chicago. I was born black and female. . . . I have been personally the victim of physical attack which was the offspring of racial and political hysteria. . . . I have . . . on a thousand occasions seen indescribable displays of man's very real inhumanity to man, and I have come to maturity, as we all must, knowing that greed and malice, and indifference to human misery and bigotry and corruption, brutality and perhaps, above all else, ignorance—the prime ancient and persistent enemy of man—abound in the world.[33]

A sensitive, ever-curious visionary, Hansberry was unable to remain aloof from the momentous social events of the 1950s and 1960s, including the beginning of the Cold War between Russia and the United States, the tumultuous roarings of the Civil Rights Movement and its ramifications, the Vietnam War coupled with the ignominy experienced by black soldiers and their families who had survived past wars, and the growing intransigence of Colored peoples across the globe.

Hansberry's life was such that she could have written little that would not have been sociopolitical. Hansberry once said, "All art is ultimately socio-political. . . . The writer is deceived who thinks he has some other choice. The question is not whether one will make a social statement in one's work—but only what the statement will say, for if it says anything, it will be social."[34] A resolute activist, Hansberry has written on a host of subjects, including the deferred dreams of African Americans, self-determination of African countries, the interconnection between Africans and African Americans, an appreciation of the beauty of things African and of things black, the evils of the slave system and its continuing impact on blacks, materialism, spiritual poverty, male chauvinism, homosexuality, bohemianism, middle-class values, nuclear holocaust, exile and isolation, women's rights, interracial friendships, the dilemma of black mothers, and the affirmation of dignity in a world that devalues integrity.

One of the most important achievements made by Hansberry was that she revolutionized the way Americans, blacks and whites, perceived Africans. Whereas Langston Hughes, Countee Cullen, and others turned a romantic eye to Africa, tantamount to a "wispy literary yearning after a lost primitivism" to be beaten out on "synthetic tomtoms," Lorraine Hansberry presented a more realistic picture of Africa and its people.[35] Asagai in *A Raisin in the Sun* and Tshembe Matoseh in *Les Blancs* are African men who are extremely literate, racially proud, revolutionary, cultured, and sensitive. With her pen, Hansberry destroyed the myth, perpetuated by the media, of the wild, savage, ugly, naked creature given to carnivorous pillaging. Asagai is held up as a handsome and proud man, particularly when Mama teases Beneatha about the pretty thing that just walked out of the apartment. Mama tells Beneatha that she understands why Africa has all of a sudden become so important. Asagai's blackness is portrayed positively. For this alone Hansberry deserves a permanent place in American theater history.

Lorraine Hansberry, born in Chicago, Illinois on May 19, 1930, was a dramatist, film and television scriptwriter, novelist, poet, book and drama critic, and essayist. This brilliant artist/activist helped usher in a new era.[36] Born to real estate broker and developer Carl A. Hansberry, and former school teacher Nanny Perry Hansberry, Lorraine and her two brothers, Carl Jr. and Perry, and her sister Mamie, were reared by educated, refined parents who provided material comfort and intellectual stimulation. Harold Isaacs points out that Hansberry's father's house "was full of books" and that when she was about nine, she started reading black poets, including Langston Hughes, Countee Cullen, and Waring Cuney, who provided her with her first and enduring images of Africa. Isaacs recalls Hansberry telling him that she "was deeply influenced by them, and their images of Africa were marvelous and beautiful."[37]

Into her parents home came such black giants as Paul Robeson, Duke Ellington, Walter White, Joe Louis, and Jesse Owens. Surrounded by black culture, politics, and economics, Hansberry watched her father, an active member of the NAACP and the Urban League, fight to get a U.S. Supreme Court decision that made segregated housing illegal in Chicago. Though de facto segregation continued to exist in housing areas in Chicago, Lorraine Hansberry learned at an early age that those who are economically secure have a duty to help those who are not. Hansberry's black consciousness was also raised by her uncle, William Leo Hansberry, a Howard University professor and internationally renowned scholar of African history.

Graduating from Englewood High School in 1948, Lorraine Hansberry enrolled at the University of Wisconsin. At the university she was exposed to and influenced by such playwrights as Strindberg, Ibsen, and Sean O'Casey whose *Juno and the Paycock* is reported to have made a tremendous impact on her. Coupled with the inspiration fostered by productions that she had enjoyed of *Othello* and *The Tempest* back in Chicago, Hansberry began thinking of theater as her medium. Performing poorly in courses related to math and science because of elementary and high school experiences in inner-city, Jim Crow schools, Hansberry left the University in 1950 without a degree and moved to New York.

It was in Harlem that Hansberry observed her people's ability to survive in oppressive surroundings. Marching on picket lines, speaking on Harlem streetcorners, and taking part in delegations to rescue persons unjustly convicted of crimes, Hansberry's commitment to civil rights and her obligation to write about the ills of society were cemented. Abramson points out that when Hansberry moved to New York in 1950, "she began hanging around little theatre groups and discovered that 'theatre embraces everything that I like all at once.'"[38] From 1950 to 1953, Hansberry wrote a host of essays and reviewed books and plays for Paul Robeson's radical black newspaper, *Freedom*. It was during her tenure at *Freedom* that Hansberry came to know and appreciate plays by Alice Childress, Loften Mitchell, William Branch, and other black dramatists.[39] Like these playwrights, Hansberry wrote of blacks' indomitable spirit of survival.

In 1953, Lorraine Hansberry embarked on an interracial marriage with aspiring writer and graduate student in English, Robert Nemiroff, that would end in divorce in 1964. Also in 1953, she resigned from full-time work at *Freedom* in order to write. From 1953 to 1956, Hansberry worked on a wealth of sociopolitical essays and plays while budgeting time for a series of part-time jobs, including typist, worker in the garment fur industry, recreation leader at the Federation for the Handicapped, and production assistant in a theatrical firm. Turning increasingly to a play that she originally entitled *The Crystal Stair,* inspired by Langston Hughes' poem "Mother to Son," Hansberry later changed it to *A Raisin in the Sun,* completing it in 1957. Hansberry's husband, Nemiroff, arranged for the play to be read to his wealthy and influential friends Burt D'Lugoff and Philip Rose who opened Broadway theater doors. With the 1959 Broadway production of *A Raisin in the Sun,* the American theater took a quantum leap in the direction of recognizing black playwrights as legitimate artists and conduits of African American culture.

From 1959 to 1964, Hansberry worked on four plays: *The Drinking Gourd, What Use Are Flowers?, The Sign in Sidney Brustein's Window,* and *Les Blancs.* Though she was diagnosed as having cancer in 1963, she continued to serve as a vital, leading spokesperson in the Civil Rights Movement. A sensitive and impassioned black activist, Hansberry never succumbed to despair and cynicism, as is apparent in her comment, "I wish to live, because life has within it that which is good; that which is beautiful and that which is love. Therefore, since I have known all of these things, I have found them reason enough—and I wish to live. Moreover, because this is so, I wish others to live for generations and generations and generations."[40] Lorraine Hansberry died of pancreatic cancer at age 34 on January 12, 1965.[41] Loften Mitchell wrote, "And a part of every Negro theatrical worker died, too."[42] Hansberry's legacy, however, lives on, particularly in *A Raisin in the Sun, The Drinking Gourd,* and *What Use Are Flowers?*

A Raisin in the Sun was first presented at the Ethel Barrymore Theatre in New York City on March 11, 1959. Essentially, this prize-winning play is about an impoverished black family whose members strive to better their estate and maintain dignity and pride in the face of economic and social inequity. Hansberry proposes that black family unity can survive only if its members, both African American and African, come together to form a fortress against any force that manipulates, threatens, or oppresses. Theophilus Lewis suggests that "If there is a message in Miss Hansberry's drama, it is that Negroes have to be tough to survive. Indeed, we see Negroes under pressure throughout the play."[43] One conclusion that is certainly insubstantial is that the play is about integration, as Harold Cruse argues in *The Crisis of the Negro Intellectual* (1968). No stronger defense of the message in *A Raisin in the Sun* can be made than Hansberry's own comments: "Moma, it is a play that tells the truth about people, Negroes and life... that we have among our miserable and downtrodden ranks—people who are the very essence of human dignity. That is what, after all the laughter and tears, the play is supposed to say. I hope, Moma, it will make you proud of me."[44]

A Raisin in the Sun takes place in the Chicago slums and revolves around what is to be done with a ten-thousand dollar life insurance check belonging to the Younger family: Lena Younger, a stalwart matriarch, wants to move her family out of the ghetto; Walter Lee, Lena's son, a thirty-five-year-old frustrated chauffeur, wants to invest in a liquor store business to give luxuries to his wife and son, Travis; Ruth, Walter Lee's wife, secretly hopes for a house, particularly since her job as a domestic will not suffice when she discovers she is pregnant, again; Beneatha, often flippant and flighty, hopes to use the money for medical school. Associated with the Younger family are the two suitors of Beneatha, Asagai, an African revolutionary and George Murchison, an African American assimilationist.

In order to keep her family together, Lena Younger, after making a $3,500 down payment on a house, entrusts Walter Lee with the remainder of the money, to put some in the bank for Beneatha's education and to invest in his liquor store business. Walter Lee gets swindled but tries to regroup by initiating steps to accept a bribe from Karl Lindner, the spokesperson for the whites who want to keep blacks out of their neighborhood. Walter Lee, at the last minute, refuses the bribe in order to preserve the family's dignity and pride and, instead, moves into the new home that no doubt will be the center of a combat zone.

A Raisin in the Sun received rave reviews from New York critics, including *The New York Times* critic Brook Atkinson, who wrote: "The play is honest. She has told the inner as well as the outer truth about a Negro family in the southside of Chicago at the present time.... *A Raisin in the Sun* has vigor as well as veracity and is likely to destroy the complacency of any one who sees it."[45] Doris Abramson best sums up the play's appeal:

A Raisin in the Sun is the first play by a Negro of which one is tempted to say, 'Everyone knows it.' Thousands of Americans have seen it on the stage in New York, in other large cities, on college campuses, and in community theatres. Many more thousands have seen it on the screen. And, finally, millions of Americans who might not seek it out have seen the movie on their television screens."[46]

Despite Hansberry's sudden rise to fame, her second play, *The Drinking Gourd* (1960), has not fared well. Hansberry was commissioned by NBC to write the first play for national television that would deal with the slavery issue from the point of view of an African American. Though scenes have been staged, *The Drinking Gourd* has yet to be professionally produced in its entirety. NBC praised the drama as superb and then placed it in a drawer.[47] Robert Nemiroff recalls trying unsuccessfully in 1965, after Hansberry's death, to secure a production of this play but was rejected: "To assorted executives at all three networks there was a new wrinkle now: *The Drinking Gourd* had become offensive. 'Well, that is, times have changed. Negroes don't want to be reminded that they once were slaves. . . . ' "[48]

Hansberry suggests in *The Drinking Gourd* that the South destroyed the way of life it sought to maintain or preserve because that way of life hinged upon the subjugation of human beings. This compelling drama is an indictment against slavery and capitalism. Margaret Wilkerson poignantly comments on Hansberry's political statements in this provocative drama. She says, "*The Drinking Gourd* explores the brutalizing effect of the U.S. slave system on all who were a part of it—master, mistress, overseer, slave. Hansberry shows how that system, set in relentless motion by greed and exploitation, is a leaderless, irresistable force that is unresponsive even to those in power who would mediate its terrifying effects."[49]

This costume drama centers around an ineffectual slave master, Hiram Sweet, who is powerless to prevent his avaricious son, Everett Sweet, from destroying what it has taken Hiram his whole life to build: a profitable plantation peopled by slaves who are supposedly treated humanely. Maria, the slave master's wife, sides with her son and helps Everett to rule without his father's knowledge and permission. Rissa, the Black Mammy and quasi confidante to Hiram, metamorphoses into a militant woman when her rebellious son, Hannibal, has his eyes gouged out—ordered by Young Master—for learning to read. Refusing to come to the aid of her master who has fallen with a heart attack, Rissa steals his gun and helps her blind son and his girlfriend, Sarah, escape to freedom. An exceptional piece of drama, *The Drinking Gourd* is unique and controversial because of Hansberry's view of the slave South as dehumanizing both black and white with its capitalistic infrastructures.

Hansberry's most experimental piece, *What Use Are Flowers?*, completed in 1962, is a fantasy play about nuclear holocaust and the possibilities for survival. In a letter to a Peking University professor, Lorraine Hansberry refers to this play by saying that it deals with an old hermit who emerges from the woods, after man has destroyed the world, and comes upon a group of children. Hansberry wrote, "The action of the play hangs upon his effort to impart to them his knowledge of the remnants of civilization which once . . . he had renounced."[50] Nemiroff argues that *What Use Are Flowers?* was Hansberry's answer to the questions of life and death, war and peace. Begun as a piece for television and then recast for the stage, Hansberry did not live to see this play produced in 1967, when three of the scenes were recorded for the radio program "Lorraine Hansberry in Her Own Words," one of which was featured in *To Be Young, Gifted and Black,* a play adapted from Hansberry's autobiography.[51] This play represents Hansberry's need to use form to express content and is the consummate example of her breadth and depth as a writer. She resisted restrictions as an artist as much as she did as an activist.

Lorraine Hansberry, reaching out to a world that was at once cruel and beautiful, broadened the boundaries of American theater to include black theater artists, playwrights, directors, actors, technical personnel, critics, and audiences. With her life and works, Lorraine Hansberry has given to the American theater what Mary McCleod Bethune offered to education, what Paul Robeson represented to acting, and what George Washington Carver bestowed upon science: a new beginning.

Seventeen years after the phenomenal run of *A Raisin in the Sun,* another play by a black woman rocked Broadway and touched the lives of blacks like no other before it. Ntozake Shange's 1976 Broadway smash hit *For Colored Girls Who Have Considered Suicide/When The Rainbow is Enuf,* the second play by a black woman to reach Broadway, marked the beginning of a new temper in American theater. Shange's *For Colored Girls* won a host of awards, including the Golden Apple, the Outer Critics Circle, the Mademoiselle, an Obie, and an Audelco, and was nominated for the Tony, Grammy, and Emmy.[52]

This box-office best seller established its author as a serious, volatile, pained American dramatist, who echoes the sentiments of women everywhere and of every race, who have been raped emotionally and physically, and who perceive themselves as exploited and unappreciated. Of the Broadway production of *For Colored Girls,* which topped *A Raisin in the Sun* with its astronomical 747 performances on Broadway,[53] Shange wrote: "the cast is enveloping almost 6,000 people a week in the words of a young black girl's growing up, her triumphs and errors, our struggle to become all that is forbidden by our environment, all that is forfeited by our gender, all that we have forgotten."[54]

Following its Broadway run, *For Colored Girls* toured London in 1977 under the auspices of the Samuel French Company and was produced as a movie for PBS in collaboration with WNET and WPBT–TV in 1982. Other plays by Shange that have been professionally produced, and will be discussed later in the chapter, include *A Photograph: A Still Life with Shadows/ A Photograph: A Study of Cruelty* (1977, 1979), *Spell #7* (1979), and *Boogie Woogie Landscapes* (1979). Shange's plays have been produced in major theaters, including the Terrace Theatre at the Kennedy Center, the Henry Street Playhouse, the Public Theatre, The Booth Theatre, Teatro de BHN in Kingston, West Indies, and the Royalty Theatre in Rio de Janeiro, Brazil.

Shange carved for herself a permanent and classic place in American theater history when she successfully broadened and redefined American theater to include the choreopoem as an acceptable, legitimate dramatic form. Not only did she popularize the choreopoem, but she brought to the American theater an art that is undeniably African. Shange's choreopoem, like African theater, is comprised of chants, poetry, dance, and rituals. With the popular appeal and commercial success of *For Colored Girls,* American theater would never be the same.

Another major achievement made by Shange is that her choreopoem encompassed so imperceptibly the particulars of black life that the substance of the piece became recognizable as universal. It is a play by, about, and for blacks, but it is also for women worldwide who need to know that they are not alone in suffering. Never before had so many women turned to a dramatic piece with admiration and support. Becoming famous overnight, Shange gave dimension and clarification to the feminist movement. Bigsby acknowledges Shange's contribution to theater when he says that "through a combination of movement, lights and music, Shange seeks to present a collage of experiences which are not the experiences of a single woman but of women in general, ranging from love to abortion to rape, from ecstasy to despair."[55]

Evoking emotional responses from across the country, her poemplays are concerned with the very peculiar or particular things that fascinate or terrify women.[56] Shange's passionate theater pieces have the power to move viewers to tears, rage, and to an undeniable rush of warmth and love. Coming from the recesses of her mutilated heart, Shange's pieces dignify women's suffering and inform females that they have a responsibility to love themselves and each other enough to resist oppression. Her female characters battle with the incomprehensible dilemma of living in a world where being female and Colored makes them twice oppressed.

Shange discovered early in life that the American patriarchy often denies injustices committed against women. She recalls her response to a reporter who tried to deny that rape exists because he had never raped anybody:

> You know, every man I meet who wants to talk about rape always wants to talk about how he never did it. Maybe we should have a congressional hearing to find out if it's the UFOs who are raping women.[57]

Denials of this type only made Shange more determined to write about, with controlled passion, women's pains, rage, anguish, and disillusionment at the hands of insensitive men who are emotionally incapable of communicating their insecurities. Written when Shange was between twenty-four and twenty-six, and after a series of failed relationships, *For Colored Girls* presents sketches of men who seem only to know how to lie, seduce, beat, rape, and abandon women.[58] Shange's stressed and often mutilated heroines band together to provide each other with the courage to become self-sufficient and self-loving to survive. Shange seems particularly disconcerted that women's suffering is not respected and insists that their lives are not only valid but valiant.[59]

The subject of much controversy, "Shange's plays not only startle and energize but also infuriate and disturb many others."[60] She seems particularly concerned for the two million children, particularly young girls, "who are abused by their parents every single year."[61] Shange's deep concern for young girls is elucidated when she says, "If there is an audience for whom I write, it's the little girls who are coming of age. I want them to know that they are not alone and that we adult women thought and continue to think about them."[62] Other themes that Shange explores include hypocrisy, racism, women's self-effacement, societal constraints on women—particularly black women—infidelity, interconnectedness of people of color, media misrepresentation of blacks, shoddy treatment of black theater artists, black middle-class values and pressures, and black spirit of survival.

Ntozake Shange (En-to-za-ke Shong-ga) was born in Trenton, New Jersey, on October 18, 1948. Playwright, novelist, poet, essayist, lecturer, educator, actress, dancer, Shange was born Paulette Williams, namesake to surgeon Paul T. Williams and Eloise Williams, a psychiatric social worker and educator. The oldest of four children, Shange's middle-class parents provided them with financial security and quality education. When Shange was eight, her parents moved to St. Louis, Missouri, where they resided for five years. St. Louis introduced her to rejection and abuse as she was bussed to a racist German-American school, but it also offered her music, dance, literature, and art. Her early struggles in St. Louis were buffered by an avid reading of her favorite authors: Mark Twain, Herman Melville, Simone de Beauvoir, and Jean Genet. Shange was also surrounded by such musicians and singers as Dizzy Gillespie, Chuck Berry, Charlie Parker, Miles Davis, Josephine Baker, and by the great intellectual, W.E.B. Dubois, all of whom were friends of her parents and directly influenced her writing.

When she was thirteen, Shange's family returned to New Jersey, where she completed high school. In her late teens she became increasingly aware of the limitations imposed upon black females in America. In 1966, at the age of eighteen, Shange attempted suicide after separating from her law-student husband. Consumed with bitterness and a deep sense of alienation, she catapulted into a series of suicide attempts, including sticking her head in a gas oven, drinking chemicals, slashing her wrist, taking an overdose of Valium, and driving her Volvo into the Pacific. These attempts were predicated upon her suppression of rage against a society that places harnesses on women.

Earning a bachelor's degree, with honors, in American studies from Barnard College in 1970, and a master's degree in American studies in 1973 from the University of Southern California, Los Angeles, Shange experienced frustration as her consciousness was being raised. While in graduate school from 1971 to 1973, she began connecting with her black literary heritage and read such authors as Margaret Walker, Ralph Ellison, Jean Toomer, Claude McKay, LeRoi Jones (Amiri Baraka), and others. In 1971, she adopted an African name. She became Ntozake (she who comes with her own things) Shange (who walks like a lion). The power of her name, perhaps, helped her redirect her life.

From 1972 to 1975, Shange taught humanities, women's and African American studies, drama, and creative writing at Sonoma State College, Mills College, and the University of California Extension while dancing and performing poetry with the Third World Collective, Raymond Sawyer's Afro-American Dance Company, West Coast Dance Works, and her own company that was then called For Colored Girls Who Have Considered Suicide.

In 1975, at the age of 27, Shange moved to New York City where her choreopoem, *For Colored Girls,* was professionally produced in New York City at Studio Rivbea in July of 1975 before moving to the New Federal Theatre, where it was produced in March of 1976, and then transferred to the Public Theatre in June of 1976, and again transferred to the Broadway Booth Theatre in September of 1976, totalling 867 performances at the four locations. Since 1975, Shange has continued to make her presence known in several genres. Author of one novella, *Sassafrass* (1977); two novels, *Sassafrass, Cypress & Indigo* (1982) and *Betsey Brown* (1985); three volumes of poetry, *Nappy Edges* (1978), *A Daughter's Geography* (1983), and *From Okra To Greens* (1984); one nonfiction book, *See No Evil: Prefaces, Essays, & Accounts, 1976–1983* (1984); and a host of critical articles in a score of journals, Shange remains associated largely with *For Colored Girls*.

A participatory theater piece resembling the style of Jean Genet, *For Colored Girls* is a compilation of twenty poems performed by seven black female characters whose names are lady in brown, yellow, orange, red, purple, blue, and green. The piece is unified by a series of shared similar experiences by characters whose names are lower-cased to represent poor, abused, self-effacing women of color. On one level, the choreopoem speaks of the physical and emotional abuse enacted against black women. On another level, however, this work is about women's possibilities, their ability to survive in the face of loneliness, rejection, pain, rape, and invalidation. The substance of the choreopoem is embedded in its title, says Shange, who feels that a rainbow, which comes after a storm, connotes the possibility "to start all over again with the power and the beauty of ourselves."[63] This theater piece that, according to Shange, is an "exploration of people's lives" provides hope for women who have known the bitterness of the storm.[64]

Shange's choreopoem is particularly enriched by several of the twenty sketches. "Now I Love Somebody More Than" and "I'm a Poet Who" speak of a black woman's need for music and dance as a means of ventillating pent-up anxieties. "Latent Rapists" centers on women who have been raped by friends—men in prominent positions—and who are afraid to press charges. "Sorry" tells of all the excuses men give when they hurt women. The most powerful poem is "A Nite With Beau Willie Brown," which deals with a maniacal wife beater who drops his two children out of the window because his mistress refuses to marry him. Finally, "A Laying on of Hands" speaks of self-love and sister sharing.

The play, in spite of its long run, received mixed reviews. Many reviewers hailed Shange's piece as provocative and poignant, including *Newsweek* critic Jack Kroll who wrote, "Shange's poems aren't war cries—they are outcries filled with controlled passion against the brutality that blasts the lives of colored girls."[65] Then there were critics like Jean Carey Bond who said, "In Shange—up to this point in her development—we have the poet's bold exploration of feeling without illumination or insight. Strewn with the corpses of failed encounters, her work is lacking in clues as to what those encounters were about in the first place and what complex human forces destroyed them."[66] One thing is certain, *For Colored Girls* touched and consoled many victimized women.

Following the long run of *For Colored Girls,* Shange published a trilogy entitled *Three Pieces,* all of which were produced but were not commercially successful. Shange's commitment to her art is apparent when she says, "These new pieces may be noncommercial, but that's what I was and still am, as far as I'm concerned—a noncommercial artist. . . . I can not allow myself to get trapped into a Broadway 'has been.' "[67]

A Photograph: Still Life With Shadows/ A Photograph: A Study of Cruelty was produced at the Public Theatre in December of 1977 and revised as *A Photograph: Lovers In Motion* for Houston's Equinox Theatre in November of 1979. In this piece, Shange explores the notion that a person's identity is not defined by things but by a belief in self. The central character is Sean David, a struggling novice photographer who is involved with a complex triad of women: Nevada is an attorney who wishes to take Sean out of the ghetto and to provide him with material comfort; Claire is a model, a cocaine addict, and a nymphomaniac who wants to possess Sean; and Michael, whom Sean chooses in the end, is a dancer who wants to help Sean fulfill his dreams. Earl, also an attorney, is a homosexual who has designs on Sean. This piece is truly lyrical and fierce. Ann Holmes of the *Houston*

Chronicle wrote; "*A Photograph* is a fascinating theatrical event in which Ms. Shange's five intertwined characters push and shove into each other's lives, making their overtures and rejections and pleas for love with seductive gestures and violent outbursts. . . . a witty, sexy, flamboyant, sometimes violent two acts."[68]

Equally as innovative is *Spell # 7,* which was produced in 1979 by Joseph Papp's New York Shakespeare Festival. Set in a bar, nine characters commiserate about racism in America, particularly in the American theater where the only roles available for blacks are degrading stereotypes, such as the neutered workhorse, the black mammy, and the promiscuous woman. *Spell # 7* is also about blacks learning to love themselves and each other. The magician casts a spell on the group telling them they are going to love being Colored. Of this powerful piece, Don Nelson of the *New York Daily News* wrote, "Ntozake Shange's *Spell # 7* is black magic. It is a celebration of blackness, the joy and pride along with the horror of it. It is a shout, a cry, a bitter laugh, a sneer. It is an extremely fine theater piece."[69]

Last in the trilogy is *Boogie Woogie Landscapes,* Shange's most experimental dramatic piece that blends surrealism and expressionism to form a fantasy world in which Layla and the other nightlife companions sing, dance, and share emotional ramifications of being black and female in America. Produced at the Terrace Theatre of the Kennedy Center in June of 1980, this piece suggests that it is not so good to be born a girl when females are infibulated, excised, clitorectomized, and are still afraid of molesters and rapists. Speaking of *Boogie Woogie Landscapes,* Anne Welsh of *The Washington Star* wrote, "Shange is a major poet, both in and out of theater."[70]

Ntozake Shange is a gifted poet/playwright. Her style, one of dazzling feminist rhetoric and evocative poetry, is fascinating, powerful, and aggressive. A definite new temper in the American theater, Shange continues to blend music, dance, and poetry to express the misery and ecstasy of being alive, female, and black in America.

Three of America's finest playwrights, Alice Childress, Lorraine Hansberry, and Ntozake Shange, came to the theater because they were compelled to speak out against the enormous disparity between the poor and rich, black and white, and women and men. Telling truths that are at once provincial and universal, each one has carved for herself a unique place on the American stage, either by slow, persistent chipping, as did Childress, or by dynamiting conventional walls overnight, as did Hansberry and Shange.

Each one has served as a vital link in the evolution of black theater in America. Their works, which are mostly full-length plays, "have taken various forms: protest dramas, comedies, tragedies, melodramas, drama of ideas, moralities, surreal fantasies, choreopoems."[71] Noted scholar, Jeanne-Marie A. Miller, argues that contemporary "black women playwrights, handed the torch from preceding generations, have continued to move forward, to develop, to expand, and to contribute to the literature of the American theater."[72]

Childress' writing career spans four decades, making her the mother of professional black theater in America. Hansberry's 1959 Broadway debut made black theater fashionable and marketable. Shange's 1976 explosive choreopoem broadened black theater to include a quest for sexual as well as racial and social identity. The dramaturgical advances made by these women are as interdependent as African Americans are to their African counterparts, a subject that is prominent in the works of all three women. It was because of Childress' pioneering spirit that Hansberry's vision could be shared with the world and Shange's new temper could appeal to women everywhere of every race.

NOTES

1. Margaret Wilkerson, *9 Plays by Black Women* (New York: New American Library, 1982), pp. xviii-xix.

2. Doris E. Abramson, *Negro Playwrights in the American Theatre, 1925–1959* (New York: Columbia University Press, 1967), p. 27.

3. Genevieve Fabre, *Afro-American Poetry and Drama, 1760–1975* (Detroit, Mich.: Book Tower, 1979), pp. 251–263.

4. Mance Williams, *Black Theatre in the 1960s and 1970s* (Westport, Conn.: Greenwood Press, 1985), p. 112.

5. Ibid., p. 113.

6. Alice Childress, Interviewed at Amherst, Mass., May 1, 1987. Unless otherwise indicated, quotes from Childress are based upon this personal interview.

7. Abramson, p. 189.

8. Alice Childress, "Knowing the Human Condition," in *Black American Literature and Humanism*, ed. R. Baxter Miller (Lexington, Ky.: The University Press of Kentucky, 1981), p. 10.

9. Biographical information on Alice Childress in this section and in sections that follow is based upon the following sources: Trudier Harris, "Alice Childress," in *DLB*, vol. 38, *Afro-American Writers After 1955: Dramatists and Prose Writers*, eds., Thadious Davis and Trudier Harris (Michigan: Gale Research Co., 1985), pp. 66–79; Doris Abramson, *Negro Playwrights in the American Theatre, 1925–1959* (New York: Columbia University Press, 1967), pp. 188–190; Dedria Bryfonski, ed., "Alice Childress," *Contemporary Literary Criticism*, vol. 12 (Detroit, Mich.: Gale Research Co., 1980), pp. 104–109; Elizabeth Brown-Guillory, "Alice Childress: A Pioneering Spirit," *SAGE: A Scholarly Journal on Black Women*, vol. 4 (Spring 1987), pp. 66–68.

10. Williams, pp. 11–12.

11. Dedria Bryfonski, ed., "Alice Childress," *Contemporary Literary Criticism*, vol. 12 (Detroit, Mich.: Gale Research Co., 1980) p. 104.

12. Trudier Harris, "Alice Childress," in *DLB*, vol. 38, eds., Thadious Davis and Trudier Harris (Detroit, Mich.: Gale Research Co., 1985), p. 69.

13. Alice Childress, *Black Scenes: Collection of Scenes From Plays Written by Black People About Black Experience* (New York: Doubleday, 1971), pp. 148–149.

14. Abramson, p. 189.

15. Loften Mitchell, *Black Drama: The Story of the American Negro in the Theatre* (New York: Hawthorn Books, 1967), p. 169.

16. Bryfonski, p. 104.

17. Honor Moore, ed., *New Women's Theatre: Ten Plays by Contemporary American Women* (New York: Vintage Books, 1977), p. 257.

18. Bryfonski, p. 105.

19. Ibid., p. 104.

20. James V. Hatch and Ted Shine, eds., *Black Theater USA: Forty-Five Plays by Black Americans, 1847–1974,* (New York: The Free Press, 1974), p. 737.

21. Alice Childress, "Mojo: A Black Love Story," in *Black World* vol. 20 (April 1971), p. 54.

22. Barbara Molette, "Black Women Playwrights: They Speak: Who Listens?", *Black World,* vol. 25 (April 1976), p. 30.

23. Bryfonski, p. 107.

24. C.W.E. Bigsby, *Beyond Broadway,* vol. 3 of *A Critical Introduction to Twentieth-Century American Drama,* (New York: Cambridge University Press, 1985), p. 433.

25. Alice Childress has a copy of the review written by Hansberry in Paul Robeson's black newspaper *Freedom* in which Hansberry credits Childress as a leading black woman playwright. Hansberry reviewed books and dramas by blacks from 1950 to 1953, a period which includes the productions of three of Childress' plays.

26. Elizabeth Brown-Guillory, "Contemporary Black Women Playwrights: A View From the Other Half," *Helicon Nine: The Journal of Women's Arts and Letters,* nos. 14 & 15, 1986, p. 121.

27. Theophilus Lewis, "Social Protest in 'A Raisin in the Sun,'" *Catholic World,* vol. 190 (October 1959), p. 33.

28. Abramson, p. 241.

29. Mitchell, p. 181.

30. Steven Carter, "Lorraine Hansberry," in *DLB,* vol. 38, *Afro-American Writers After 1955: Dramatists and Prose Writers,* eds. Thadious Davis and Trudier Harris, (Detroit, Mich.: Gale Research Co., 1985), p. 124.

31. Ibid., p. 125.

32. Paula Gidding, "'Raisin' Revisited," *Encore,* vol. 4 (July 1975), p. 29.

33. Lorraine Hansberry, *To Be Young, Gifted and Black,* (New Jersey: Prentice Hall, 1969), pp. 5–6.

34. Lorraine Hansberry, "The Negro Writer and His Roots: Toward a New Romanticism," *The Black Scholar,* vol. 12 (March/April 1981), p. 5.

35. Harold Isaacs, "Five Writers and Their African Ancestors," *Phylon* vol. 21 (Fourth Quarter 1960), p. 329.

36. Biographical information on Lorraine Hansberry in this section and in sections that follow is based upon the following sources: Doris Abramson, *Negro Playwrights in the American Theatre, 1925–1959* (New York: Columbia University Press, 1967), pp. 239–266; Lorraine Hansberry, *To Be Young, Gifted and Black,* adapted by Robert Nemiroff (New York: New American Library, 1969); Elizabeth C. Phillips, *The Works of Lorraine Hansberry: A Critical Commentary* (New York: Monarch Press, 1973), pp. 1–141; Steven Carter, "Lorraine Hansberry," *DLB,* vol. 38, *Afro-American*

Writers After 1955: Dramatists and Prose Writers, eds. Thadious Davis and Trudier Harris, (Detroit, Mich.: Gale Research Co., 1985), pp. 120–134.

37. Isaacs, p. 334.

38. Abramson, p. 240.

39. Loften Mitchell, Interviewed at Amherst, Massachusetts, May 1, 1987.

40. Hansberry, "The Negro Artist and His Roots: Toward a New Romanticism," The Black Scholar, vol. 12 (March/April 1981), p. 11.

41. Hansberry's biographer Margaret B. Wilkerson, in her paper "The Dark Vision of Lorraine Hansberry," presented at the University of Massachusetts on May 1, 1987, revealed that Hansberry died of pancreatic cancer.

42. Mitchell, p. 203.

43. Lewis, p. 35.

44. Lorraine Hansberry, *To Be Young, Gifted and Black,* adapted by Robert Nemiroff (New York: New American Library, 1969), p. 109.

45. Brooks Atkinson, "A Raisin in the Sun," in *On Stage: Selected Theater Reviews from The New York Times, 1920–1970,* eds. Bernard Beckerman and Howard Siegman (New York: An Arno Press, 1970), p. 402.

46. Abramson, p. 241.

47. Robert Nemiroff, ed. *Lorraine Hansberry: The Collected Last Plays* (New York: New American Library, 1972), pp. 143–162.

48. Ibid., p. 160.

49. Margaret Wilkerson, "Lorraine Hansberry: The Complete Feminist," *Freedomways* (A Lorraine Hansberry Issue) vol. 19 (1979), pp. 188–189.

50. Nemiroff, p. 223.

51. Ibid., p. 226.

52. Biographical information on Ntozake Shange in this section and in following sections is based upon the following sources: Elizabeth Brown, "Ntozake Shange," *DLB,* vol. 38, *Afro-American Writers After 1955: Dramatists and Prose Writers,* eds. Thadious Davis and Trudier Harris, (Detroit, Mich.: Gale Research Co., 1985) pp. 240–250.; Charles Moritz, ed. "Ntozake Shange," *Current Biography* (New York: The H. W. Wilson, Co., 1978), pp. 380–383.

53. Allen Woll, *Dictionary of Black Theatre,* (Westport, Conn.: Greenwood Press, 1983), p. 65.

54. Ntozake Shange, *For Colored Girls Who Have Considered Suicide/When The Rainbow Is Enuf* (New York: MacMillan Co., 1977), p. xv.

55. Bigsby, pp. 411–412.

56. Claudia Tate, *Black Women Writers at Work* (New York: Continuum, 1983), p. 153.

57. Ibid., p. 159.

58. Ibid., p. 170.

59. Ibid., p. 156.

60. Sandra L. Richards, "Conflicting Impulses in the Plays of Ntozake Shange," *Black American Literature Forum,* vol. 17 (Summer 1983), p. 73.

61. Tate, p. 158.

62. Ibid., p. 162.

63. Moritz, p. 381.

64. Tate, p. 171.

65. Moritz, p. 382.

66. Jean Carey Bond, "For Colored Girls Who Have Considered Suicide," *Freedomways* vol. 16 (Third Quarter 1976), p. 191.

67. Pepsi Charles, transcriber, "Ntozake Shange Talks With Marcia Ann Gillespie," *Essence,* May 1985, pp. 122–123.

68. Ntozake Shange, *Three Pieces* (New York: St. Martin's Press, 1981). Excerpts from reviews of Shange's plays are found on the dust cover of this publication.

69. Ibid.

70. Ibid.

71. Jeanne-Marie A. Miller, "Black Women Playwrights from Grimke to Shange: Selected Synopses of Their Works," in *All the Women are White, All the Blacks are Men, But Some of Us Are Brave,* eds. Gloria T. Hull, Patricia Bell-Scott, and Barbara Smith (Old Westbury, N.Y.: The Feminist Press, 1982), p. 289.

72. Ibid., p. 290.

3

Tonal Form: Symbols as Shapers of "Theater of Struggle"

Any serious discussion of the plays of Alice Childress, Lorraine Hansberry, and Ntozake Shange must include a study of form. C. Hughes Holman defines form as "the pattern or structure of organization which is employed to give expression to content."[1] Fred B. Millet and Gerald Eades Bentley in *The Art of the Drama* place dramatic form into four categories: genres, (tragedy, comedy, melodrama, and farce); aesthetic modes or styles (classical, romantic, realistic, etc.); technical elements (plot, character, dialogue, and setting); and conventions (presentation of characters as types, the tone or mood, and the style of dialogue).[2] Noted drama critic Stanley Vincent Longman, in *Composing Drama for Stage and Screen* narrows the number of dramatic form categories to two: tonal form and structural form, the latter of which will be treated in a subsequent chapter.[3]

There are no clear-cut delineations between tonal and structural form. Longman argues that "nothing is fixed in all this" and that both tonal and structural form "are ultimately determined by attitude" (Longman, *Composing Drama . . .* , p. 119). Some degree of circularity is inevitable, especially since both tonal and structural form combine to advance the ideas of a play. On the subject of the importance of examining form, Longman says, "It is impossible to conceive of a play without some sense of its form nor of a form without some feel for its probable content" (Longman, p. 119).

To date, tonal form has not been examined in the plays of Childress, Hansberry, and Shange. Tonal form, using Longman's definition, is "the author's attitude toward the play's experience, its characters and the overall world of the play" (Longman, p. 119). Longman's contention is that "tonal form is closely tied to tradition and audience expectation. The attitude of the playwright, which he of course hopes to inspire in the audience as well, leads to patterns of shaping the play" (Longman, p. 120). What Longman does not point out is that tonal form, to a very large degree, is shaped by the author's development of symbols. These building blocks of tonal form "expand the play beyond its own action into profundity."[4]

Kenneth M. Cameron and Theodore J. C. Hoffman maintain, in *The Theatrical Response,* that "any play so devoid of difficulty and ambiguity as to be completely clear in character, language, and total meaning, without the use of great supporting symbols, is overclear and oversimple."[5] For Cameron and Hoffman, symbols are the "source of vitality" and do much to shape a play.[6] Other critics have voiced similar opinions about tonal form. Famed New York drama critic Walter Kerr calls for "shape" in a play. One of Kerr's most frequent complaints about contemporary theater is its thinness of invention and its failure to handle the play's material imaginatively.[7] Roderick Bladel, in *Walter Kerr: An Analysis of His Criticism,* says that Kerr "likes the audience to have the pleasure of drawing inferences from a play."[8]

Inferences can be drawn from two types of symbols: those that embody within themselves universal suggestions of meaning, as water suggests baptism or purgation, and those that secure suggestiveness from the way they are used in a given work and usually offer meaning on a number of different levels. It is in examining symbols that conjectures can be made about the author's perceptions and perspectives about the world mirrored in the play.

A study of symbols in selected plays by Childress, Hansberry, and Shange reveals a shared vision: blacks must struggle together to secure political, social, and economic gains. What emerges as one examines the macrame of symbols in these plays is a conscious effort on the part of these dramatists to illuminate the condition of blacks in patriarchal America, one of constant struggle to survive against overwhelming odds. In this "Theater of Struggle," where battles are frequent, black resiliency and spirit of survival are heralded. These dramatists have very definite and similar views about racism, poverty, education, politics, and sexism. The symbols in these plays serve as an index to the authors' attitudes about these and other subjects.

The contention thus far is that meaning, thoughts, or ideas in plays can be elucidated via an analysis of tonal form that depends very heavily upon symbols for its shape. Accordingly, this chapter will study symbols while simultaneously drawing parallels between the authors' personal values, commitment, and experiences, and those embedded in the texts. The worlds that these authors have created in their plays are very much a product of the worlds out of which they have come. The shape or tonal form in their plays is an extension of their viewpoints or perspectives, which are distinctively and inextricably black and feminine. Their own personal struggles are mirrored in this "Theater of Struggle."

Alice Childress' brilliance, her intense and microscopic penetration into life, matches such great twentieth-century dramatists as Anton Chekhov, August Strindberg, Jean Anouilh, Sean O'Casey, Sholem Aleichem, Noel Coward, Tennessee Williams, and the Pulitzer Prize winning African dramatist, Wole Soyinka. Childress' decision to write was prompted by two factors: racism and a feeling that she was somewhat alone in her ideas.[9] Of her experiences as a writer Childress has written, "Being a woman adds difficulty to self expression, but being Black is the larger factor of struggle against odds. Black men and women have particular problems above and beyond the average, in any field of endeavor."[10] Particularly resembling O'Casey and Soyinka, Childress uses her keen mind to address the struggle of her people with the aim of effecting social change.

One who takes great pride in serving as a spokesperson for poor and uneducated blacks, Childress commented in 1968, "The plaster now slapped on our wounds is welfare and poverty programs. . . . This society tells us they would rather support us as charity cases than open the doors and let us win or fail, live or die, as full citizens of this country.[11] Almost twenty years later, Childress' view of American society has not changed. She continues to perceive that black Americans are "besieged with accusations of inferiority in learning skills."[12] On the subject of education, she poignantly reminds America that blacks were the only racial group in the United States ever forbidden by law to read and write, and to enter libraries, concert halls, theaters, and public schools.[13]

Summing up her concern for society's most shoddily treated people and issuing a warning to black artists, Childress remarks, "It is a serious self-deception to think that culturally ignoring those who are poor, lost, and/or rebellious will somehow better our image. . . . Black writers cannot afford to abuse or neglect the so-called ordinary characters who represent a part of ourselves, the self twice denied, first by racism and then by class difference."[14] She urges writers to be wary of those who tell them to leave the past alone and confine themselves to the present moment. Childress argues that "our story has not been told in any moment."[15] Childress contends that "today we hear so much about the 'New Negro.' As though we had never breathed a protest until a few years ago. But the story of the 'Old Negro' has not been told."[16] Labeled controversial because her works confront social and political issues in depth, Childress believes that all art is and must be political. Firm and articulate about her philosophy of art, Childress admits that "even when a writer seeks to evade all that is political, because it is politic to do so, that then becomes political."[17]

The tone of Childress' work reflects her belief that African Americans live in a world where they are not free from the emotional shackles of slavery and Jim Crow. A veteran of the struggle, Childress brilliantly brings together the crux of her philosophy about the black experience in America:

A part of the Black Liberation struggle is to constantly evaluate, or to re-evaluate ground we have covered, making sure that we are not judging our

struggle by appearances; substituting appearance for struggle . . . dashiki, jew-
elry, language, stance, attitudes, music preferences, soul food, . . . used in place
of concrete action, or used as delaying action because we may not know
exactly what to do at the moment. Knowing we are in trouble and knowing
we do not exactly know what to do . . . is true knowledge and gives us a clean
slate to start with. We are varied people and our ideas are bound to clash . . .
but I remind myself frequently that symbols may trick us.[18]

Childress is an incisive thinker, a dramatist whose ideas are no less complex
than the form she uses to express her thoughts. A writer who constantly
evaluates her beliefs and craft, Childress has commented, "I try to bend
my writing form to most truthfully express content; to move beyond . . .
politically imposed limitations."[19] One need only examine the symbols in
Childress' *Florence, Trouble in Mind,* and *Mojo* to conclude that she skillfully
manipulates tonal form to express content.

Florence,[20] set in the waiting room of a small Southern railway station,
is fraught with potent symbols and symbolic gestures that serve as signposts
to the play's main idea, which is, according to Samuel Hay, that "Black
people—not white liberals—must struggle if there is to be real political and
economic equality."[21] Childress' symbols point out that blacks must not
turn over to white liberals the responsibility of nurturing young, black
dreamers but must encourage their children to fight to reach their fullest
potential in spite of racial biases.

One very important symbol are the signs that divide the railway waiting
room. "Colored" and "White" signs hang over the doorway entrances to
each side. The division is further emphasized by the hanging of "Colored
women" and "Colored men" and "White ladies" and "White gentlemen"
over the restroom doors. Hay argues that the signs are significant because
they are both signs and symbols.[22] Referring to Susanne K. Langer's landmark book *Feeling and Form,*[23] Hay concludes that, "They are signs because
they 'serve to make us notice the situation'; they are symbols because 'they
help us understand the situation.'"[24] The signs in this Jim Crow railway
station are symbols because they point to the separate and unequal treatment
of blacks.

Racial inequity is signaled by the very use of the words "ladies" and
"gentlemen" on the restroom doors designated for whites. These titles,
which suggest grace, culture, wealth, or royalty, do no appear on the
restroom doors for blacks, an implication that Colored men and women
are a cut below White ladies and gentlemen. Another example of Childress'
orchestration of this sign–symbol occurs when the porter tells Mama that
should she need to use the restroom, she must use the Colored men's because
the other one is out of order. It is illegal for Mama to step into the "White
ladies" restroom, so she will have to demean herself and risk having her
privacy invaded in the Colored men's restroom.

The out-of-order restroom becomes a symbol of the black woman's historical burden in America, that of struggling to keep together the family that slavocracy plotted to destroy. This play on words hints that for Colored women, there is no room for rest. Childress implies that the Colored woman, as Zora Neale Hurston once said, is the mule of the world. On another level, Childress' symbol suggests that the American societal structure is out-of-order, nonfunctioning for African Americans. Childress mirrors a society that is and will remain out of order as long as people are judged by the color of their skin.

In addition to the obtrusive signs that bar whites and blacks from crossing lines, a low railing divides the waiting room. This railing serves as a physical and emotional barrier between whites and blacks and is the symbol around which the central idea of the play is developed. Conversations and actions are structured around this dividing line that reminds the audience that there are special limitations placed on blacks and whites. Childress moves both the black and white characters toward or away from this low railing to suggest racial constraints. She ingeniously demonstrates that the railing prevents both blacks and whites from crossing into each other's territory. On one level, the bar symbolizes the need for blacks to fight against the harnesses of racism and to cross the line to secure those privileges in life that belong not just to whites but to all human beings. On another level, the railing suggests that segregation breeds ignorance. Childress illustrates that the Jim Crow laws that were set in place to restrict blacks also kept whites from interacting with blacks. The point is that when whites are barred from firsthand knowledge about blacks, they are forced to imagine, which leads to the creation of stereotypes.

The play opens with Mama waiting to board a train for New York where she is going to convince her daughter, Florence, to come back South. Florence left the South when her husband was lynched for voting. While Mama waits, her daughter, Marge, details for her the rules for traveling safely to the North. The railway becomes a symbol of escape, conjuring up the Underground Railroad that helped runaway slaves get to the North.[25] Later, when the white actress, Mrs. Carter, arrives at the railway station, she announces, "I can't leave this place fast enough. . . . These people are still fighting the Civil War" (p. 39). Childress paints a picture of the South as a racist and ignorant place from which to escape.

As Marge says her good-bys to her mother in this little railway station, the low railing serves as a constant reminder of existing racial constraints. Marge unconsciously wanders upstage to the railing but stops as she tells her mother to buy coffee when the waiter passes through the Jim Crow cars because she will not be able to go to the segregated diner. In this instance, the audience is reminded that just as Marge cannot cross the railing, blacks are unable to cross lines in other establishments and can only achieve what is prescribed for them by white supremacists. While still at the railing, Marge pleads with her mother to force Florence to come home from New York because, "She got notions a Negro woman don't need" (p. 35).

A while later, Marge nears the railing but stops when she tells Mama that Florence must think she is white, pursuing a career in which typically only whites had succeeded. She also reminds Mama of the time Florence went to Strumley's asking to be a sales girl, knowing that blacks were not hired for such positions. Marge actually crosses over the line and onto the "White" side of the stage just as she says, "there's things we can't do cause they ain't gonna let us" (p. 36). Once on the forbidden side, Marge sarcastically comments that it does not feel any differently. This crossing over suggests that blacks feel harnessed in their struggle against oppression and, perhaps, envious of the privileges and rights accorded whites. Marge steps back over to the "Colored" side just as she tells her mother that she must not give Florence any money but must, instead, bring her back home. This synchronized movement to the "Colored" side symbolizes Marge's internalization of her designated place in society.

Mama, like Marge, seems to know her place until Mrs. Carter enters and provokes her into realizing that blacks cannot afford to give up the struggle for equality. This struggle is illustrated as Childress catapults both Mama and Mrs. Carter back and forth across the dividing line. Childress seems to be working with a symbol within a symbol, i.e., a trip within a trip. The cross-country trip that the women are going on parallels the cross-cultural trip that they take each time the railing is crossed. These women step in and out of each other's cultures as they try to communicate their limitations. Childress suggests that the railing, representing segregation, has left Mrs. Carter and white liberals like her ignorant and insensitive to blacks. By the same token, the railing serves as a driving force behind black achievement; racial bars must be torn down in order for blacks to be free to succeed.

The cross-cultural trip begins when Mrs. Carter gradually moves near the dividing line to tell Mama about her brother's struggle to capture the lives of black people. Almost on the rail, Mrs. Carter boasts of her brother's novel, "It's profound. Real . . . you know. It's about your people. . . . He suffers so with his characters" (p. 40). Leaning on the rail, Mrs. Carter proceeds to tell of the mulatto who, with tears rolling down her cheeks, jumps from a bridge to her death saying, "Almost! Almost white . . . but I'm black! I'm a Negro" (p. 41). Childress' disdain for stereotypes is plain, particularly the tragic mulatto. Mrs. Carter's brother is held up as a white liberal who means well but who knows little about what he writes.

Outraged by the white author's stereotyping of blacks, Mama tells Mrs. Carter, "That ain't so! Not one bit it ain't" (p. 41). At this point, Mrs. Carter backs away from the railing while Mama, citing cases of mulattos who did not kill themselves, works her way around the bar until she crosses about a foot over to the "White" side and is face to face with Mrs. Carter. Crossing the railing in this instance suggests Mama's refusal to accept myths about blacks. Mama moves back to the "Colored" side when she looks up and sees the sign "White ladies." The inference is that only "White ladies" or naive, white liberals would believe that blacks kill themselves for wishing to be white. Also, Childress demonstrates that in 1950 blacks and whites were painfully aware of racial bars. Mama cannot exchange ideas with Mrs. Carter without being reminded that she must remain in her place on the "Colored" side.

Like a skilled checker player, Mrs. Carter hesitantly makes the next move. She approaches the rail to apologize to Mama. This gesture, however, is deflated when Mrs. Carter says, "This whole thing is a completely controversial subject. If it's too much for Jeff [her brother the author]... well naturally I shouldn't discuss it with you" (p. 42). Mrs. Carter does not realize that she is condescending in her assumption that Mama is too simple-minded to understand the issues surrounding the poor reviews given the book. The apology, then, becomes a false sign and instead becomes another indicator of Mrs. Carter's racism.

Mrs. Carter crosses over to the "Colored" side as she tells Mama, "You know I try but it's really difficult to understand you people. However... I keep trying" (p. 42). When Mama remains unmoved, Mrs. Carter retreats back to the "White" side and offers another sign of her love and respect for blacks, "I know what's going on in your mind... and what you're thinking is wrong. I've... I've eaten with Negroes" (p. 42). This gesture is symbolic because as Hay puts it, "Eating together has been for Mama and many Blacks the symbol of equality, not only because of the biblical references but also because the Southern oligarchy made it so by outlawing breaking bread together."[26] Hay argues that to Mrs. Carter, eating together is by no means a representation of equality. Hay's contention is that Childress offers Mrs. Carter's acknowledgment that she has eaten with blacks as a symbol to point out that "the fight of the forties and fifties to eat with whites was assigned too much importance."[27]

Mrs. Carter insults Mama again during their discussion of Florence's dream of becoming a dramatic actress. Unaware that she is condescending, Mrs. Carter assures Mama that blacks are far better suited to entertainment, such as singing spirituals like "Steal Away" and "Swing Low, Sweet Chariot." Mrs. Carter tells Mama that Florence stands little or no chance in New York, especially since she is without contacts. Mama, genuinely moved by Mrs. Carter's concern for Florence, asks her to help the struggling actress. Knowing that Mama has in mind an acting job, Mrs. Carter instead offers to contact a director friend of hers who will take on Florence as a domestic.

The dividing line takes on significance once more as Mrs. Carter crosses over to the "Colored" side to give Mama the address and phone number of her director friend and to reassure Mama that Florence will be in good hands if she is dependable and trustworthy. Reaching out, Mama clutches Mrs. Carter's arm almost pulling her off balance. It is at this point that Mama understands that white liberals should not be counted on for helping blacks in the struggle because racism in America has blinded and desensitized them. Mrs. Carter cannot empathize, nor understand Florence's determination to succeed at acting, or at any other career that has been typically open only to whites, because she is a product of the railing that has kept her ignorant about blacks. Mama realizes that she, and all blacks, must contribute to the empowerment of her people by offering continued encouragement to their children. Realizing that she is hurting Mrs. Carter, Mama unclutches her and snaps, "You better get on over on the other side of that rail. It's against the law for you to be here with me" (p. 46). Mrs. Carter goes scurrying across the line, rubbing her wrist and not fully understanding why Mama has reacted violently.

Keeping her eyes on the dividing line after Mrs. Carter exits to powder her nose in the "White ladies" room, Mama assures the porter that "Marge can't make her turn back, Mrs. Carter can't make her turn back" (p. 47). She writes a note to Florence telling her to keep trying and that she has a right to be or do anything she wants in this world. Mama's linking Marge to Mrs. Carter is significant because both women believe that Florence does not know her limitations.

One comes away from this drama sensing Childress' outrage that blacks are forced to live in a world that prescribes positions or careers for them. Childress also levels an indictment against white liberals who claim to be experts about black life but who are both presumptuous and blind. She does, however, credit white liberals for at least trying to interact with blacks. Mrs. Carter makes several attempts at reaching out to Mama, albeit those attempts show her to be racist. One alarming thought that emerges from this play is that if white liberals hopelessly misunderstand blacks, how much less do ultraconservative whites know about blacks? Childress uses the railing to show that whites are barred from knowing blacks. She insists that blacks are victimized or oppressed by the dominant race because of this unfamiliarity with black life.

Produced five years after *Florence, Trouble in Mind* treats similar issues: racial stereotyping both in and outside of the theater, the presumptuousness and insensitivity of white liberals, and blacks' struggle for equality.[28] It is not surprising that strong parallels can be drawn between these two plays, given that they were written during Childress' tenure as an active member— playwright, actress, director, and lobbyist for equity standards—of the American Negro Theatre. As is the case in *Florence,* the tone of this work is serious. Childress allows the audience to extricate meaning that is embedded in what Baudelaire has termed a "forest of symbols."[29] The symbol that Childress uses to develop the main ideas and also to set the tone of the play grows out of her creation of metadrama in *Trouble in Mind.*

Richard Hornby defines metadrama as "drama about drama," suggesting that "it occurs whenever the subject of a play turns out to be, in some sense, drama itself."[30] There are, according to Hornby, five types of metadrama: the ceremony within the play, role playing within the play, literary and real-life reference, self reference, and the play within the play, the latter of which appears in *Trouble in Mind* and serves as the controlling symbol.[31]

Crediting Shakespeare as one of her favorite playwrights, Childress successfully manipulates the play within the play.[32] As does Shakespeare in "The Mousetrap" in *Hamlet,* Childress uses the "inset" type of a play within a play, one in which the performance is set apart from the main action with the cast of the primary play recognizing the existence of a secondary play.[33] A master craftsperson, Childress establishes herself as a serious and gifted creator of metatheater, a technique that has appeared in relatively few plays since the Renaissance.[34] Only the most extraordinary playwrights have been able to create successful metadrama. Hornby, writing in his *Drama, Metadrama and Perception,* is of the opinion that "great playwrights tend to be more consciously metadramatic than ordinary ones, and their plays to employ metadramatic devices more obviously because the great playwright conceives his mission to be one of altering the norms and standards by which his audience views the world, and is thus more likely to attack those norms frontally" (Hornby, p. 32). Indeed, Childress' aim is to revolutionize the way society views people of color.

The play within the play is used as a means of discovering truth, and is "expressive of its society's deep cynicism about life" (Hornby, p. 45). For Childress, truth is that society is out-of-order because it does not function for African Americans. In order to illustrate this brokenness, Childress works toward achieving "ostraneniye," wherein the audience is made to feel a sense of estrangement or uneasiness about the issues of the play.[35] Thus, in *Trouble in Mind,* the play within the play, *Chaos in Belleville,* serves as the symbol of blacks' struggle in America, mirroring Childress' disappointment, which she hopes will also become the audience's attitude about the level of racism, sexism, and poverty in America. This play within a play is a "private symbol" and represents African Americans as the stepchildren of American society.[36] It becomes the vehicle by which Childress comments on the various ways blacks survive in racist America.

Childress uses *Chaos in Belleville,* a black play written, directed, and funded by white men, to point out much that is out-of-order in America. With this technique, Childress reinforces and elucidates the ideas contained in the primary play. *Chaos in Belleville* centers around whites in an imaginary town who form a mob because a young, poor, Southern black man, Job, dared to vote. Job's incredulity at the lynch mob's anger at him is shown when he says, "I wasn't even votin' for a black man, votin' for somebody white same as they" (p. 161). With the mob approaching his house, Job runs to his sharecropping parents who passively chastise him for not knowing his place and tell him that the only thing left for him to do is give himself up to the law for safekeeping. These poor blacks are portrayed as too underprivileged and uneducated to know enough to come to the aid of their son who will meet certain death.

Wiletta, veteran actress and mouthpiece for Childress, argues that the scene is all wrong, saying that no black mother and father would sit idly by and watch as their child was lynched, nor would they turn the child over to the law, because history has taught blacks that the law is powerless against the lynch mob, and sometimes the law is the lynch mob. She pleads with the director, Al Manners, to request that the author revise the script, calling for the young man, since it seems he must die, to be killed while running away or to be dragged out of the house with his parents fighting every inch of the way. Childress dramatizes that education has little to do with parental instinct and that poor blacks are just as dignified and self-respecting as anyone else. Childress' belief in the nobility of the poor and in struggling is seen in her treatment of Wiletta, who has no formal training but who exhibits a great deal of common sense, integrity, and grace, especially in her insistence that the poor blacks in *Chaos in Belleville* are misrepresented. Manners ignores Wiletta, however, and tells her that she should stick to acting and leave the writing to the author and the interpretation to him.

Manners, when Wiletta refuses to be silenced, tells her that since no one in the cast has ever seen a lynching, each must only imagine as did the playwright. The world of the play within the play is connected to the world of the primary play and the real world when Sheldon steps out of his character in *Chaos in Belleville* and tells of the lynching he witnessed when he was a boy living in the South. The occurrence that Sheldon describes is diametrically opposite to that which the playwright of *Chaos in Belleville* offers as truth concerning blacks and lynchings.

In perhaps the most poignant moment of the play, Sheldon describes the lynching. He recalls, "The screamin' comin' closer and closer ... and the screamin' was laughin'. . . . Horse just pullin along ... and then I saw it! Chained to the back of the wagon, draggin' and bumpin' along ... The arms of it stretched out ... a burnt, naked thing that once was a man" (p. 166). Sheldon goes on to tell how he screamed but no sound would come out. Later he found out that the murdered man was Mr. Morris, a person looked upon by the black community as generous and loving but who was known to speak his mind to whites. Sheldon's description of the lynching stirs Manners to say, "When I hear of barbarism ... I feel so wretched, so guilty" (p. 166). Instead of agreeing to ask for script changes, however, he merely tells the cast to break for lunch.

The violence in *Chaos in Belleville* is symbolic because it parallels the violence taking place in the outside world. Childress, serving as historian, as she so often does in her writing, highlights black struggle by having primary cast members discuss the causes of racial tensions. Wiletta speaks of the Little Rock incident wherein stones were thrown at innocent children for trying to get a quality education. Later, Sheldon refers to the Montgomery, Alabama bus boycott. The cast also discusses segregated housing, once a cause of inner-city race riots. The issue of separate and unequal housing surfaces when Sheldon asks Bill O'Wray, a white actor who boasts of his comfortable apartment, if there are any Colored people living in the building. When Bill hesitantly answers that he has not seen any but will inquire, Sheldon assures him that no blacks live there if he has to check. Black struggle permeates every layer of *Trouble in Mind*.

Childress' resentment of racial stereotyping goes beyond the lynching scene in *Chaos in Belleville*. She pokes fun at stereotypical names given to black characters, the exaggeration of religiosity among blacks, and the invalidation of blacks, all of which have counterparts in the primary play. For example, the black women in *Chaos in Belleville* are named Petunia and Ruby. These names are held up as stereotypical in the primary play when Wiletta teases Millie, a co-worker, about having played all the flowers in the garden, including Gardenia, Magnolia, and Chrysanthemum. Millie, not wishing to be outdone, reminds Wiletta that she has played all the jewels, including Crystal, Pearl, and Opal.

Childress makes a strong case against white authors who categorize blacks as passive and religious. The lynching scene in *Chaos in Belleville*, for example, is one in which the father merely whittles a stick and sings a spiritual and the mother wrings her hands and repeatedly calls on the Lord for mercy while their son's life hangs in the balance. Similarly, Wiletta and Millie in the primary play commiserate about the inaccurate portrayals of blacks. Wiletta shares with the cast that she refused to tell her relatives about the last show she was in because all she did was shout "Lord, have mercy" for almost two hours (p. 141).

Another concern of Childress' is the invalidation of blacks as persons. She seems especially critical of whites who either ignore the presence of a black, (i.e., talk as if a black person is not in the room), or who ignore or dismiss comments made by blacks. *Chaos in Belleville* contains a scene wherein a white liberal shows her racism by telling the black woman that she does not want to leave her alone in the face of the ensuing lynch mob. Sheldon, from the primary play, breaks character and tells the director that an error has been made because Ruby is not alone; two black servants are in the room with her. What the young white woman means is that she does not want to leave the black woman alone without the protective arm of a white person. The point that Childress is making is that whites do not consider blacks as people or as equals.

The primary play also treats the invalidation of blacks. Manners' constant waving of his hand to silence his cast is symbolic. In addition to indicating to them that he does not want to hear comments about inaccurately drawn sketches of blacks, his gesture represents the silencing or ignoring of blacks in America. Several times when Sheldon questions inconsistencies, Manners hastily tells him not to interrupt or emphatically waves him into silence. At one point, when Wiletta tries to express to Manners that she thinks the third act of *Chaos in Belleville* is not the natural outcome of the first, he waves her into silence and tells her, "Make me a solemn promise, don't start thinking" (p. 157). Another case in point is Manners' ordering danish when the cast agreed that they would like to have jelly doughnuts. Manners says that jelly doughnuts are a horrible thought and then summarily instructs the stage manager to order danish.

Childress also addresses the issue of invalidation of women. Judy, a young white actress who plays the part of a timid girl dominated by a Southern planter father in *Chaos in Belleville,* is humiliated many times by Al Manners who represents the worst of patriarchal America. Judy makes the mistake of boasting that she is a graduate of the Yale drama course. From that point on Manners, apparently intimidated by her credentials and perhaps insecure about his own ineptness, ridicules Judy in a manner that suggests sexism. Manners orders Judy around, constantly shouting at her, "Yale, please!" (p. 147). Becoming very nervous because of Manners' harsh treatment of her, Judy gets confused and cannot remember stage positions. Immediately, Manners descends upon her like a condor, grabs her by the shoulders, and speedily leads her around the stage to the various positions. It never occurs to Manners to treat any of the males with such condescension and aggressiveness. Childress depicts the blatant sexism that women of the 1950s were forced to tolerate both on and off the American stage.

Taking its title from the blues song of the same name, *Trouble in Mind* seriously examines the shoddy treatment of the poor, of blacks, and of women. Tonal form in this Obie award winning play is shaped by the play within the play that symbolizes black struggle. For Childress, this struggle is a painful but necessary one. Fearing that she will be fired for insisting upon script changes, Wiletta says at the end of the play, "Divide and conquer . . . that's the way they get the upper hand" (p. 173). Childress seems to be suggesting that blacks must struggle together or continue to be victimized together.

The symbols in Childress' *Mojo: A Black Love Story* are as equally effective in shaping tone as are those found in *Florence* and *Trouble in Mind*.[37] A series of symbols are strung together, making it clear that Childress seems saddened by the suffering of blacks in America. A great deal of pain is evoked as the symbols take shape and suggest meaning. The play opens with Teddy, a black racketeer, talking to his white girlfriend, Berenice, from what he considers to be the ultimate in apartment living. Later, he admits that Berenice decorated his apartment, which is described by Childress as an overdone room, one with too much crystal, too many figurines, and too many pieces of satiny, overstuffed furniture. These things represent to

Teddy success, the good life. He thinks that he has arrived and is better than less fortunate blacks because of the "expensive junk" that he owns. In fact, he defines his manhood by the things he has been able to buy and by the fact that he sports around with a white girlfriend. Hay says that "Teddy removes himself geographically and fills his space with the cultural 'gadgets' of his white girlfriend's culture."[38] It is not until Irene, his former wife, comes back into his life that he learns that things do not define his manhood.

When Irene tells Teddy that she has cancer and must undergo an operation, these two black people are able to open up to each other for the first time. She discloses to Teddy that the day the doctor told her of her illness she went to the bathroom, "a place full of echoes. . . . I leaned my head against the cold, tile wall . . . it was yellow tile . . . big square, yellow tiles . . . and I cried out the fullness of my feeling" (p. 64). The yellow tile symbolizes not only Irene's fear of dying but of living. Yellow, with its suggestiveness of cowardice, takes on meaning as Irene tells Teddy that she secretly had his baby and gave it up for adoption because she feared she would lose her mind or physically harm the baby. She reveals that she has spent the last eighteen years of her life worrying about what has become of the daughter she gave up for adoption. Irene says of her fears, "Instead of one child . . . I had thousands" (p. 72). Each time she saw a raggedy child on the street, she worried that it was her daughter. As the years passed, she began to imagine that her daughter was one of the baby-faced prostitutes she passed on the streets. Like a caged animal, Irene has spent her life surrounded by cold, yellow, square, tile walls that remind her that as long as she lives, she will fear that her daughter did not fare well.

Attached to the notion of fear is Teddy's tale of the rats that terrorized him when he was a child. Teddy reminisces that when he was a boy, he accompanied his father in the blistering cold to pull garbage out of the shafts of tenement buildings. He vividly recalls the gigantic rats who did not back off but instead walked around like they were invincible. The rats represent the violence, despair, and pain associated with poverty. Childress uses the rat symbol to suggest that blacks are forced to scratch out a living. She also shows that it is very difficult to communicate or caress in circumstances that rob people of their dignity. Telling of the frightening noises made as the rats ransacked the walls of the building where he lived, Teddy shares that his home was no place for love talk. The rats point to the turmoil and degradation associated with poverty.

Similarly, Irene has known poverty all of her life. Irene reminisces about the years she worked as a restroom attendant in segregated hotels for the affluent. She reminds Teddy that over half of her life has been spent "in white folks' toilets, smellin' their funk and grinnin' in their face" (p. 74). Irene tells of the countless times that she wiped up the floor behind sick drunks, washed away tears, or laughed at "Jew" and "Darky" jokes. She recalls listening to white women tell her how to feel about the race problem.

The toilet is symbolic of the liberties that white women have taken with Irene's life. Irene and the toilet are one, both function as repositories of society's wastes. Childress suggests that Irene and millions of blacks like her are demeaned as they struggle to survive on menial jobs that require them to grin and wear the mask.

The main symbol in *Mojo* is Africa, which stands for love, hope, togetherness, and security. Irene comes to feel that she cannot survive cancer surgery without a piece of Africa, something black to sustain her. She says to Teddy, "I want a good Blackness like some of the young people feel . . . clean Black—a Blackness I never knew" (p. 80). Telling Teddy that she cannot go into surgery lying on white sheets and surrounded by white doctors and white nurses wearing white masks without his strength and the power of her ancestral African spirits, Irene concludes, "I got to take to the hospital with me . . . a little of this Africa" (p. 81). Irene and Teddy agree that she needs a mojo, which is a reference to African witchdoctors who could cast either good or bad spells. This good luck charm is one way in which Childress links Teddy and Irene to each other and to their counterparts in Africa. The need for blacks to struggle together is best represented in Childress' epigraph at the beginning of the play: "She found in her time of trouble, the beauty in her man and in Blackness that once she had misplaced" (p. 54). Childress suggests that this love of things black or of Mother Africa represents wholeness and survival for Irene and people of color around the world.

Childress' tone in *Mojo* is consistent with her attitudes expressed in both *Florence* and *Trouble in Mind*. She uses symbols to express her disappointment in America's injustice toward blacks. She has written that "the twisted circumstances under which we live is grist for the writing mill."[39] This perceptive dramatist makes no apology for the traditional subjects she treats because in her opinion racism, sexism, and poverty are not dead. Of her role as an African American artist, Childress says that her aim is to find "new handles for old pitchers."[40] She is serious but not pessimistic.

Childress believes that there is hope for blacks but that they must band together to demand equality. In all three of the plays, Childress cautions blacks about turning over responsibility for their survival and success to white liberals. It is Hay's contention that these three plays document Childress' progressive ideas concerning black well-being over a period of twenty years. Mama in 1950 was merely asking Mrs. Carter to help Florence survive. Wiletta in 1955 was insisting that Manners allow black people to control their images. By 1970, Irene and Teddy were turning to things African as a coping mechanism and as a means of carving out a future for themselves, one in which the white liberal plays a minimal role.[41] Neither caustic nor saccharine, Childress tells the truth about the deaf ears that America continues to turn to blacks.

Hansberry, like Childress, believed that the black artist has a responsibility to tell the truth about the miseries that afflict the peoples of the world, particularly people of color. Hansberry, in "The Negro Writer and His Roots," outlines her philosophy about art: "I believe in the truth of art and the art of truth and the most painful exigency of cultural and social life will not be exempt from exploration by my mind or pen."[42] Hansberry announced that she was going "to tell the truth from all its sides, including what is the still bitter epic of the black man in this most hostile nation" (Hansberry, "The Negro Writer..." p. 10). For Hansberry there were several truths that she felt compelled to tell: all art is social and must make a statement; art must examine the source of human anguish and behavior; and there is not an inexhaustible period of time before oppressed blacks will rise to wrest those privileges guaranteed them by the U.S. Constitution (Hansberry, pp. 4–6). Of the latter, Hansberry had much to say.

She believed that an unequivocal "no" must be the answer given to three crucial questions concerning African Americans: Are blacks free citizens in the United States? Do blacks enjoy equal opportunity in the most basic aspects of American life, housing, employment, franchise? Are blacks free of the most primitive, savage, and intolerable of customs: lynching? (Hansberry, p. 10). Hansberry's pain over the lynching issue is best illustrated when she says, "Every mother's child of us knows that they are still murdering Negroes in this country, with and without rope and faggot, in all the old ways and many new ones. Lest we forget, I give you the name of an American boy, Emmett Till" (Hansberry, p. 10). The kidnapping and lynching of Emmett Till for whistling at a white girl in 1955[43] led Hansberry to believe that the Negro writer has the role of shaming the conscience of a government that allows such inhumanity to go on unchecked.[44]

Hansberry's disappointment in the American government is best summed up in her autobiography, *To Be Young, Gifted and Black,* "Quite simply and quietly as I know how to say it: I am sick of poverty, lynching, stupid wars and the universal maltreatment of my people and obsessed with a rather desperate desire for a new world for me and my brothers."[45] Hansberry wanted a world where blacks could breathe. To achieve this, she argued that blacks would have to involve themselves in every single means of struggle, even if they must "harass, debate, petition, give money to court struggles, sit-in, lie-down, strike, boycott, sing hymns, pray on steps— and shoot from their windows when the racists come cruising through their communities."[46]

What was so extraordinary about Hansberry was that though she was inundated with pain, both from the cancer that plagued her body and the cancer that she felt was absorbing American society, she turned her vision inward to celebrate the joy of living and struggling together. She was a realist, struggling to "chisel out some expression of what life can conceivably be."[47] Hansberry was eternally optimistic and held the view that the world could be reconstructed. Shortly before she died, Hansberry wrote

that the United States was "a great nation with certain beautiful and indestructible traditions and potentials which can be seized by all who possess
imagination and love of man. . . . There is no reason why dreams should
dry up like raisins or prunes or anything else in America."[48] She was committed to capturing the human spirit that swings between despair and joy.
Hansberry's tone in her works reflects this bittersweet philosophy of life in
America.

Symbols in *A Raisin in the Sun*[49] and *The Drinking Gourd*[50] suggest that
Hansberry, though she was angered by the oppression of blacks, continued
to believe in life's possibilities and people's ability to "embrace the stars."[51]
Hansberry uses several symbols to set the tone of *A Raisin in the Sun*.
Margaret Wilkerson notes that Hansberry "carefully orchestrates the moods
of the play, using highly symbolic, nonrealistic actions when needed" to
guide readers through "a maze of emotional and humorous moments."[52]
The play opens with an important symbol. The furnishings on stage symbolize the shabbiness, drabness, and desperation of the ghetto. Hansberry
once wrote, "We must come out of the ghettos of America, because the
ghettos are killing us; not only our dreams . . . but our very bodies."[53] The
furnishings, which are described as "tired" from having had to sustain the
living of too many people for too many years, suggest the weariness of the
inhabitants of this Southside of Chicago apartment where roaches and ro-
dents share the family's living space. The furnishings suggest two things:
the struggle and deferred dreams.

Like the furniture that sags, so does a little plant belonging to Mama.
The feeble plant growing doggedly in a pot on the window sill represents
the suffering and disillusionment that Mama and other poor blacks experience when they find themselves entrenched in deplorable living conditions.
Throughout much of the play, Mama tends to this withering plant that
suffers because the apartment has only one, small window, through which
comes a minimal amount of sunlight. The paucity of sunlight represents
the modicum of hope that propels blacks to keep searching for personal
and political freedom. Whereas the sunlight battles its way through the tiny
window to get to the plant, the Youngers struggle to find an exit from the
ghetto. Mama compares the plant's resiliency to the spiritedness of her
children and goes on to say that the plant expresses her. That little plant is
the symbol of hope for a family determined to escape the squalor and
violence of the ghetto. Linked to the plant is the garden that Mama envisions
whenever she thinks of the new house. Mary Louise Anderson, in "Black
Matriarchy: Portrayals of Women in Three Plays," suggests that the garden
is a symbol communicating that the house will be the place where the family
can grow and flourish in better conditions. It is fitting that her family would
give her gardening tools and a gardening hat, symbolizing the tools she
needs to nurture them and help their dreams grow."[54]

Hunger is often associated with ghetto living. Hansberry uses food to symbolize the emotional or spiritual deprivation that results when dreams are thwarted. One of the early scenes centers around Ruth insisting that Walter Lee eat his eggs. Each time Walter Lee attempts to talk to his wife about his dreams of becoming an entrepreneur, she tries to circumvent the issue by offering him eggs. When Walter Lee complains, for example, that black men are yoked to a race of narrow-minded women, Ruth disinterestedly tells him that he should eat his eggs and be quiet. Later, when Walter Lee comes home inebriated because Mama will not give him money to invest in a liquor store, Ruth offers him hot milk. Lashing out at her, Walter Lee demands to know why Ruth keeps trying to feed him. Ruth despondently replies, "What else can I give you, Walter Lee Younger?" (p. 74). Ruth cannot satisfy her husband's yearnings to excel, so she tries to satiate him with food. Hansberry again uses food to suggest yearning or emotional hunger in the nickname given to Beneatha by the African intellectual, Asagai. He refers to Beneatha as "Alaiyo," translating into "One for whom Bread—Food—is Not enough" (p. 52). Hansberry demonstrates that even the poorest of people hunger and thirst for a dignified existence, one in which they are validated as human beings and full citizens in America.

Carl Lindner, chairperson of the Clybourne Park Improvement Association, represents white supremacy and all that is entailed in this mentality. Lindner becomes the gatekeeper whose function is to bar blacks out of white neighborhoods, where the houses are less expensive than in comparable black residential areas. Lindner does not come to the Youngers robed in a Klansman's hood nor does he overtly threaten violence; instead, he speaks softly and talks about the need for blacks and whites to work together peacefully. He insists that the reason why there is a race problem is because blacks and whites do not sit down together and try to understand each other's problems. Lindner proceeds gently to tell the Youngers that the whites of his community have spent their lives working to keep it a certain way. This community is linked to Civil War whites who fought to maintain a way of life predicated on the labor of black slaves. Lindner's racism is magnified, indeed made laughable, as he tells the Youngers that his offer to buy them out has nothing to do with race prejudice.

Tied into Lindner's assumption that blacks are happier when they live in their own communities are other myths that Hansberry hopes to dispel. Hansberry, like Childress, was passionate in her resentment of black stereotypes perpetuated by whites. Hansberry believed that whites are confounded when blacks cannot seem to find themselves in inaccurate images created by whites.[55] There are two crucial references in *A Raisin in the Sun* to stereotyping. When Mama notices that Ruth is not feeling well, she offers to call Ruth's white employers to tell them that she has the flu. Ruth questions Mama's choice of the flu as an excuse only to have her explain that unless whites are told that blacks are stricken with what whites consider a "respectable" illness, they will assume that their domestic help has been cut up or beaten.

Even more representative of Hansberry's disappointment with stereotyping is Walter Lee's plan to shuffle and grin in order to get money from Lindner. Walter Lee, once he loses the family's inheritance, decides that he will give Lindner what white America expects from blacks: subservience and buffoonery. Hansberry pokes fun at whites who mutilate black speech. Walter Lee tells his family that he will put on a grand performance by crawling on the floor when Lindner arrives and by saying to him, "Captain, Mistuh, Bossman . . . A-hee-hee-hee! . . . just gi' ussen de money, fo' God's sake" (p. 124). These references point to Hansberry's outrage over racial stereotyping that stems from ignorance about blacks.

Believing that if man is "as small and ugly and grotesque as his most inhuman act, he is also as large as his most heroic gesture," Hansberry felt that blacks had the potential for epic magnitude.[56] She believed that the insularity of black struggle was a major reason for their continued oppression. For Hansberry, the key to liberation for blacks, in America and around the world, was political power, which could be attained through solidarity.[57] Hansberry uses Africa in *A Raisin in the Sun* as a symbol of black struggle and freedom. Asagai, an African revolutionary, models for Beneatha the attitudes and commitment needed in order for blacks to secure full citizenship in America and the world. Hansberry sets him up as a link between Africans and African Americans. Asagai tells Beneatha that he would like to take her back to their ancestral home: Nigeria. He tells her that once they are home they would pretend that there were never three hundred years of separation. Hansberry makes it clear that African Americans and their counterparts in other parts of the world are family members who must unite in order to reconstruct a world that looks upon people of color with hostile eyes.

Hansberry's revolutionary spirit is again displayed in her second play, *The Drinking Gourd,* set in the slave South. Hansberry felt quite comfortable writing about the South and considered it her homeland. Her maternal and paternal grandparents and many relatives were Southerners whose sagas of the South's violence did not leave Hansberry unscathed. She was never allowed to forget that her uncle was one among others lynched in the infamous Elaine, Arkansas riot of 1919. Stories of this and other atrocities in the South haunted Hansberry. Hansberry's vision was particularly shaped by the cruelties of the 1950s, including the legal lynching of Josephine Grayson of the "Martinsville Seven" and the gouging out of the eyes of Mrs. Westry's son by policemen who subsequently fatally shot him on the operating table.[58]

Almost a decade later, Hansberry wrote about another son whose eyes are gouged out in *The Drinking Gourd.* She captures the revolutionary spirit of the 1950s and 1960s in the defiant and courageous Hannibal, who resembles the legendary African general of the same name. Hannibal's life changes when he finds freedom in literacy; he becomes contemptuous of the world he sees. Hannibal's insight leads him to disdain the constraints of slavery and to yearn for a better life. Dispelling the myth of the contented slave, Hannibal tells his mother that the only kind of slave he could stand to be is a bad one. When the son of the plantation owner, Everett, discovers that Hannibal has learned to read and to write, he says to him, "There is only one thing I have ever heard of that was proper for an educated slave . . . when a part is corrupted by disease—one cuts out the disease" (p. 732). The overseer is ordered to use the butt end of his whip to hollow out Hannibal's eyes.

Eyes are the windows of the world, and Everett attempts to bar Hannibal from the free world that lies outside of the parameters of slavery. Furthermore, Everett takes away Hannibal's sight for fear that this insurrectionist's vision will corrupt other slaves. Though Hannibal's body is broken, his spirit is not. The play ends with Hannibal escaping to freedom with the aid of his girlfriend, Sarah. This blinding of Hannibal represents the inhumanity heaped upon blacks in the struggle for freedom. Wilkerson contends that the gouging out of Hannibal's eyes suggests the moral bankruptcy of slavery.[59] One might even conjecture that Hansberry uses this play to argue against present day institutional racism, which is rooted in slavery. Hansberry's feeling heart led her to encourage blacks not to accept quietly injustices that began during slavery and continue to be the focus of the struggle. She made good her promise to tell the truth. Hansberry wrote about the world as it is and as she thought it should be.

Ntozake Shange resembles Childress and Hansberry in her commitment to telling the truth. One senses Shange's intensity when she says, "I can't live around a whole bunch of lies. . . . I cannot sustain lies. . . . I refuse to be part of this conspiracy of silence. . . . I'm tired of living lies."[60] Shange, like Childress, Hansberry, and black writers since the colonial period, argues that lies are being told about racism, sexism, poverty, and imperialism. She feels that much of the suffering that women and black people experience goes unrespected in America.[61] Her aim has been to evoke an emotional response as the lives of these walking wounded are laid bare for all to see. She emphatically insists that all of her work is an exploration of people's lives. Shange maintains that she writes about the roughness and the rawness of human life, a perspective shaped by her own personal struggle to survive in America as a black woman.[62]

Her first choreopoem, For Colored Girls Who Have Considered Suicide/ When the Rainbow is Enuf addresses the emotional and physical abuse heaped upon women in America.[63] Shange incisively expresses her commitment to women and children when she says, "There are dead children out here, desperate women out here, the sky is falling and I am choking to death, it

has not always been this way."[64] Shange insists that though there are millions
of American women and children who are abused every year, the American
public refuses to take responsibility for protecting them.[65] Her anger is
evident in her definition of treason, which for her is "when you abuse
countrymen or countrywomen in this country because she or he is a child
or because she is your wife or because she is just a woman on the street
and you feel violent that night and you want to rape somebody."[66]

The tone of this work angered many men, particularly black men, but
incited women of all color from everywhere to hail Shange as a heroine
and as a major American artist. Martin Gottfried of the *New York Post*
describes Shange's tone in *For Colored Girls* as "bitter, funny, ironic, and
savage; fiercely honest and personal."[67] Unequivocally, Shange's first choreopoem presents men as instruments of pain. Sensing the antagonism that
her work stirred up, Shange admits that she is capable of writing "very
pernicious, nasty, awful, terrible, cruel, virtually sadistic things."[68]

Shange, however, has grown since the Broadway production of *For Colored Girls*. She seems less hostile and more consciously aware of the need
to people her theater pieces with dimensional characters who feel as well
as search for reasons for their behavior. Shange reveals herself to be highly
intellectual, immensely skillful and diverse in terms of craft, and acutely
globally oriented. *Three Pieces,* a collection of three dramas, demonstrates
that Shange is as much concerned with the plight of black people as she is
with women's rights. The question of sexual identity does not dominate
over racial identity in *Three Pieces*. In fact, sexism is treated as a manifestation
of racism. Shange's perspective in works beyond *For Colored Girls* shows
her to be multifaceted in her approaches to the world. She resents what she
considers the systematic cultural attack on black people, one which prop-
agates the misconception that black artists can easily be categorized and
placed in a narrow corner.[69]

Recalling that writing *Three Pieces* left her with fury and homicidal desires,
Shange reveals that "in addition to the obvious stress of racism or poverty/
afro-american culture ... has minimized its emotional vocabulary to the
extent that admitting feelings of rage, defeat, frustration is virtually impossible outside of a collective voice."[70] She asserts that the characters in
Three Pieces are "afflicted with the kinds of insecurities and delusions only
available to those who learned themselves thru the traumas of racism."[71]
Though it was not commercially successful, *Spell # 7,* included in *Three
Pieces,* is an excellent example of Shange's breadth as an artist.[72] One can
only surmise that the American public still does not want to be told the
truth about the struggling lives of millions of black people in America.

A gifted poet/playwright, Shange orchestrates symbols both in *For Colored Girls* and in *Spell # 7*. These indices to tonal form advance meaning
in Shange's choreopoems. One symbol in *For Colored Girls* that legitimizes
women's vision is the array of colors worn by the seven women, including

brown, yellow, red, green, purple, blue, and orange. These colors of the rainbow suggest the diversity of women, the limitless possibilities. Shange uses the rainbow myth—presumably a pot of gold can be found at the end of a rainbow—to illustrate that these Colored women are moving toward something good, liberating, and dynamic. Shange also uses the elusiveness and ephemeral nature of the rainbow to demonstrate the mystery of life, particularly of the lives of her women who have been marred by strangers and acquaintances alike. There is a certain amount of illusory hope expressed by these women who do not always understand why they have been victimized. With names lower cased, suggesting self-effacement, invisibility, and a lack of self-confidence, these women battle the storm before they can enjoy the quiet of the rainbow.

Another important symbol is the tagging that occurs as the play opens. The seven women stand motionless until lady in brown tags each one. This touching invigorates each woman who comes alive to share her experiences with the world. This gesture is significant because it stands for the networking that women must involve themselves in if they are to have the strength to survive the blows leveled at them in a sexist world. The tagging also suggests a spiritual and cultural communion among women.

Shange ends the choreopoem with a gesture that is more powerful than the tagging. The seven women experience a laying on of hands, chanting that they have found God in themselves and they love Her fiercely. This locking of hands represents a cementing of spirits and sensibilities. These women celebrate their wholeness. They form an impenetrable circle that stands for the shield they must wear to buffer against the pain and to empower themselves with the courage to begin again. This closure represents freedom to move beyond the anguish and pain. Shange emphasizes that women must be about the business of nurturing and protecting each other, and that women must turn inward to the God in themselves for sustenance.

Dancing is another symbol that shapes tonal form in this choreopoem. Resembling a catharsis, dancing is a freeing agent for these Colored girls. Shange's female characters also use dancing as a defense mechanism. While whirling around on the stage, lady in yellow says, "we gotta dance to keep from cryin" (p. 15). Similarly, lady in brown retorts with, "we gotta dance to keep from dyin" (p. 15). There is a sense of desperation and outrage in Shange's tone as she flings these characters across the stage to dance out the pain of their lives. The dancing also suggests exploration. The characters come to know their bodies and invariably their souls through dancing. Of her love for dancing, Shange wrote, "With dance I discovered my body more intimately than I had imagined possible . . . pulling ancient trampled spirits out of present tense Afro-American dance."[73] Shange uses dancing in "Graduation Nite" to suggest initiation into womanhood. The lady in yellow tells how she danced "nasty ole tricks" frenetically, reminiscent of an African tribal ritual, just before giving up her virginity in the back seat of a Buick on graduation night (p. 9). Choreographing both their vulnerability and resiliency, Shange portrays the spirit of survival of these Colored girls.

Dancing is also symbolic in Shange's *Spell # 7*. Shange uses dancing and music to suggest linkages. She believes that black playwrights should not be allowed to work without dancers and musicians because "black people have some music and movement in their lives."[74] Operating from this principle, Shange links her characters by having them, at one point, engage in a series of steps or dance routines that identify every period of African American entertainment, including acrobats, comedians, tap-dancers, Calindy dancers, Cotton Club choruses, and Apollo Theater du-wop groups. The characters' friendships are tested and strengthened in *Spell # 7* as they reenact, through dancing, the various stories of their lives and the lives of a host of black heroes, including Muhammad Ali, Ishmael Reed, Marcus Garvey, the Commodores, Bob Marley, Stevie Wonder, and the Miracles. Through dancing, the characters develop a sense of familiarity and family, a shared cultural heritage. The dancing becomes a cultural communion, with the participants deriving spiritual nourishment and a sense of impenetrable solidarity.

Spell # 7 is a theater piece that treats a multitude of intellectual disciplines, including psychotherapy, philosophy, and foreign languages and countries. Equally diverse is its treatment of the subjects of racism and sexism. Shange imaginatively develops the mask as a symbol. A huge black-face mask hanging from the ceiling is lowered and raised at several intervals in *Spell # 7*. This larger than life mask represents the misrepresentations of black life both on and off the American stage. Shange's characters in *Spell # 7*, like the persona in Paul Laurence Dunbar's "We Wear the Mask," reveal that they have had to lie, grin, and hide the truths about their lives in order to survive in America. With the mask looming, the play opens with a magician who promises to cast a spell on black America. As if to counter all that the mask has done to shape blacks' attitudes about themselves and each other, the magician announces that he is going to make them love being colored.

When the magician casts his spell, the characters tear off their black-face masks, representing their freedom to reveal secrets, fantasies, nightmares, and hope. They become uninhibited and begin to tell truths about the journey of blacks in America. The magician then commands the hideous, gigantic mask to disappear. Though the mask rises, it is never hidden from the audience's view. Shange does not want the audience to forget that the mask is symbolic of oppression. She makes this clear by linking the raising of the mask to the preceding lynch mob scene. The menacing shouts, cries, and laughter of the mob cement the cast to the floor while the unmasking frees them.

Like Childress and Hansberry, Shange levels an indictment against the American stage, which mirrors ideas tainted by racism. Under the watchful eye of the hovering mask, the characters voice their anger at the stereotypical roles that are offered to them. They express contempt at being forced to squabble over such degrading roles as mammy, prostitute, and buffoon. Bettina, a struggling actress, says, "if that director asks me to play it any blacker/i'm gonna have to do it in a mammy dress" (p. 14). Trying to comfort Lily, a fellow actress who complains that the only roles she can find are ones that call for blacks to sing and dance or shuffle, grin, hum, and pray, Bettina says, "at least yr not playin a whore/if some other woman comes in here & tells me she's playing a whore/ i think i might kill her" (p. 23). Lily teases Bettina, telling her that she would kill the woman and then take the part for herself. The scarcity of realistic, dramatic roles for blacks has been a serious concern for Shange and for countless other artists, particularly because the stereotyping continues both on and off the American stage.

Shange, armed with quick and bitter wit, tears away at racially biased myths about black women. Shange claims that black women are unloved, unwanted and unattended because of these myths. Lou, one of the black male characters, says, "nobody loves the black woman like they love farrah fawcett-majors. the whole world dont turn out for a dead black woman like they did for marilyn monroe" (p. 36). In another scene, a black man recently back from Europe sits in awe of a black woman who reads Nietzsche, speaks several foreign languages, and talks about global issues. The man tells her several times that she is not like any black woman he has ever met. Shange argues that this is one of the lies that racist America has fed to black men. Her message is that there are millions of black women who are intellectuals, and that black women for too long have been assigned restricting labels.

If there is any question that Shange views sexism as an outgrowth of racism, one need only examine the scene that pokes fun at white women who accept and promote these myths about blacks. Shange ridicules white women by depicting them as gullible, frivolous, artificial, and emotionally weak. Natalie, a not too successful performer, announces that she is going to be a white girl for a day. She tells the cast that the first thing a white girl does when she wakes up in the morning is to give thanks that she is not black, and then she flings her hair and waters her plants. Shange depicts white women as paranoid of blacks, thinking that black men plot to beat, rape, murder, or marry them. Also coming under attack are whites who write about blacks. The persona says, "after all, gertrude stein wanted to know abt the black women/alice adams wrote *thinking abt billie*/joyce carol oates has three different black characters all with the same name/i guess cuz we are underdeveloped individuals or cuz we are all the same" (p. 48).

Shange is clearly resentful in her treatment of the white female liberal.

Natalie points out that there are some white women who castigate themselves because they were not born black. Natalie says, "yes, i'm sorry they
were born niggahs. But then if I cant punish myself to death for being
white/i certainly cant in good conscience keep waiting for the cleaning lady"
(p. 49). Shange's most severe indictment against white female liberals is her
denouncement of them as women who have to take twenty Valium a day
to contend with their ignorance of the world, ERA, and men. Unlike *For
Colored Girls,* which seems to focus on the common suffering of women,
Spell # 7 singles out black women as victims at the hands of white men
and white women.

Spell # 7 is not without elements of hope. Shange challenges blacks to
rise above injustices and particularly to avoid hurting each other. Natalie
says, "surviving the impossible is sposed to accentuate the positive aspects
of a people" (p. 51). The play ends as it began, with the magician casting
a spell to make blacks love themselves. So as not to imply that the struggle
is over, Shange has the huge minstrel mask lowered while the cast sings
"colored & love it" (p. 52).

It is not surprising that Childress, Hansberry, and Shange chose to write
about racism, sexism, and poverty. These are problems that seriously affect
the quality of life for African Americans. These contemporary playwrights
have taken up the cross once carried by black women playwrights who
wrote before 1950. Whereas the early mavericks often trod gently and spoke
softly, these contemporary black women playwrights have lifted their voices
in order to raise consciousness in this "Theater of Struggle." The authors'
tones, shaped by the skillful development of private and public symbols,
range within each play from disappointment to outrage.

These women could not look upon America and the world and feel
anything but outrage at society's inhumanity. Unable to escape into a world
of racelessness, these dramatists wrote candidly about blacks and their struggle in America. Each of these playwrights wrote about the extraordinary
spirit of survival of blacks and offered encouragement. Each believed mightily in the capability of individuals to make the world a better place. Though
each has her own brand of humor, wit, and wrath, the messages are the
same: African Americans must struggle together in order to make substantial
social, political, and economic gains.

NOTES

1. C. Hughes Holman, *A Handbook to Literature* (New York: The Bobbs-Merrill
Co, Inc., 1972), p. 231.

2. Fred B. Millet and Gerald Eades Bentley, *The Act of the Drama* (New York:
D. Appleton-Century Company, 1935), pp. 4–5.

3. Stanley Vincent Longman, *Composing Drama for Stage and Screen* (Boston,
Mass.: Allyn and Bacon, Inc. 1986), p. 119.

4. Kenneth M. Cameron and Theodore J.C. Hoffman, *The Theatrical Response* (New York: The Macmillan Company, 1969), p. 237.

5. Ibid., p. 236.

6. Ibid., p. 237.

7. Roderick Bladel, *Walter Kerr: An Analysis of His Criticism* (Metuchen, N.J.: The Scarecrow Press, Inc., 1976), pp. 30–37.

8. Ibid., p. 39.

9. Alice Childress, "A Candle in a Gale Wind," in *Black Women Writers (1950–1980)*, ed. Mari Evans (New York: Anchor Press/Doubleday, 1984), p. 115.

10. Ibid.

11. Alice Childress, "Black Writer's Views on Literary Lions and Values," *Negro Digest*, vol. 17 (January 1968), p. 86.

12. Childress, "A Candle in a Gale Wind," p. 113.

13. Ibid.

14. Alice Childress, "Knowing the Human Condition," in *Black American Literature and Humanism*, ed. R. Baxter Miller (Lexington, Ky.: The University Press of Kentucky, 1981), pp. 9–10.

15. Alice Childress, "The Negro Woman in American Literature," *Freedomways*, vol. 16 (First Quarter 1966), p. 16.

16. Ibid., p. 19.

17. Childress, "A Candle in a Gale Wind," p. 113.

18. Alice Childress, "Interjections," in *Black American Writers Past and Present: A Biographical and Bibliographical Dictionary*, eds. Theresa Gunnels, Carol Fairbanks, and Esther Spring (Metuchen, N.J.: The Scarecrow Press, 1975), p. 151.

19. Childress, "A Candle in a Gale Wind," p. 114.

20. Alice Childress, "Florence," in *Masses and Mainstream*, vol. 3 (October 1950), pp. 34–47. All quotes and references to the play are based upon this source. Also, see chapter two for synopsis and additional analysis of *Florence*.

21. Samuel A. Hay, "Alice Childress' Dramatic Structure," in *Black Women Writers (1950–1980)*, ed. Mari Evans (New York: Anchor Press/Doubleday, 1984), p. 119.

22. Ibid., p. 117.

23. Hay refers to a book by Susanne K. Langer, *Feeling and Form* (New York: Scribner's, 1953). Langer is considered by many to be a leading scholar on the nature of form in drama.

24. Hay, p. 117.

25. The Underground Railroad and its significance to black people concerned Childress, as is evidenced by her writing of the play *Harriet Tubman*, (New York: Coward, McCann, Geoghegen, 1976).

26. Hay, p. 118.

27. Ibid., p. 118.

28. Alice Childress, "Trouble in Mind," in *Black Theatre: A Twentieth Century Collection of the Works of its Best Playwrights*, ed. Lindsay Patterson (New York: Dodd, Mead, and Co., 1971), pp. 137–174. All quotes and references to the play are based upon this source. Also, see chapter two for synopsis and additional analysis of *Trouble in Mind*.

29. Holman, p. 521.

30. Richard Hornby, *Drama, Metadrama, and Perception* (Lewisburg, Pa.: Bucknell University Press, 1986), p. 31.

31. Ibid., p. 32.

32. Dedria Bryfonski, ed. "Alice Childress," *Contemporary Literary Criticism* (Detroit, Mich.: Gale Research Co., 1980), p. 104.

33. Hornby, p. 33. See this source for a detailed explanation of "inset" versus "framed" types of the play within a play.

34. Ibid., pp. 40–45. See this source for a chronicling of the appearance of the play within a play technique in plays since the Renaissance.

35. Ibid., p. 45. See this source for a detailed definition of "ostraneniye."

36. Definitions of public and private symbols can be found in Stephen Minot, *Three Genres: The Writing of Fiction, Poetry, and Drama* (Englewood Cliffs, N.J.: Prentice-Hall, Inc. 1965), p. 307.

37. Alice Childress, "Mojo: A Black Love Story," in *Black World* vol. 20 (April 1971), pp. 54–82. All quotes and references to the play are based upon this source. Also, see chapter two for synopsis and additional analysis of *Mojo*.

38. Hay, p. 126.

39. Childress, "A Candle in a Gale Wind," p. 115.

40. Ibid., p. 115.

41. Hay, p. 127.

42. Lorraine Hansberry, "The Negro Writer and His Roots: Toward a New Romanticism," *Black Scholar*, vol. 12 (March/April 1981), p. 11.

43. For more information about the lynching of Emmett Till and about recorded occurrences of thousands of lynchings in the United States, see the following sources: Lerone Bennett, Jr., *Before the Mayflower: A History of Black America* (Baltimore, Md.: Penguin Book, 1966), and Albert P. Blaustein and Robert L. Zangrando, eds. *Civil Rights and the Black American* (New York: Washington Square Press, 1968).

44. Hansberry, "The Negro Writer and His Roots," p. 10.

45. Lorraine Hansberry, *To Be Young, Gifted and Black*, adapted by Robert Nemiroff (New York: New American Library, 1969), p. 103.

46. Ibid., p. 222.

47. Lorraine Hansberry, "A Challenge to Artists," *Freedomways*, vol. 3 (Winter 1963), p. 32.

48. Hansberry, *To Be Young, Gifted and Black*, pp. 129–130.

49. Lorraine Hansberry, "A Raisin in the Sun," in *A Raisin in the Sun and The Sign in Sidney Brustein's Window* (New York: New American Library, 1966), pp. 11–130. All quotes and references to the play are based upon this source. Also, see chapter two for synopsis and additional analysis of *A Raisin in the Sun*.

50. Lorraine Hansberry, "The Drinking Gourd," in *Black Theater U.S.A.: Forty-Five Plays by Black Americans, 1847–1974*, eds. James V. Hatch and Ted Shine (New York: The Free Press, 1974), pp. 714–736. All quotes and references to the play are based upon this source. Also, see chapter two for synopsis and additional analysis of *The Drinking Gourd*.

51. Hansberry, *To Be Young, Gifted and Black*, p. 41.

52. Margaret Wilkerson, "The Sighted Eyes and Feeling Heart of Lorraine Hansberry," *Black American Literature Forum*, vol. 17 (Spring 1983), p. 11.

53. Hansberry, *To Be Young, Gifted and Black*, pp. 131–132.

54. Mary Louise Anderson, "Black Matriarchy: Portrayals of Women in Three Plays," *Black American Literature Forum,* vol. 10 (Spring 1976), pp. 93–94.

55. Hansberry, *To Be Young, Gifted and Black,* p. 210.

56. Hansberry, "The Negro Writer and His Roots," p. 12.

57. Ibid., p. 9.

58. Robert Nemiroff, "From These Roots: Lorraine Hansberry and the South," *Southern Exposure,* vol. 10 (September/October 1984), pp. 33–34.

59. Wilkerson, p. 66.

60. Claudia Tate, ed. *Black Women Writers At Work* (New York: Continuum, 1983), p. 158.

61. Ibid., p. 155.

62. Ibid., pp. 156–171.

63. Ntozake Shange, *For Colored Girls Who Have Considered Suicide/When the Rainbow is Enuf* (New York: Bantam Books, 1977). All quotes and references to the play are based upon this source. Also, see chapter two for synopsis and additional analysis of *For Colored Girls Who Have Considered Suicide/When the Rainbow is Enuf.*

64. George Greenfield Associates, 217 East 82nd Street, New York, New York, serving as Shange's agent in 1982, circulated a flyer advertising Shange's availability for lectures, readings, and workshops.

65. Pepsi Charles, transcriber, "Ntozake Shange Talks with Marcia Ann Gilespie," *Essence,* May 1985, p. 203.

66. Ibid., p. 203.

67. Ntozake Shange, *For Colored Girls Who Have Considered Suicide/When the Rainbow is Enuf* (New York: Bantam Books, 1977). Gottfried's comments about Shange's tone appear on the first page of this edition.

68. Tate, p. 165.

69. Ibid., p. 164.

70. Ntozake Shange, *Three Pieces* (New York: St. Martin's Press, 1981), p. xii.

71. Ibid., pp. xiv-xv.

72. Ntozake Shange, "Spell # 7" in *Three Pieces* (New York: St. Martin's Press, 1981). All quotes and references to the play are based upon this source. Also, see chapter two for synopsis and additional analysis of *Spell # 7.*

73. Shange, *For Colored Girls Who Have Considered Suicide/When the Rainbow is Enuf,* pp. xv-xvi.

74. Ibid., p. x.

4

Structural Form: African American Initiation and Survival Rituals

Structural form has evolved considerably since "the period of dramatic experimentation," an era that includes such playwrights as Aeschylus (525–456 B.C.), Sophocles (495–406 B.C.), Euripides (480–406 B.C.) and Aristophanes (448–380 B.C.).[1] During this early period, it was not uncommon for stage plays to run an entire day.[2] Between 975 A.D. and the seventeenth century, structural form underwent a series of revolutions to accommodate the moves from the miracle or mystery play, to the morality play, to the interlude or nonreligious-based plays.[3]

Dramatic structure varied during these centuries to please the tastes of the crowds at given periods. Shakespeare, however, popularized the five-act structure that was believed by Gustav Freytag to correspond to the five-part dramatic structure: an act of exposition, an act of rising action, an act of climax, an act of falling action, and an act of catastrophe.[4] Commenting on changes that have taken place in mechanical divisions of dramatic structure, Longman asserts, "For several centuries, the five-act structure was regarded as essential. For much of the present century, the three-act play has been the norm, recently replaced by the two-act structure.[5]

More important than the mechanical divisions is the logical progression of thoughts and action in plays. Frederick J. Hunter, in *The Power of Dramatic Form*, emphasizes that the aim of structural form is to advance meaning or thoughts in a play. He claims that structural form allows playwrights to express the truth about justice, freedom, love, beauty, peace, fame, fortune, generosity, selfishness, economy, waste, marriage, sex, larceny, and big business.[6]

Though radical changes have occurred in certain aspects of the theater over the centuries, many European conventions dating back to the ancients continue to influence contemporary American theater. The fundamental dramatic structure seems impervious to change, as evidenced by a survey of current scholarship. Stuart Griffiths, in *How Plays are Made*, argues that dramatic structure is shaped by action, tension, and characters that live.[7] Raymond Hull, in *How to Write a Play*, contends that dramatic structure is based on "the rule of the six C's": conflict, characters, complications, crisis, catastrophe, and conclusion.[8] Longman, in *Composing Drama for Stage and Screen*, asserts that the typical phases of dramatic action include precipitating context, the emergence of the driving force, resistance, crux, and denouement. Longman points out that these phases serve to structure action, giving the play "a coherence, a system of relative values, by which the audience knows what has import and what does not."[9] The ideas about structural form expressed by Griffiths, Hull, and Longman are not very different from concepts expressed in Freytag's Pyramid of epitasis or rising action, tragic force or climax, and catastasis or falling action.[10]

American theater has not only been influenced by European models but by non-European ones as well. It has been affected, in varying degrees, by Japanese Noh and Kubuki plays, Chinese Ching Hsi drama, Indian Sanscrit drama, and traditional African drama, all of which contain elements of mime, dancing, stylized gestures, song, and instrumental music.[11] An examination of the plays of Pulitzer Prize winning Wole Soyinka reveals that plays by contemporary African American women strikingly resemble Africa's methexic drama, containing songs, drums, dance, rituals, masks, chants, music, and the call and response.

Childress, Hansberry, and Shange have adapted traditional structural form to express black culture and history. With the continual broadening of the American stage, it is not surprising that these black playwrights have redefined American theater to include African myths, rituals, and conventions. Acceptance of cultural diversity and a tolerance for experimentation in the American theater seem to be the trend of the last several decades. Walter Kerr asserts that since 1959, play structure has become increasingly flexible. Kerr argues that "the familiar boundaries are shot to blazes, and every young playwright is obliged to invent his own form."[12]

Kimberly Benston concurs that structural form is less rigid and that artists, particularly black playwrights, have enriched the American theater with their African traditions. Arguing that little attention has been paid to the structural dimension of plays by blacks, Benston contends that "black drama's aesthetic describes a curve which moves dialectically from quasi-naturalism and overt rage against Euro-American institutions toward the shaping of uniquely Afro-American mythologies and symbolisms, flexibility of dramatic form, and participatory theater within the Black community."[13] For Benston, European drama, which is basically mimetic—an imitation or representation of an action—amounts to "the spectacle observed," whereas African American drama grows out of rituals that dissolve "traditional divisions between actor and spectator, between self and other."[14] Alvin Goldfarb and Edwin Wilson note that "while western theatre and drama have emphasized separation of audience and actor, individual creativity, and a set text from which little variation is permitted, African theatre has emphasized audience participation, group creativity, and improvisation. The result is that while the purpose of the European theatre is to entertain and to teach, that of the African is to embody and affect, and to be."[15]

It is too simplistic and not altogether accurate to treat black plays as an imitation of either Europe or African models. An examination of Childress' *Wedding Band* and *Wine in the Wilderness*, Hansberry's *A Raisin in the Sun*, and Shange's *A Photograph: Lovers in Motion* reveals a unique brand of theater in which many heritages come together, functioning side by side, to produce theater that is engaging, provocative, and diverse. These dramatists, particularly Childress and Hansberry, and to a lesser degree Shange, have retained traditional dramatic structure but with some very important modifications. The dramatic action in these plays is inextricably linked to and is defined by the experiences of African Americans, which are rooted in African rituals. The bulk of this chapter examines the structural form in black women's playwriting as it is shaped by African American initiation and survival rituals. Female characters in these plays journey through several stages of psychological growth. Each stage is a complete infrastructure that advances the action of the play. Parallels can be drawn between these stages of growth and the progression through the phases of exposition, complication, and resolution. The progression, however, is undeniably linked to African American struggle for survival and wholeness.

These stages of growth are similar to those discussed by Carol Pearson and Katherine Pope in *The Female Hero in American and British Literature*, wherein the archetypal journey of the heroine is broken into three stages: the departure, the initiation, and the return. Pearson and Pope cite Joseph Campbell's study *The Hero with a Thousand Faces*, in which Campbell emphasizes that the heroine returns to her community as a whole person only after having entered the world of chaos where she must confront and slay dragons that paralyze her. In slaying these dragons, she wins "the ultimate boon of inexhaustible life, joy, and wholeness" and returns to the community not only to facilitate or cement her wholeness but to rejuvinate the community as well.[16]

In selected plays by Childress, Hansberry, and Shange, the female characters undergo a personal and sometimes political odyssey or search for wholeness as they progress through six stages: koinonia, logus, metanoia, kerygma, didache, and eucharistia.[17] These stages, which have their equivalency in Freytag's Pyramid, are terms based on Koine Greek, the marketplace or common man's Greek spoken during the Hellenistic through Roman periods. Lending themselves to broad interpretations these terms are herewith defined and placed in the context of African American initiation and survival rituals.[18]

Koinonia means fellowship, to be united in something deeply, family, to be inextricably bound by common grounds or experiences, a sharing of life's moments, a foundation, values imparted to a person via her community, a fellowship that helps to define and positively affirm a person's sense of self. In short, the koinonia is a person's beginnings, and there can be no exit or departure that Pearson and Pope speak of unless there is a koinonia. Reverend Victor Cohea contends that koinonia, as it applies to blacks in America, is a stage of growth that does not generally build in racial bias as a buffer. Cohea argues that parents of black children generally do not teach them about racism and, in fact, do their best to shield them from prejudice. According to Cohea, black children become very vulnerable when they go out into the world that is inundated by racism.[19]

Credence is given to Cohea's comments about blacks' vulnerability when in the second stage, the logus, blacks are shocked, sometimes marred permanently, by the racism that they encounter. Blacks often experience anything from disappointment to rage as they move out into a world that lets them know almost daily that blacks are considered second class citizens, if indeed, citizens at all. In the narrow sense, logus means "the word of Jesus," but in its broader interpretation logus can be defined as an awareness moment, a revelation that sets things in motion, a "loss of innocence." Logus parallels what Lindsay Patterson in *Black Theater* refers to as the "Nigger Moment." Patterson makes the following assertion:

> But there comes a time in life when one loses his innocence and is pushed boldly into the real world . . . I mean by lost innocence that specific moment when a black discovers he is a 'nigger' and his mentality shifts gears and begins that long, uphill climb to bring psychological order out of chaos. It's not a moment, however, easily detected. All of black literature is more or less unconsciously preoccupied with precisely pinpointing and defining it. It is an elusive, complex moment, with complex reactions and can occur at four or forty.[20]

The logus serves to bring on confusion and doubt. Lucius Guillory claims that "Logus is that testing element which determines if a person can withstand the subtle and overt racist-based derision. Logus is the pain one feels at having to admit that black people are victimized because of skin color. It is when a black person realizes that his poverty or illiteracy or exclusion from or failure in a given field is a direct result of racism. Unfortunately, blacks frequently causes other blacks to experience a nigger moment."[21]

The metanoia, the third stage of growth, involves a turning away or turning around, a quest to understand and be saved from the confusion and disappointment, a struggle to cope with the oppression, a coming to terms, an uphill climb accompanied by a series of trials and errors. Cohea asserts that "the metanoia occurs when the person discovers that the 'nigger moment' was a hoax . . . that he or she is a worthy human being and deserving of equitable treatment."[22] The kerygma generally follows the metanoia. This stage of growth centers around the heroine's compulsion to speak. It is when she lashes out and tells her agitator, usually a naive loved one, that she will not stand being treated shoddily. It is an irrefutable "telling off" or "slaying of the dragon." Kerygma suggests explosion, sometimes verbal but oftentimes physical. Pearson and Pope suggest that "the hero who is an outsider because she is female, black, or poor is almost always a revolutionary."[23]

The didache, the fifth stage, is a summation, the bottom line of a formal message that the heroine passes on to blacks. It is her legacy to the young or the naive who may have condemned her or some other black person for some error in judgment. The message, or didache, serves as a catalyst for those who have sat in judgment and catapults the heroine into the final stage of growth. The eucharistia, stage six, is a combining of inner wholeness with outward community. This wholeness or completeness leads the heroine to cement a family, whether it is a consanguineous or spiritual one, that has been torn apart. Oftentimes, the heroine rejoins her immediate family, or lover, or significant other, or community to celebrate her renewed faith in the nutritive value of solidarity. Lucius Guillory points out that "the community reaffirms his or her newfound positive sense of self."[24] Eucharistia is a rejoicing at the commonness that the community shares; it is a celebration of self, life, and community wholeness and strength. The heroine comes to some sort of decision about the course of the rest of her life and finds peace in that choice. Reverend Cohea contends that "there can be no eucharistia if there is no koinonia."[25]

Julia in Childress' *Wedding Band* sets out on an odyssey that culminates in emotional growth.[26] Julia's first stage of growth, koinonia, provides readers with a clear sense of her past, both immediate and ancestral. She recalls her beginnings by telling of her father's back-breaking years as a brick mason. Her pride in his contributions to his community magnifies her sense of family solidarity. Boasting of her father's accomplishments, Julia says, "My father was somebody. He helped put up Roper Hospital and Webster Rice Mills after the earthquake wiped the face-a this Gawdforsaken city clean" (p. 331). Julia's respect for her father's years of working to make ends meet for the family is apparent by her reference to the fact that he gave his absolute best in spite of the fact that he earned one-third of what white brick masons on the same projects were paid.

More is learned about Julia's roots when she confides to Herman, her white lover and best friend, that she is descended from a generation of poor people. Annoyed because her boyfriend tries to elicit sympathy by telling her that his family did not have a big name and was not from the aristocracy,

Julia quips, "Poor! My gramma was a slave wash-woman bustin' suds for free. Can't get poorer than that" (p. 332). When Herman insists that his family had it just as hard as hers, Julia digs deeper into her past to demonstrate that hers was one of enslavement and his was not. She tells him that regardless of what he considers as his family's hardships, they are miniscule compared to her beginnings. Deriving a sense of strength and courage from reliving the collective past of blacks in America, Julia reminds Herman that her people built the pretty white mansions and the fishing boats, made the clothes, and raised and cooked the food for whites for free. As if summoning up dead African spirits, Julia says, "All-a my people that's been killed . . . It's your people that killed 'em . . . all that's been in bondage—your people put 'em there—all that didn't go to school—your people kept 'em out" (p. 332). Herman's protestations go unheard as Julia tells him that all the dead slaves in South Carolina continue to serve their masters well because their hearts' blood nourishes the cotton crops. Julia links herself to African slaves when she says that the roots of the cotton are tangled and wrapped around her bones.

Julia's koinonia is also shaped by the immediate community in which she lives. As the play opens, Julia has just moved into a backyard where four houses are owned by a black woman entrepreneur, Fanny. Childress holds Julia up as a part of a diverse community. Margaret Wilkerson, in *9 Plays by Black Women*, comments that "in the backyard communities where Julia and Herman meet, there is pettiness, racial ugliness, jealousy, and exploitation—from the blacks as well as the whites; but there is also nobility, gentleness, pride, and love."[27] Though each woman has her own peculiar problem, she is so very much like the next one in terms of struggling to survive. One of Julia's neighbors, Mattie, is alone because her husband is away serving as a merchant marine. Coupled with the difficulty of raising a child alone, Mattie has to cope with the fact that the bureaucracy refuses to honor her common-law marriage and withholds her husband's check. Often left with a mere quarter in her coffers, Mattie is typical of Childress' empathy for impecunious folk. Another neighbor of Julia's is Lulu, whose husband used to beat her so mercilessly that one day while she was telling her troubles, her only baby son wandered off and was killed on the railroad tracks. To atone for what she considers is her sin, Lulu adopted Nelson, who has a pail of dirty water dumped on him by an angry mob because he dared to wear his U.S. Army uniform while on furlough. Fanny, the neighbor Julia likes least, adds spice to the community as she goes around complaining about the terrible burden of always having to be a credit to her race. She, too, has known the pain of loneliness as has Julia, a woman who has moved from one secluded place to another to keep neighbors from interfering in her affair with a white man. All four of these women are united by their common experiences in white America and, later in the play, become the group to which Jullia returns to share her wholeness or completeness.

Childress makes several references to Julia's second stage of growth, the logus or nigger moment that apparently left emotional scars. At two points in the play, Julia recalls that her Aunt Cora raised her after her parents died. She reminisces with pain and bitterness about the fact that her Aunt Cora sent her off on a live-in job in the best years of her youth. Sharing the degradation she felt as a black youth working in the kitchen of a white woman who denigrated her every action, Julia tells Herman that Miss Bessie was "one mean white woman" (p. 286). When Herman tells her simply to say that Miss Bessie was a mean woman, Julia snaps, "Well, yes, but she was white too" (p. 286). Clearly, Julia is trying delicately to tell Herman that part of the reason why Miss Bessie was so mean to her was because of racism.

For most African Americans, each time an incident involving racial prejudice occurs, the logus or nigger moment is evoked, analogous to a recurring nightmare wherein a black person's sense of self-worth is assaulted. The result is that blacks do not merely have one nigger moment but a chain of them as they journey through life. There are at least two instances when Julia is reminded that society views her as a nigger. The first occurrence is when The Bell Man, a white man who goes door to door selling stockings, lingerie, and sheets, boldly propositions Julia. He walks into this woman's home whom he has never met, sits on her bed, bounces up and down, and says, "Sister, Um in need for it like I never been before. Will you 'commodate me? Straighten me, fix me up, will you?' " (p. 271). The vulgar gesture is exacerbated when he tells Julia that he is as quick as a jack rabbit and the sex act would not last more than five minutes. Not noticing the repulsion on her face, The Bell Man tells Julia that he is as clean as the Board of Health because he does not believe in dipping into everything. As a further sign of his invalidation of her personhood, he offers her stockings as payment because he says he could not afford to pay for her services with cash. When Julia screams at him to leave, he exits muttering, "She must be goin' crazy. Unfriendly, sick-minded bitch" (p. 272). The Bell Man never realizes the impact of his insult and violation of Julia because he is a product of a tradition that devalues black women's bodies and minds. His philistine denial of Julia's personhood magnifies his backwardness.

A second reference to Julia's logus is made when she and Herman reminisce about the good and bad times of their ten-year affair. Herman mourns the fact that he has not been able to give Julia his name and protection because of South Carolina laws forbidding mixed marriages. He also feels trapped because in ten years he has not been able to pay back his mother the three-thousand dollars she lent him to open up the bakery that is floundering during war time. Herman tells Julia to look to the day when they can escape to the North, Philadelphia or New York, to get married. Herman's words fall upon deaf ears because Julia has heard these ineffectual promises before. While he imagines a world where he will be free to love her, Julia's thoughts fly to the albatross of their relationship: his mother. Julia tells Herman that she will never forget his mother's words to his sister, "Annabelle, you've got a brother who makes pies and loves a nigger" (p. 285). At this juncture, *Wedding Band* "forces the audience to confront fully the historical baggage of racial antipathy."[28] Herman, pulled very swiftly from his fantasy world, asks her how is it that she can remember these things from seven or eight years ago, and accuses her of harboring anger. She tells Herman that she is not angry but that she does remember. It is the memory of a logus or nigger moment that often propels blacks to reconstruct the course of their lives.

Julia moves into the third stage of growth, the metanoia, once the illusion that she is equal in American society is shattered. Julia's quest to understand why Herman's mother and other whites in her community say and do hateful things to blacks leads her to make discoveries about herself. She realizes that she needs to be around people who will not make her feel dirty. She also tells Herman about the loneliness she has known since she cut herself off from the black community in order to maintain her relationship with him. When he asks her why she moved into somebody's backyard, Julia tries to make Herman understand that she desperately needs other people, especially of similar background. She reminds him that she does not go anywhere nor does she know anybody. The more articulate she becomes about not liking her illicit liaison with Herman and about her severed ties from the black community, the less appealing the relationship looks to her. The uncertainty that Julia begins to feel about her relationship with Herman develops into newfound strength as she comes to terms with the fact that Herman is a weak man and may never extricate himself from his mother's clutches. Julia's uphill climb takes the form of her turning away from Herman's promises and looking for solace in things black.

Julia's epiphany or metanoia is apparent when she accepts an invitation from Fanny to attend a religious ceremony in the backyard. Though Herman protests that the women in the neighborhood only want to make fun of her, and though he conveniently announces that he will on Monday morning buy Julia the much talked about ticket to New York, Julia seems resolved. She quickly kisses Herman on the cheek and tells him that it has been a long time since anybody invited her anywhere and that she intends to go to the prayer meeting. Once there, among her sisters in the struggle, Julia transforms into a woman who is not afraid to embrace her community. She stands before peers who disapproved of her affair with Herman and tells them that she is sorry for past sins and that from here on in she intends to live in dignity according to the laws of God and man. Julia recognizes, perhaps for the first time, that she has a right to feel good about her life and that she has the responsibility of not giving anyone easy access to humiliate her.

Armed with this new awareness, Julia moves into the fourth stage of growth, the kerygma. When Herman's mother, Frieda, alias Miss Thelma, comes with horse and buggy to pick up her son who has fallen ill with the flu in Julia's bed, she at first pretends that Julia is not there. She commands Fanny to go through Julia's dresser drawers to locate Herman's belongings, flaunting that she will burn them. Without acknowledging Julia's presence, Herman's mother asks him where is his money and did he give it to her [Julia]. When Miss Thelma finally speaks to Julia, she accuses her of thievery and lowlife. Julia, trying hard to control her temper, tells Miss Thelma that she will not match words with her because "I'm too much of a lady" (p. 313). Miss Thelma shouts to Julia that a lady "oughta learn how to keep her dress down" (p. 312).

Julia explodes and commences to slay the dragon who dares to come into her house and tell her that she is filth. Julia tells Miss Thelma, "I'm your damn daughter-in-law, you old bitch" (p. 317). Julia tells Miss Thelma that she is the "black thing" who has secretly cared for her during the past ten years, buying a hot water bottle to ease her rheumatism, purchasing a flannel gown to warm her mean, old body, selecting the lace curtains for her parlor, and sewing the shirtwaist that she now wears. Furious that Julia has embarrassed her by telling of unmatched acts of kindness, Miss Thelma flings at Julia, "Nigger whore . . . he used you for a garbage pail . . . Dirty black nigger" (p. 318). Julia, with the ultimate insult flung into her face, shouts to Miss Thelma and Herman, "Out! Out! Out! And take the last ten years-a my life with you and . . . when he gets better . . . keep him home. Killers, Murderers . . . Kinsmen! Klansmen! Keep him home" (p. 318). As if someone has taken control of her body, Julia rushes into her house and returns with an armful of bedding. As she pitches the linen, she says that she wants to clean the whiteness out of her house and be left to her black self.

Julia's journey into the next stage of growth, the didache, comes shortly after this purging of everything white around her, including her lover. The next afternoon, Julia joins the group of women who are cautiously eager to bring up the past evening's explosion. Not knowing how to broach the subject, one of the women, Lulu, mentions to Julia that Uncle Greenlee, who works in Herman's mother's livery stable, seems to be "well-fixed." Julia thinks that Uncle Greenlee is an Uncle Tom in the most pejorative sense. When Lulu approves that Uncle Greenlee cleans up behind horses in a uniform and wishes that her adopted son, Nelson, could land such a safe job after the war, Julia sends out a message. She tells Lulu that the only kind of safe jobs for black men are the ones that require them to become informants and betrayers of their race. Julia's plea is for dignity, which involves relying on the strength and heroism of one's heritage. When Lulu tells Julia that blacks have to be three times as good as whites or be killed,

Julia tells her that whites still find ways to kill blacks. Her point is that black men will never be free until they arm themselves with the courage of their past. She tells Lulu that murdered black and bloody, silent slaves gathered last night at the foot of her bed as a reminder of what has been done to the black race in America. For Julia, only dignity can sustain blacks as they move through the social minefields of America.

When a dying Herman returns to try to make amends with Julia, he discovers that he has really lost her. He admits to Julia that he has put his mother, his sister, the bakery business, the law, and ignorance before her while she waited faithfully for ten years. Julia forgives Herman and even helps him to take his last breath in her arms. She can make this gesture, however, because she has moved into the final stage of growth, the eucharistia. Julia could not have been so forgiving had she not found the dignity that she had recently preached to her neighbors. It is in going back to her community that she discovers that the key is not to spend one's life consumed with hate but to struggle together to make life better, to show courage and resiliency in the face of bigotry. This outlook on life is celebrated as Julia and Lulu engage in a "Carolina folk dance passed on from some dimly remembered African beginnings" (p. 324). As the music plays, Julia calls for self-respect, singing that blacks must rise up higher than the dirt around them. The entire backyard community comes together as Julia tells Nelson a series of harmless lies to give him encouragement as he goes off to war. She tells him that his efforts in the war will make him a Colored hero and because of him, blacks will be able to go to parks, band concerts, museums, and libraries. Julia knows full well that Nelson's efforts in 1918 would guarantee few, if any, of the above-mentioned rights and privileges. What is important, however, is the sense of togetherness shared in the backyard. The blacks rally around each other as they grapple for means of survival. Julia shares her inner wholeness with the outer community when she announces, "I'm so happy! I've never been this happy in all my life! I'm happy to be alive, alive and living for my people" (p. 320).

Tommy, in *Wine in the Wilderness*, is as equally receptive to growth as Julia is in *Wedding Band*.[29] She is no staunch, stoic, sexless matriarch; nor is she a defiled, broken, delicate woman who crawls off into some corner to suffer from a nervous breakdown and spend the rest of her life condemning men for her emotional and physical bruises. Instead, she is a vulnerable yet resilient woman who steadily moves in the direction of wholeness. Hatch and Shine note that Childress endows this defiant and diverse heroine from the depths of the black community with "warmth, compassion, inner dignity, and pride."[30] In *Wine in the Wilderness*, Tommy is pitted against Bill Jameson, Cynthia, and Sonny-man, three middle-class blacks who despise their heritage and castigate grass-roots blacks. Regardless of the fact that her bourgeois acquaintances almost destroy her sense of self-worth, Tommy reaches a state of completeness.

Information about Tommy's koinonia is provided via flashbacks. Her background is one of poverty, as was Childress', who argues that if black writers ignore the poor, tantamount to denying their humanity, they are failing to see themselves.[31] Tommy tells Cynthia, a social worker, that she comes from poor people. The similarities are reinforced between Childress and her heroine when Tommy reminds Cynthia that people in her field talk endlessly about poverty but that she knows all the nuances of living from month to month on a crust of bread. Recalling the abject poverty she and her mother experienced, Tommy tells Cynthia that it was considered a feast if they were fortunate enough to have grits, or bread and coffee. She painfully recalls her mother tying up her stockings with strips of rags because she could not afford garters. Tommy's hardship as a child is best illustrated when she comments, "We didn't have nothin' to rule over, not a pot nor a window" (p. 745).

More is learned about Tommy's beginnings when she tells Bill, a struggling artist, that there were many people who made her feel loved, worthy, and rooted. She shares that she was born in Baltimore, Maryland and was raised in Harlem. She goes on to tell of her mother's family, particularly her mother's father who was a Mason. She is aware of her past as she tells Bill that her great-great-grandparents were slaves. Tommy's personal history is very skillfully linked to the larger black community as she and Bill talk about such black heroes as Frederick Douglass, Harriet Tubman, Monroe Trotter, Martin Luther King, and Malcolm X. They also discuss whites who have been sympathetic to black struggle, such as John Brown, Elijah Lovejoy, and Adam Powell. Tommy's comments demonstrate her strong ties to her family and to both her immediate and at-large community. Childress skillfully gives Tommy a rooted past before she sends her out into a world that often devalues black history or treats it as a separate entity unrelated to American history.

Tommy's logus occurs during adolescence, coming into it as do the youths in Margaret Walker's poem, "For My People," who chant, "We discovered that we were black and poor and small and different and nobody cared and nobody wondered and nobody understood."[32] Tommy recalls, in a touching conversation with Bill, the moment she realized that blacks were oppressed in America. She tells him of the painful moment in her life when her uncle and fifteen-hundred blacks went to jail for wearing the "Elk" emblem on their coat lapel, an insignia that only whites at that time were allowed to wear. Dispelling the myth that blacks are a passive people, Childress writes about the tenacity of blacks who would rather be incarcerated than tolerate an infringement of their rights. Tommy expresses her disconcertedness about the fact that the blacks obtained the copyright first, but were taken to court and barred from using the name. She reveals that the white Elks are called The Benevolent Protective Order of Elks and the blacks are referred to as The Improved Benevolent Protective Order of Elks of the World. This nigger moment leads to Tommy's curiosity about white/black relationships in her community and her subsequent confusion about her own place in America. Thus, the quest begins.

Tommy's third stage of growth, the metanoia, is characterized by her searching for a niche. She seeks solace in church, as do so many blacks who have difficulty living in a society where one's very survival hinges upon an adeptness at dodging racial barbs and bars. Tommy tells Bill that she pledged herself to the African Methodist Episcopal Zion Church early in life. In the church, Tommy found partial sustenance, but not enough to shield her from the rawness she encounters during the journey. One sees Tommy trying to make sense out of the anger and violence of the Harlem streets where a riot is raging as the play opens. Her apartment, located atop a grocery store, has been burned and ransacked by looters and padlocked by policemen. Seeing the rioters as desperate men battling against the tenacles of racism, she tries to escape her own poverty by turning to her bourgeois companions for validation. This choice, however, precipitously leads Tommy to engage in a series of emotional boxing matches. An inherent part of the metanoia involves going through a series of trials and errors before resolving the genesis of the confusion. Tommy, during the bulk of the action of the play, tries hard to emulate and be accepted by these supposedly sophisticated blacks who are as mean to her as some of the whites who have dehumanized her.

Determined to get their stamp of approval, Tommy lays bare her soul to the insensitive, insipid Cynthia. Begging Cynthia to tell her what is wrong with her, Tommy reassures her that she will not get angry at her. She genuinely wants to make herself appealing to her newly found middle class acquaintances. Tommy's pain goes unassuaged, and she is no closer to a positive sense of self when this refined black woman points out her shortcomings. Cynthia superciliously warns Tommy that she is too brash, too used to looking out for herself, and that she must give black men back their manhood by letting them do the chasing and talking, by asking their opinion, by waiting for them to open the door, and by concentrating on looking sexually attractive. When Cynthia finishes chipping away at Tommy's self-confidence, Bill commences. Bill resembles Walter Lee in Hansberry's *A Raisin in the Sun* in his penchant for accusing black women of retarding the progress of black men. Bill's inflated sense of self allows him to mouth a host of "the trouble with black women is . . . " refrains, including that they want to eat before they do anything; they all want to be great brains; they do not know anything about being feminine; they are too opinionated; and they always want to latch onto or secure a permanent relationship.

Perhaps the single most important impetus for Tommy's turning away from these undeserving mentors is her discovery from Oldtimer, an elderly grass-roots black man, that she is to be represented on Bill's triptych as the dregs of society. When Tommy points out to Oldtimer that she is to be portrayed as a beautiful, African queen, he inadvertently tells her "No, you gonna be this her last one. The worst gal in town. A messed-up chick that— that—" (p. 752). At this point in Tommy's growth, she realizes that the people she wanted most to be like are emotional and social cripples, and she completely reevaluates her earlier decision to emulate these "wine-sampling" blacks.

Tommy clearly moves into the fourth stage of growth, the kerygma, when it is confirmed that she is merely being studied like a guinea pig. She snaps, stops accommodating, and explodes as she hurls, "Trouble is I was Tommin to you, to all of you, . . . 'Oh, maybe they gon' like me' . . . I was your fool, thinkin' writers and painters know moren' me, that maybe a little bit of you would rub off on me" (p. 752). She looks them in the face and, with the emotional fervor of a protestant minister, tells them that she was lost but now is found and that she was blind but now can see. When Bill tells everyone to clear the room, she tells them they had better not leave her alone with him because she might kill him. Tommy's anger is exacerbated by the fact that her discovery of Bill's plans for the triptych comes shortly after she and Bill had consummated their relationship. When Bill asks her if she can be generous enough to forgive him, Tommy seethes with anger, saying, "Nigger, I been too damn generous with you already" (p. 753). She cogently argues that she has been their fool and tells them that there is something inside of her that says she is not supposed to let anybody play her cheap.

Tommy's adrenalin does not ebb until she delivers her message in its entirety. In an unanticipated move that offends their sensibilities, Tommy calls them phoney niggers. She berates them by telling them that they only have love and admiration for black people who are in a history book, printed on a pitcher, or drawn on a painting. No holds barred, she tells them that when they run into the living and breathing blacks in the ghetto, they bitterly complain that grass-roots blacks are untogether. Tommy verbally slaps them hard across the face when she accuses them of hating blacks, themselves and her. A stronger, more confident Tommy emerges as she tries to enlighten those 'pseudointellectuals' about what she has just been able to piece together because of their hideous treatment of her. Tommy's formal message is best summed up when she comments:

You treat me like a nigger, that's what. I'd rather be called one than treated that way . . . When they [whites] say 'nigger' just-dry-long-so, they mean educated you and uneducated me. They hate you and call you 'nigger,' I called you 'nigger,' but I love you. (pp. 753–754)

Tommy tells these shallow, bourgeois blacks that perhaps they hate her so much because she reminds them too much of their own mothers who sacrificed to make a better life for them. Additionally, she argues that if the masses of blacks are so untogether it is because the ones with education have forgotten what it is like to be black and have joined forces with those whites who castigate blacks. This epiphany serves as a catalyst for them and launches her into her final stage of growth.

Tommy wades into eucharistia when she firmly resolves that she will not let anyone, black or white, make her feel small or half-human ever again. In this stage of growth, she realizes that her nigger moment was a hoax. She knows intuitively that she is not inferior in any way. All of the past wounds are healed once she asserts herself. She announces that she is going back to the nitty gritty crowd "where the talk is we'ness and us-ness. I thank you 'cause I'm walkin out with much more than I brought in" (p. 754). Tommy walks out with a positive sense of self, one that will help her to relate better to the masses of blacks who are downtrodden. She tells them that if she can go through life other-cheeking white folks, she can do the same to any blacks who consider themselves superior to grass-roots people. For some, a positive experience brings them into wholeness, into humanity, but Tommy's eyeopener stems from negative treatment by blacks who themselves are not whole. A strong, whole woman rises as does the phoenix to tell these "Buppies"—black, urban, professionals—that she is the true wine in the wilderness, "cussin' and fightin' and lookin' out for my damn self 'cause ain' nobody else round to do it, dontcha know" (p. 754).

Tommy's celebration of self is infectious; the once "phoney niggers" join in and affirm her metamorphosis. Together they celebrate the cessation of Tommy's quest, a journey that has, presumably, benefited them as much as her. Commenting on Tommy's eucharistia and its impact on her associates Hatch and Shine aptly note, "When she undergoes a metamorphosis before his eyes, he [Bill Jameson] suddenly becomes aware that she is the source of inspiration that he and the others so desperately needed to find themselves, and their blackness."[33] Thus, Tommy does become that wine, with its biblical resonances, that will revive, nourish, and nurture her black counterparts.

Jacqueline Fleming, author of *Blacks in College*, contends that "people are the sum total of the conditioning they have been given."[34] Fleming argues that negative conditioning breeds failure. She stresses, however, that there are some cases where people survive and succeed without the benefit of positive reinforcement. Childress apparently concurs with Dr. Fleming. Tommy, for example, metaphorically gives birth to herself in order to survive whole. Childress' heroines typically are not fragmented, irreparably wounded, caustic women but are at once courageous, discerning, vulnerable, insecure, and optimistic. In short, they are human, real. Childress is that new thought, that breath of fresh air, that possibility in the American theater. More than just a wine in the wilderness, Alice Childress is the bread and the song.

A Raisin in the Sun,[35] now recognized as an American classic[36] by a politically sophisticated black woman and humanist, is a play in which practically all of the characters undertake a journey.[37] Genevieve Fabre in Drumbeats, Masks and Metaphor contends that Hansberry has been acclaimed by some to be the Clifford Odets of the new generation, particularly since she idealized the image of the working class.[38] Unlike Odets, Hansberry writes sensitively about working–class blacks whose quest leads them inevitably to certain discoveries or conclusions. George R. Adams in "Black Militant Drama" points out that the Youngers in A Raisin in the Sun come to recognize that "Black Americans have a social right (to move out of the ghetto into the white suburbs), a psychological necessity (to direct frustration outward into healthy aggression, manifested as self-assertion and hard work), a social duty (to reinforce the values of mature citizen responsibility and the American democratic ethic), an economic responsibility (to invest money wisely), and a personal and familial obligation (pride in oneself and one's forebears)."[39]

Mrs. Lena Younger or Mama in A Raisin in the Sun moves through the six stages of growth as she and her children learn together the value of give and take in familial relationships. Commenting on Mama's pivotal role, Wilkerson notes that "She, who embodies the race's will to transcend and who forms that critical link between the past and the future, articulates and transmits the traditions of the race to the next generation."[40] Wilkerson argues that although Mama may appear to be merely conservative, it is she who is the mother of revolutionaries and it is she who makes possible the change and movement of the new generation.[41]

Mama's koinonia manifests itself in the form of her sharing life's moments with Ruth, her daughter-in-law. She discloses to Ruth that she and her husband, Big Walter, were a close-knit family. She shares with her the difficulties she and Big Walter experienced before they uprooted and moved North. Characterizing the South as a place that suffocates poor blacks, Mama reveals that the North was in many ways more cruel to a struggling black couple. Mama nostalgically recalls that she and Big Walter had only been married two weeks when they moved in the now rodent- and roach-infested, dilapidated tenement. She reveals that they had only planned to remain there a year before buying a house in Morgan Park with a backyard for gardening. There is a certain amount of remorse as Mama, looking back on her youth, describes the abject poverty that she and Big Walter weathered. She reflects on the countless nights that Big Walter came home slumped over, having only enough energy to look back and forth from the rug to her with eyes weighted down by a sense of hopelessness. Speaking of the infant she lost to poverty, little Claude, Mama shares that Big Walter worked unyieldingly to forget the pain, but carried this grief with him to an untimely grave.

Both Mama and Big Walter wanted the absolute best for their children, to give them something that would sustain them as they journeyed through life. Mama remembers that Big Walter often remarked that it seemed that God did not see fit to give blacks anything but dreams. Mama's reflections on yesteryears provide the audience with insight into her tenacity. She has clung for nearly forty years to her dream of extricating her family from the ghetto. Additionally, Mama's sense of family is expressed in her remarks to Walter, her son, and Beneatha, her daughter, about ingratitude and irreverence, respectively. Mama chastises Walter Lee for not being satisfied or proud of the fact that she and Big Walter sacrificed to provide them with a home, clothes, food, and spiritual guidance. When Beneatha becomes iconoclastic, Mama reminds her that she and Big Walter brought her up in the church and that she had better remember the values and morals they tried to teach her. There is ample evidence in the play that Mama is spiritually rooted in African American culture and traditions.

The action of *A Raisin in the Sun* is advanced as Mama refers to her nigger moment. Mama informs her children that when she was a youth, there were many real horrors that tormented blacks. Recognition on Mama's part that society looks upon her as a nigger is evident when she tells Walter Lee, "In my time we was worried about not being lynched and getting to the North if we could and how to stay alive and still have a pinch of dignity" (p. 61). From this statement, one can infer that Mama not only experienced one, but probably a series of nigger moments throughout her life. At one point, she tells Walter Lee that it is because of people like her and Big Walter that he does not have to ride to work on the back of anybody's streetcar.

In another sense, Mama's logus or loss of innocence can be defined in terms of her interaction with Walter Lee. There is an awareness moment of a different kind when Mama realizes that she has helped to emasculate her son. When Mama, without consulting Walter Lee or anyone else in the family, puts a downpayment on a house in a white neighborhood, Walter Lee sees his dream of becoming a liquor store tycoon wither up like a raisin in the sun. So battered by what he perceives as his mother's betrayal of him, Walter Lee abandons his job for long drives and walks in the country, and nights at the Green Hat Lounge, becoming inebriated with liquor and music. Mama listens as he tells of the seductiveness of the music in the club. For the first time, Mama recognizes his desperation and the role she has played in unraveling him. In one brief moment, she becomes aware that "I've helped to do it to you, haven't I son? Walter, I been wrong" (p. 86).

Mama's acknowledging her guilt, or at least her part in emasculating Walter Lee, leads her to stage three in her growth. The action of the play is propelled by Mama's metanoia, which involves her relinquishing power to Walter Lee. This turning away from her established pattern of behavior, that of making all decisions without any input from the adults of the household, illustrates the impact of the logus. Mama moves to try to make Walter Lee whole by entrusting him with sixty-five hundred dollars, the balance of which she had placed as a downpayment on a home. Mama desperately wants Walter Lee to succeed, and so in addition to the money, she tells him that not only does she love him very much but that she trusts him as well.

Walter Lee's rash judgment to entrust every remaining penny of his family's inheritance to a con artist causes Mama to explode verbally and physically. In this fourth stage, the kerygma, Mama, blinded by rage, beats the thirty-five year old Walter Lee senselessly in the face to express her disgust that he has lost the family's means of escaping the ghetto. Mama's disappointment in her son is evident when she tells him that night after night she watched her husband drag his broken body home with red showing in his eyes and veins throbbing in his head. She tells Walter Lee that his father grew thin and old before he was forty by working like somebody's old horse to save them from the ravages of the ghetto. Mama has a difficult time containing herself because Walter Lee gave away in one day his father's life's earnings.

Unlike earlier when she had tried to pound some sense into her son's head, Mama is calm and deliberate when she tells Walter Lee that she sees things differently now. She tells her family that sometimes people have to give up on some things and hold on to what they already own. Mama pleads with them to accept the reality that they may never leave the ghetto and to put their heads together to try to spruce up a sagging physical and emotional household.

A short time later, however, when Mama discovers that Walter Lee plans to allow the white neighborhood association to buy them out in order to recoup the lost money, she regains her courage and moves into another stage of growth, the didache. Free of the depression and perhaps self-pity that plagued her earlier, Mama draws herself up to teach Walter Lee a lesson. Mama tries to instill pride in her son by reminding him of their family history when she says, "Son—I come from five generations of people who was slaves and sharecroppers—but ain't nobody in my family never let nobody pay 'em no money that was a way of telling us we wasn't fit to walk the earth. We ain't never been that poor. We ain't never been that dead inside" (p. 123). Her message to Walter Lee is that the Youngers are hardworking people who have dignity and cannot be bought at any price.

Mama also teaches Beneatha a lesson when the young girl says that her brother is not a man but a toothless rat. Mama chastises Beneatha for thinking that she is better than Walter Lee. She wants to know who gave Beneatha the privilege of writing Walter Lee's epitaph, just as the rest of the world has done. When Beneatha tells her mother that there is nothing left to love in Walter Lee, Mama has a message for her. She instructs

Beneatha that there is always something left to love. More importantly, she teaches Beneatha that the time to love someone is not when that person has done good and made things easy for everybody, but "It's when he's at his lowest and can't believe in hisself 'cause the world done whipped him so" (p. 125). In a very poignant moment, Mama cautions her naive daughter that when she starts measuring somebody, she should measure that person right by taking into consideration what hills and valleys that poor soul has traversed before getting to rock bottom.

Not only does Mama grow, but she serves as a catalyst for the maturation of her son and daughter. When Walter Lee attempts to send his son out of the room so that he can bow and scratch to the white representative, Carl Lindner, Mama blocks Travis' path. She tells Walter Lee that he has to let his son see how low their five generations in America have sunk. Peter Hays argues that it is Mama's leading and pushing that steers Walter Lee into his manhood.[42] Mama's last attempt serves to cement the Younger family, thereby initiating the eucharistia. Walter Lee can not find it in his heart to show his son, the sixth generation, that the Youngers are without dignity. Instead, he tells Mr. Lindner that the family will move into the house as planned and that they will try to be good neighbors.

Walter Lee, to a large degree, is responsible for restoring Mama's faith in her dreams of leaving the ghetto. His actions complete Mama's growth. Mama's wholeness is evident when she tells Lindner not to try to appeal to her because her son, the head of the house, has firmly decided. There is little evidence of Lloyd Brown's contention that the Youngers' "main achievement lies in an incipient (rather than full-blown) self-esteem."[43] The Youngers definitely do experience a renewed faith in the nutritive value of solidarity and come to recognize the power of a positive sense of self-worth. As the play ends, the Youngers celebrate the dignity and nobility of their family, regardless of the fact that they will probably be met with opposition as they move into an all-white neighborhood. The fact that Mama carries her withering plant with her to the new house suggests that the weariness of living in America is not over but will be transferred to a new location. In spite of the uncertainty of their future, these blacks steadfastly celebrate the mending of a family that had literally been torn apart.

Lorraine Hansberry strove for wholeness in her characters, particularly the heroines. Her aim was to capture the fervor of their lives and demonstrate that they could survive whole in spite of all the responsibilities heaped upon the black woman's back. In the theater, Hansberry could mirror not only the quagmires but the fullness of these women's lives. Wilkerson says of Hansberry, "The theatre was a working laboratory for this brilliant woman whose sighted eyes and feeling heart caused her to reach out to a world at once cruel and beautiful."[44]

Ntozake Shange, taking the lead from Hansberry, seems preoccupied with broadening the American theater to include African rituals. Shange's theater pieces generally do not conform to traditional dramatic structure, making it difficult to detect a noticeable progression of action, or to identify characters' stages of growth. Addressing the issue of dramatic structure in Shange's pieces, Sandra L. Richards asserts, "By constructing most of her plays as a series of poetic monologues, occasionally interrupted by conventional dialogue, she takes advantage of the telegraphic, elusive quality of poetry to encourage audiences to listen with close, critical attention."[45] Richards argues that Shange most often does not write "tidy plays in which a crisis is resolved within the structure of the play" but rather "attempts to create a liberated stage space supportive of Black self-expression."[46] Characterizing Shange's dramas as structurally episodic, Richards contends that Shange minimizes an audiences' empathetic tendencies by denying them a chance to experience rounded or dimensional characters.[47] James Haskins, in *Black Theater in America*, argues that Shange's pieces are without formal structure and comments that she is "something besides a poet, but she is not—at least not at this stage—a dramatist. More than anything else, she is a troubadour."[48]

Shange's redefinition of what constitutes theater in America caused a great deal of controversy, particularly since her verse drama is antithetical to that of such established writers as Maxwell Anderson, Robert Lowell, and James Scheville. Wilkerson notes that "Shange is critical of the artistic constraints imposed by the professional theatre on black writers and performers."[49] C.W.E. Bigsby points out that Shange views the originality of her dramatic form as a "necessary gesture of revolt of models of drama which she saw as alien to her own situation."[50]

Shange's theater pieces, beyond the commercially successful *For Colored Girls Who Have Considered Suicide/When the Rainbow is Enuf*, have gone virtually unnoticed in critical studies. One case in point is Shange's *A Photograph: Lovers in Motion*,[51] a drama that "comes closest to play form in that there is a logical progression of action and dialogue, with some detectable growth in at least one of the five characters."[52] Though the stages of growth are not as readily detected as in plays by Childress and Hansberry, Michael in *A Photograph: Lovers in Motion* does embark on a journey that results in her wholeness. Shange's integrity as a dramatist who seeks to "transcend or bypass through music and dance the limitations of social and human existence" is not compromised in this theater piece, but rather is enhanced by the depth of these characters.[53] Not only is *A Photograph: Lovers in Motion* an exploration of lives, but it is a drama that answers some of the whys of human behavior as the heroine grows and becomes a catalyst for the growth of her lover.

Michael, a dancer who is in love with the struggling photographer, Sean, is culturally and spiritually grounded. Evidence of Michael's koinonia or beginnings is presented as she shares with Sean the strength of her ancestors. Michael tells Sean that her people—grandparents and uncles—took care of themselves and fought for every breath each and every day of their lives. When Sean attempts to deflate Michael's sense of self by telling her that black people are not as courageous as she imagines because he only knows of "welfare/the white folks/heroin & whores," she describes a vulnerable but resilient grandmother who carried a shotgun to protect her offspring from racists and who sat on the porch telling stories about Marcus Garvey, W.E.B. Dubois, Jack Johnson, and the colored horse soldiers (p. 80). Michael not only has the strength of her grandparents to rely upon, but also the stories of black heroes who offer hope to young blacks as they journey through life in America. Michael reminds Sean that her history is one filled with "alla the blood & the fields & the satchels dragging in the dust" (p. 81). Shange roots Michael by connecting her to her immediate and distant fore-bears who represent tradition, shared experiences, and community spirit of survival.

Michael's logus came early in her life. She shares with Sean an incident that traumatized her and shaped the lives of her entire family. Michael painfully recalls for Sean the details of her grandfather's savage lynching in the Carolinas. She tells him that it was at that point in her grandmother's life that she started carrying a shotgun to ensure that no more of her children would be brutally murdered by a white mob that had no respect for black life. Michael connects her own nigger moment to what she perceives is Sean's. She berates Sean for allowing Nevada, a bourgeois lawyer who is passionate about Sean, to dehumanize him. Sean allows the jealous Nevada to destroy at whim several of his photographs because she is subsidizing his career. Michael tells Sean that she is disappointed that he thinks that "being a nigger is being nothin" (p. 80). She is repulsed by the fact that he allows Nevada to buy him with her money and tells him that she did not come from people who tolerated being treated like niggers.

The action of *A Photograph: Lovers in Motion* is advanced as Michael moves into the third stage of growth, the metanoia. At this juncture, Michael informs Sean that she wants to end the relationship, one which includes his sexual involvement not only with her but with Nevada and Claire, a model. Michael comes to the realization that she must turn away from Sean in order to keep her own dignity intact. This awakening is prompted by a visit from Nevada who offers to help Sean get a show at a museum. Though Sean turns down Nevada's invitation to help him, he does accept a very expensive lens for his camera from her. When Nevada leaves, Sean gleefully intimates that he has scored one on Nevada. Michael decides that she no longer can tolerate Sean's manipulation of women and his own self-de-basement. Recognizing that he is a parasite and a coward, among other things, she tells him "i'm leaving . . . it'll keep me loving myself" (pp. 83–84).

Michael journeys into the fourth stage of growth when she and Sean argue about his lack of self-confidence. She tries to tell him that he is capable of great things as an artist, but that it is his fear of failing that prevents him from putting his photographs on exhibit. Sean's defense mechanism is to shout obscenities at Michael, doing his best to make her feel small, dumb, and helpless. He accuses her of not knowing anything about him except that he is perpetually making love to her "never get enuf ass" (p. 85). Michael is hurt by Sean's verbal blows to her self-esteem. His sense of inadequacy is infectious and Michael begins to question her own worth. However, when Sean asserts that Michael is a "stupid bitch" who can be appeased, like all females, by sexual pleasure, Michael goes into a fit of rage. She regains her own sense of self-worth as she slays the dragons that plague Sean: insecurity and indecisiveness. Michael's kerygma comes full circle when she verbally retaliates with, "i dont like thinking that you think yr dick means more to me than yr work" (p. 86). Michael tells Sean that he is not a man, somebody who loves in the world. She mirrors for him his own emptiness and callousness.

Michael shows her love for Sean by refusing to give up on him, in spite of the fact that he abuses her emotionally. She does not stop chipping away at Sean's layers of insecurities until she helps him to recognize that it is less important to be the greatest photographer in the world than it is for him to be the best photographer that he can be. Her message, or didache, comes in the form of her teaching him that he must learn to love his art, regardless of whether the Washington critics or anybody else tells him that his photographs are without quality. When he pushes her down on the bed because he does not want to hear her message, she tells him that she is not afraid. Though Sean grabs her and wrestles her down to silence her, she continues to spread the news to him, telling him "when you work on yr pictures like you worked on me/i'll believe you/right now I think yr fulla shit & i'm ashamed cuz I believed you at least loved photography" (p. 87). Michael prepares to leave but Sean regresses to his boyhood, during which his father loved a pet monkey more than he did Sean. Shange portrays two people who are missing something that only the other can supply: a love that satiates. Michael's growth is inextricably linked to Sean's.

Michael's reaching out to him not only heals the wounds left by his father's abuse but cements her relationship with Sean. Michael stands by Sean and is made whole by his love for her and by the fact that she could reach out and convince the man she loves of his own self-worth. He chooses her, discarding Nevada and Claire, because she believes in him and forces him to risk sharing his work with the public, and to dare to love her without fear of being hurt. This rejoining of two lovers points to Michael's eucharistia, which is characterized by her celebration dance. As the play closes, Sean tells Michael, for the first time, that he loves her. Her response is to dance, suggestive of the joy and peace she has found in her relationship with a black man who so desperately needs, and can now reciprocate, understanding and tenderness.

Ntozake Shange's originality revolutionized the American theater. Her works are interdisciplinary, often focusing on the lives of musicians, dancers, visual and performing artists, etc. Her use of poetry, dance, music, and choreographed lighting is her way of bringing to the American theater the heart and soul of African American traditions. Blacks have traditionally turned to singing and dancing as coping strategies because those areas were open to blacks in white America. Shange's dramatic structure is exciting and innovative and, in at least one play, A Photograph: Lovers in Motion, the poet/playwright merges traditional dramatic structure with identifiable African American self-expression.

Childress, Hansberry, and Shange all chose to write about the pitfalls and progress that their heroines experience as they undergo a personal and often political odyssey. The six stages of growth that appear in these plays reflect life for many African Americans. In a recent Essence interview, the outstanding actress and television talk-show host Oprah Winfrey speaks of her koinonia when she says, "You know, as Black people we all share the same kind of emotional roots. Spending the first six years with my grandmother [in the South] instilled a kind of strength and a belief system in me that I didn't know I had."[54] At another point in the interview, Winfrey again refers to her koinonia by commenting, "I know and understand that I am where I am because of the bridges that I crossed over to get here. Sojourner Truth was a bridge. Harriet Tubman was a bridge. Ida B. Wells was a bridge. Madame C. J. Walker was a bridge. Fannie Lou Hamer was a bridge. Every day that I'm out there I see myself as a resurrection of those women. I feel very strongly about black womanhood."[55] The interview goes on to provide information about the other stages of growth through which Winfrey journeyed.

Childress, Hansberry, and Shange, in varying degrees, structured their plays around the initiation and survival rituals of African American women who struggle mightily to make their peace with what class bias, sexism, and racism have wrought in their lives. These dark and lovely heroines strive to make themselves whole in spite of the forces that seek to negate their personhood. There are no easy resolutions for these African American women, only continual growing and becoming.

NOTES

1. Raymond Hull, How to Write a Play (Cincinnati, Ohio: Writer's Digest Books, 1983), pp. 9–10.

2. Stanley Vincent Longman, Composing Drama for Stage and Screen (Boston, Mass.: Allyn and Bacon, Inc., 1986), p. 120.

3. Hull, p. 13.

4. C. Hughes Holman, A Handbook to Literature (New York: The Bobbs-Merrill Co., 1972), pp. 173–174. The relation of these parts (the five-part dramatic structure)

is sometimes represented geographically by the figure of a pyramid, called Freytag's Pyramid, the rising slope suggesting the rising action or tying of the knot, the falling slope the falling action or resolution, the apex representing the climax.

5. Longman, p. 120.

6. Frederick J. Hunter, *The Power of Dramatic Form* (New York: Exposition Press, 1974), p. 68.

7. Stuart Griffiths, *How Plays are Made* (London, England: Heinemann Educational Books, 1982), p. 11.

8. Hull, p. 31.

9. Longman, p. 110.

10. Holman, pp. 173–174.

11. Seymore Reiter, *World Theater: The Structure and Meaning of Drama* (New York: Dell Pub. Co., 1973), pp. 57–74.

12. Walter Kerr, *New York Herald Tribune*, May 29, 1960, Section 4, p. 1.

13. Kimberly W. Benston, "The Aesthetics of Modern Black Drama: From Mimesis to Methexis," in *The Theatre of Black Americans*, vol. I, ed. Errol Hill (Englewood Cliffs, N.J.: Prentice Hall, Inc., 1980), p. 62.

14. Ibid., pp. 62–63.

15. Alvin Goldfarb and Edwin Wilson, *Living Theater: An Introduction to Theater History* (New York: McGraw-Hill Book Co., 1983), p. 413.

16. Carol Pearson and Katherine Pope, *The Female Hero in American and British Literature* (New York: R.R. Bowker, 1981), pp. 3–4.

17. Details about the Koine Six stages of growth are based upon personal interviews with Lucius M. Guillory, educational consultant and principal of St. Gabriel's Catholic School in New Orleans, La., and Reverend Victor Cohea, M.Div., Pastor of St. Monica's Catholic Church, New Orleans, La., July 1985.

18. A minimal portion of this chapter, now revised, and expanded, was previously published as "Images of Blacks in Plays by Black Women," *Phylon*, vol. 17 (September 1986), pp. 230–237.

19. Cohea, personal interview.

20. Lindsay Patterson, *Black Theater: A Twentieth Century Collection of the Works of Its Best Playwrights* (New York: Dodd, Mead and Co., 1971), pp. ix–x.

21. Guillory, personal interview.

22. Cohea, personal interview.

23. Pearson and Pope, p. 9.

24. Guillory, personal interview.

25. Cohea, personal interview.

26. Alice Childress, "Wedding Band: A Love/Hate Story in Black and White," in *New Women's Theatre: Ten Plays by Contemporary American Women*, ed., Honor Moore (New York: Vintage Books, 1977), pp. 257–337. All quotes and references to the play are based upon this source. Also, see chapter two for synopsis and additional analysis of *Wedding Band*.

27. Margaret B. Wilkerson, ed. *9 Plays by Black Women* (New York: New American Library, 1986), p. 71.

28. Ibid., p. 71.

29. Alice Childress, "Wine in the Wilderness," in *Black Theater U.S.A.: Forty-Five Plays by Black Americans, 1847–1974*, eds. James V. Hatch and Ted Shine, (New

York: The Free Press, 1974), pp. 738–755. All quotes and references to the play are based upon this source. Also, see chapter two for synopsis and additional analysis of *Wine in the Wilderness*.

30. Hatch and Shine, p. 737.

31. Alice Childress, "Knowing the Human Condition," in *Black American Literature and Humanism*, ed. R. Baxter Miller (Lexington, Ky.: The University Press of Kentucky, 1981), p. 10.

32. Margaret Walker, "For My People," in *Black Voices*, ed. Abraham Chapman (New York: New American Library, 1968), p. 459.

33. Hatch and Shine, p. 737.

34. Jacqueline Fleming, "Success and the Black College Student," Dillard University Faculty Inservice, New Orleans, La., 16 August, 1985.

35. Lorraine Hansberry, "A Raisin in the Sun," in *A Raisin in the Sun and The Sign in Sidney Brustein's Window*, (New York: New American Library, 1966), pp. 11–130. All quotes and references to the play are based upon this source. Also, see chapter two for synopsis and additional analysis of *A Raisin in the Sun*.

36. Wilkerson, p. 41.

37. David E. Ness, "A Writer of Penetrating Vision and Truth," *Freedomways*, Vol. 12 (Third Quarter 1972), p. 246.

38. Genevieve Fabre, *Drumbeats, Masks, and Metaphor: Contemporary Afro-American Theater* (Boston, Mass.: Harvard University Press, 1983), pp. 13–14.

39. George R. Adams, "Black Militant Drama," *The American Image*, vol. 28 (Summer 1971), p. 114.

40. Margaret B. Wilkerson, Introduction to *Lorraine Hansberry: The Collected Last Plays*, ed. Robert Nemiroff (New York: New American Library, 1983), p. 11.

41. Ibid., p. 11.

42. Peter L. Hays, "*A Raisin in the Sun* and *Juno and the Paycock*" *Phylon*, vol. 33 (Summer 1972), p. 176.

43. Lloyd W. Brown, "Lorraine Hansberry as Ironist: A Reappraisal of 'A Raisin in the Sun,' " *Journal of Black Studies*, vol. 4 (March 1974), p. 246.

44. Margaret B. Wilkerson, "The Sighted Eyes and Feeling Heart of Lorraine Hansberry," *Black American Literature Forum*, vol. 17 (Spring 1982), p. 13.

45. Sandra L. Richards, "Conflicting Impulses in the Plays of Ntozake Shange," *Black American Literatures Forum*, vol. 17 (Summer 1983), p. 75.

46. Ibid.

47. Ibid.

48. James Haskins, *Black Theater in America* (New York: Thomas Y. Crowell, 1982), p. 160.

49. Wilkerson, *9 Plays by Black Women*, p. 241.

50. C.W.E. Bigsby, *Beyond Broadway*, vol. 3 of *A Critical Introduction to Twentieth-Century American Drama* (New York: Cambridge University Press, 1985), p. 412.

51. Ntozake Shange, "A Photograph: Lovers in Motion," in *Three Pieces* (New York: St. Martin's Press, 1981), pp. 55–108. All quotes and references to the play are based upon this source. Also, see chapter two for a synopsis and additional analysis of *A Photograph*.

52. Elizabeth Brown, "Ntozake Shange," in *Afro-American Writers After 1955: Dramatists and Prose Writers*, vol. 38, of *Dictionary of Literary Biography*, eds. Thadeous Davis and Trudier Harris (Detroit, Mich.: Gale Research Co., 1985), p. 249.

53. Richards, p. 73.

54. Susan L. Taylor, "An Intimate Talk With Oprah," *Essence* (August 1987), p. 57.

55. Ibid., p. 58.

5

Mirroring the Dark and Beautiful Warriors: Images of Blacks

Alice Childress, Lorraine Hansberry, and Ntozake Shange have created a multiplicity of realistic images of black men and women. The picture of black life that these dramatists offer is decidedly different from that portrayed by white female or black or white male dramatists between the 1950s and 1980s. Viewing black life from a special angle, these playwrights have worked to redefine the American stage that has traditionally been populated with stereotypes of blacks. These dramatists have literally reshaped American theater to include their visions of blacks, an especially difficult task because of the narrow and particularistic portraits of blacks that have dominated the stage.

Many well-meaning white dramatists between the 1920s and 1930s, such as Ridgely Torrence, Marc Connelly, Paul Green, and Eugene O'Neill, chose blacks as subject matter. Alvin Goldfarb and Edwin Wilson, in *The Living Theatre*, argue that "though many of the plays of these white dramatists are now considered condescending to blacks, they were not racist in intent, nor were they so regarded at the time, and they reflected a growing, if naive, interest in black life among whites."[1] These and other white writers, however, added to the list of stereotypes of blacks because their experiences and their racial background could not prepare them to interpret black life accurately. They were outsiders looking in and, as such, created peripheral characters.

The Negro character appeared in literature long before Ridgely Torrence's popularization of the Negro as subject matter. Jean Fagan Yellin, in *The Intricate Knot*, contends that a study of the characterization of black figures in American literature might begin with Thomas Jefferson's essay of 1781, "Notes on Virginia," wherein he argues that a black man's reasoning is inferior and his imagination is dull, tasteless, and anomalous. Jefferson believed that blacks had a talent for music and religion and were basically benevolent, grateful, loyal, and subservient.[2] Others of similar mind helped to create one-dimensional images of blacks that found their way into early American literature. As early as 1795, the servile Sambo character appeared in plantation fiction and has since given birth to a host of stereotypes of black men and women.

Goldfarb and Wilson best sum up the appearance of the Negro in early American literature.:

> American playwrights were not slow to see the comic possibilities of the 'darkie' servant, and they set about writing dialogue for this character in a dialect thick with malapropisms . . . The writers gave the character a slow shuffle, made him stupid, and laughed at the ill-fitting livery they had clothed him in. As a final insult, he was invariably played by white actors in blackface.[3]

Goldfarb and Wilson insist that countless white minstrels earned immense sums of money by mimicking, distorting, and ridiculing black music, black speech, black dance, and black culture, a practice that extended through the mid-twentieth century.[4]

A survey of the scholarship on images of blacks in literature as well as films reveals a frustration at the American public's encouragement and acceptance of myths about blacks. Jeanne-Marie A. Miller, in "Black Women Playwrights from Grimke to Shange," has observed that "early in American drama, white playwrights used misshapen Black images to help justify slavery; in the post-Civil War period, they used them to rationalize this nation's unfair treatment of blacks."[5] Sterling Brown, in *Negro Poetry and Drama and The Negro in American Fiction*, argues that it is imperative that black writers reclaim their own experiences from the white man's falsifications, and that they must counteract such stereotypes as "the exotic primitive, the comic stooge, and the tragic mulatto."[6]

The American film industry must take its share of responsibility for distorting black life. Donald Bogle's extensive study *Toms, Coons, Mulattoes, Mammies, and Bucks: An Interpretive History of Blacks in American Films* examines the pre–1920 images of blacks in American films, such as the tom, the coon or buffoon, the tragic mulatto, the mammy, and the brutal black buck; the black jester or comic Negro of the 1920s; the servants of the 1930s; the entertainers, the new Negroes in serious roles, and the problem people of the 1940s; the black stars of the 1950s and the problem people who turn militant in the 1960s.[7] Bogle argues that the five basic stereotypes of the pre–1920s appear in the films of the 1970s and that films about black people remain distorted and far from satisfying.[8]

Author of *Black Macho and the Myth of the Superwoman*, Michele Wallace states that black men for decades have been portrayed as infantile, happy-go-lucky, and predominantly sexual in orientation.[9] Miller, in "Images of Black Women in Plays by Blacks," argues that "in American literature, then, including the drama, Blacks had been depicted most often as . . . the contented slave, the wretched freeman, the comic Negro, the brute Negro, . . . the local color Negro, and the exotic primitive."[10] Noted sociologist Robert Staples, in writing about black masculinity, has observed that "his cultural image is usually one of several types, the sexual superstud, the athlete, and the rapacious criminal."[11]

Historically, black women have not fared much better in American literature and films. Author of *I Know Why the Caged Bird Sings*, Maya Angelou points to the plethora of stereotypical images of women: "Called Matriarch, Emasculator, and Hot Momma. Sometimes . . . Auntie, Mammy, and Girl. Called Unwed Mother. Welfare Recipient and Inner City Consumer. The Black American woman has had to admit that while nobody knew the troubles she saw, everybody, his brother, and his dog, felt qualified to explain her, even to herself.[12] Mary Helen Washington, in "Black Women Image Makers," comments that blacks "must not allow whites to create our images for us."[13] Washington cautions blacks to work to destroy the legendary and romanticized images of the black woman as "Superwoman— bad talking and ball-busting, strong enough to sustain her family and herself through the hardest conditions."[14]

Lynora Williams, in "Violence Against Women," blames the high rate of physical and emotional abuse of black women on the "sexist media images which portray Third World women as exotic sex tigresses."[15] Actress Cynthia Belgrave contends that black females are placed in a special bind: "If you're strong and stoical, you're a matriach, and if you're weak and sensual, you're a whore. Of course there are no equitable gradations in between. The Black woman is at the mercy of everybody. When we finish kicking people, let us kick the Black woman again."[16] Mae C. King, in "The Politics of Sexual Stereotyping," suggests that the American society has generally decreed the black woman as invisible with its debilitating images of her as "the non-feminist, the depreciated sex object, and the loser image."[17] Edward Mapp, in his landmark "Black Women in Films," argues that a tragic history of stereotyping has occurred, resulting in a "steady procession of mammies, maids, miscegenists, matriarchs, madams, and assorted 'make-it-for-money' types . . . The black female as 'seductress' is as old as the motion picture medium itself."[18]

Mapp contends that the film industry has carried the insidious message that black women yearn for interracial romantic alliances at any price.[19] Much has been said and written about the white man's exploitation of black women in both American literature and criticism, but none as powerful as the indictment leveled by black political leader W.E.B. DuBois. Champion of women's rights, DuBois believed that white men created stereotypes of black women in order to justify their exploitation and rape of black women during and after slavery. Perhaps DuBois' comments in *Darkwater* best sum up the anger and disappointment that many blacks feel toward both the myths perpetuated about black women as well as the genesis of those myths:

> I shall forgive the South much in its final judgement day: I shall forgive its slavery, for slavery is a world-old habit; I shall forgive its fighting for a well-lost cause, and for remembering that struggle with tender tears; I shall forgive its so called 'pride of race,' the passion of its hot blood, and even its dear, old, laughable strutting and posing; but one thing I shall never forgive, neither in this world nor in the world to come: its wanton and continued and persistent insulting of the black womanhood which it sought and seeks to prostitute to its lust.[20]

Some of the stereotypical images of blacks that have appeared on the American stage have been created by a nominal number of the pre-revolutionary black writers who echoed the sentiments of well-meaning whites in order to gain acceptance by mainstream audiences. Cato in William Wells Brown's *The Escape* (1858), Rufus in Garland Anderson's *Appearances* (1925), and George in Willis Richardson's *The Idle Head* (1927) are stereotypes that did not go against the status quo.[21] It was not until the 1950s that blacks began to demand realistic images of themselves. Black male writers, particularly such dramatists as Ossie Davis, James Baldwin, Amiri Baraka, and Ed Bullins, rose to meet the needs of black people by portraying blacks as rational, sensitive, hardworking, intelligent human beings. Many of their plays, however, have dealt with the black male experience in America, painting only sketchy or uninteresting portraits of black women. Sandra Hollins Flowers' in "Colored Girls: Textbook for the Eighties," calls for a rethinking of the African American literature canon, which is top heavy with male writers. Flowers points out that "the works which usually comprise Afro-American literature curricula and become part of general reading materials, for instance, show the position of the black man in America; but generally we see black women only peripherally as the protagonist's lover, wife, mother, or in some other supporting or detracting role."[22]

Like black male playwrights, black women dramatists since 1950 have written almost exclusively about the black experience in America. Their images of black men, however, are not paragons as found in William Branch's *In Splendid Error* (1954), Amiri Baraka's *The Slave* (1964), or Ted Shine's *Herbert III* (1974).[23] Nor do they resemble the one-dimensional black mammies that appear in many works by white writers. Outraged by the popular stereotypes of blacks, Lorraine Hansberry remarked in 1959 that "One night, after seeing a play I won't mention, I suddenly became disgusted with the whole body of material about Negroes. Cardboard characters. Cute dialect bits. Or swinging musicals from exotic sources."[24] Six years later, however, in 1965, Hansberry commented, "I think that American writers have already begun to believe what I suspect has always been one of the secrets of fine art: that there are no simple men."[25] Hansberry's call for multidimensional characters did not go unheard. Black women playwrights took up the pen to express their realities.

Jeanne-Marie A. Miller contends that black women dramatists have a unique perspective on black life and that their visions must be carefully studied. Miller argues that

> their themes and their treatment of Black women characters, however, have differed from those of other playwrights. Often in plays by Black men, the happiness of Black women or their 'completeness' in life depends upon strong black men. In contrast to white authored dramas, where Black women have usually appeared as devoted servants to white families, as matriarchs, or as dumb, incompetent people, Black women playwrights have told the Black woman's story—from slavery to freedom—from her point of view.[26]

Miller points out that black women's plays generally center on the black woman's tragedies, struggles, ambitions and dreams, family and race.[27] Miller argues that images created by black women "are usually positive, and their female characters, for the most part, have great moral strength."[28] Mary Helen Washington, in *Black-Eyed Susans*, makes a strong case for studying black women writers:

> What is most important about the black woman writer is her special and unique vision of the black woman ... One of the main preoccupations of the black woman writer has been the black woman herself—her aspirations, her conflicts, her relationships to her men and her children, her creativity ... That these writers have firsthand knowledge of their subject ought to be enough to command attention.[29]

A study of the images of blacks in plays written between the 1950s and the 1980s by Childress, Hansberry, and Shange is important because the portraits chronicle not only the literary and intellectual history but the changing social history of these decades as well.[30] These dramatists are concerned with the verities that cut across all boundaries, and their depictions ring with authenticity and verisimilitude. Several individualized portraits of black men and women appear in the plays, including "the black male in search of his manhood," "the black activist," "the black assimilationist," "the evolving black woman," "the chauvinist," and "the black mother."

Anger, frustration, and ambivalence characterized the 1950s, a decade that witnessed the Korean War, McCarthyism, the Civil Rights Movement, namely the 1954 *Brown v. Board of Education* decision to desegregate public schools. Concomitantly, riots against racial discrimination sprang up across the country, including such places as Chicago, Illinois; Montgomery and

Birmingham, Alabama; Tallahassee, Florida; Little Rock, Arkansas; Mansfield and Sturgis, Texas; Clay, Kentucky; and Oklahoma City, Oklahoma. In 1951, Governor Adlai Stevenson called out the National Guard to quell rioting in Cicero, Illinois, where on July 12, 3,500 persons attempted to prevent a Negro family from moving into an all-white city. The year 1952 was the first year in seventy-one years that no lynchings had been recorded in the United States. The reprieve was not to be a lasting one. Particularly disturbing was the lynching of two black men in Mississippi in 1955 and 1959: Emmett Till and Mack Parker, respectively. It was the decade when Martin Luther King founded the Southern Christian Leadership Conference (SCLC). In general, the era was one in which the contributions of many blacks went ignored, particularly the unheralded war veterans.

The frustration experienced by blacks of the 1950s manifested itself in the form of insecurity, and thus the image of "the black man in search of his manhood" found its way onto the American stage. Feeling disinherited, he struggles to realize who he is and what his function in life is to be. In his essay, "Visions of Love and Manliness in a Blackening World: Dramas of Black Life from 1953–1970," Darwin T. Turner makes the following observation about the ambivalence experienced by black men of the 1950s: "Ironically, as black dramatists examine their characters more critically, often they seem less polemical and more compassionate because, in the black world, they perceive not only individuals searching for manhood and love but even more pathetic figures too impotent to search for manhood or to achieve a relationship of love."[31]

Plays by Childress and Hansberry substantiate Turner's claim because the image of the black male in search of his manhood is shown either as a creature who is in the process of becoming a mature human being, or one who is too incapacitated to move in that direction. His insecurity with his own identity and his values renders him generally passive. Like the character in Ralph Ellison's *Invisible Man*, the black man in search of manhood wants desperately to be recognized as a courageous and determined adult. He vacillates between integration and separatism. He has yet to establish a philosophy about how to succeed or to cope in American society. As he strives to overcome personal problems and to achieve responsible maturity, the searching black male may castigate blacks and opt to align himself with whites whom he feels will validate his manhood. The black male reaches maturity or moves in the direction of manhood when he realizes that his manhood does not hinge upon his acceptance by whites, but upon himself. Adam David Miller in "It's a Long Way to St. Louis," argues that "what Negroes need to know is not that they are needed by whites but that they are needed by one another. They need to be shown by their playwrights how to reach out to one another across the need . . . to see themselves in their complexity."[32] Childress and Hansberry do, in fact, demonstrate that in order for black males to develop a positive sense of self, they must realize that manhood is contingent upon an ability to be nurturing, understanding, firm, persistent, self-respecting, and assertive.

John Nevins in Alice Childress' *Trouble in Mind* (1955) typifies the black male in search of his manhood.[33] A male in his early twenties, John hopes to prove his manhood by becoming a successful actor. He wants a chance to show himself to be a quality black man. Almost immediately when he walks onto the stage, he condescendingly lets the cast know that he is better than they because of his determination to succeed. He boasts that he knows what he wants in the theater and plans to go right to the top. His boasting does not mask the fact that he is extremely unsure of himself. A novice among his veteran-actor co-workers, John dreams of making money, regardless of what must be sacrificed. It is his insecurity that makes him retaliate when Wiletta tries to tell him how to succeed in the white man's theater. Though he chastises Wiletta for telling him that to succeed in the theater means sacrificing one's dignity, John immediately becomes a yesman when the white director, Al Manners, arrives. John mouths quite obsequiously the sentiments he perceives will ingratiate him to the man in charge.

An example of John's fawning and lack of courage is his quickness to agree with everything Al Manners says. During the rehearsal of *Chaos in Belleville*, when Al Manners asks John if he can object in an artistic sense to the word "darkies," John placatingly replies, "No, I don't object. I don't like the word but it is used, it's a slice of life. Let's face it, Judy wouldn't use it, Mr. Manners wouldn't . . . " (p. 147). Struggling to achieve at any cost, John eagerly compromises his opinions to keep his role in *Chaos in Belleville*. He feels that he has an opportunity to excel where apparently his colleagues have failed.

When it becomes apparent that the more experienced cast members do not want his suggestions about script interpretation, John aligns himself with one of the white actresses, Judy, hoping that she will give him the stamp of approval that he seeks. They take breaks together, dine privately, agree on script interpretation, and bask in the fact that they are eminently equipped to succeed in the theater because of their acting classes. John attracts attention to himself every chance he gets. He offers suggestions to Judy about line delivery and so on, all of which make Judy become quite familiar and affectionate toward this black male in search of his manhood.

Later, Wiletta tries to teach John that her earlier lesson to him was a mistake. She begs him to forget that she told him to exchange dignity for commercial success. Wiletta reaches out to John in an attempt to help him to become a man. Like Sister Margaret in James Baldwin's *The Amen Corner* (written 1955, produced 1965), Wiletta is challenged with the dilemma of treating John as a man and at the same time protecting him from "the bloody consequences of trying to be a man in this society."[34] She tries to tell John that if he is not careful about his friendliness toward Judy, he may get lynched. When she tells him that it is demeaning to bow and scrape, John devalues her remarks by saying arrogantly, "Wiletta, my dear, you're my sweetheart, I love you and I think you're wonderfully magnificent" (p. 167).

John begins to understand Wiletta's advice only after Al Manners inadvertently dehumanizes him. During an argument over interpretation, Al Manners unwittingly implies that John could not be compared to his son because John is black and his son is white. Under pressure from Wiletta to recognize the stereotypes he is forcing them to play, Al Manners angrily quips, "Don't compare him with my son, they've got nothing in common . . . not a Goddam thing!" (p. 171). The implication is that white men cannot be placed in the same category as black men because black men are not men, or people for that matter. He blatantly reminds John that he is invisible, at best. Angered by Al Manners' remarks and encouraged by his black co-workers to assert himself, John reevaluates his values and decides that racial pride means more to him than success in a play that degrades blacks. Boldly John declares, "They can write what they want but we don't have to do it" (p. 172). In making this choice to stand up, courage intact, John moves in the direction of manhood.

Whereas John eventually asserts himself, Sheldon Forrester, one of John's co-workers, typifies the image of the black who is too impotent to search for manhood. An elderly man, Sheldon has been worn down by years of accepting second-class citizenship. He laughs, cries, hums, and shuffles on cue. He ingratiates himself to the white director by giving him what he expects of blacks: total subservience. Sheldon has no self-respect, and he chastises those blacks who affirm themselves. This extremely malleable male feels that it is futile for a black man to assert his manhood in the American society. Ironically, Sheldon defines his manhood in terms of his success at projecting that he is not a man among white men. He brags to his co-workers that his denial of self has helped him to survive in the world. Sheldon's impotence is apparent when he lashes out at Wiletta for angering the white director who may decide to cancel the black show written by a white playwright. He tells her that he allows himself to be demeaned because he knows that his bills will not get paid with pride. Sheldon's whole life has been spent exchanging his dignity for minor roles, albeit stereotypical ones, on the American stage.

Walter Lee Younger in Lorraine Hansberry's *A Raisin in the Sun* (1959) is a black male in search of manhood.[35] A man in his mid-thirties and the father of a ten-year-old boy, Walter Lee very often behaves immaturely. Living in a cramped, run-down apartment with his mother Lena, Walter Lee allows himself to be ordered around by his mother as though he were a child. He is frustrated because he can not provide for his family the luxuries that are to him a sign of manhood. Walter Lee deemphasizes genuine human values by believing that his manhood hinges upon securing large sums of money. When it appears that he will not be able to use his mother's ten-thousand-dollar insurance check to invest in a liquor store business, Walter Lee throws a tantrum in which he accuses his family and white America of preventing him from being a man. Like Bigger Thomas in Richard Wright's *Native Son* (1940), Walter Lee shifts blame for his failure onto others without accepting responsibility for the errors in judgment that he has made in life. He castigates blacks and implies that whites are to be emulated for their shrewdness in business matters. He suggests that black men cannot be men "cause we all tied up in a race of people that don't know how to do nothing but moan and pray and have babies" (p. 73).

His antics so displease Mama that she eventually does entrust a substantial amount of money to Walter Lee. He naively loses the money, however, to an unscrupulous business partner. Walter Lee's need to redeem himself in his family's eyes leads him to come up with what he thinks is a foolproof strategy. In desperation, he decides to degrade himself by accepting a bribe from whites who do not wish to accept blacks in their neighborhood. In many respects, Walter Lee is like Sheldon in *Trouble in Mind*, a man who can be bought. With the help of his mother, Walter Lee comes into his manhood. At the crucial moment when Walter Lee has to choose between money, and love of family and pride of race, he chooses the latter. He sheds the garments of the id-centered, irresponsible person and moves in the direction of maturity as the play closes.

Though *A Raisin in the Sun* was produced on Broadway in 1959, it foreshadowed much of the emotional climate of the 1960s. The volatile 1960s saw 250,000 people march on Washington D.C. in 1963 to protest housing, school, and job discrimination. One year earlier, James H. Meredith, escorted by federal marshals, had registered at the University of Southern Mississippi, first in a long line of white colleges to protest the admission of black students. This decade gave way to the burning and bombing of a rash of Negro churches and homes, including the murder of four little black girls who were victims of the bombing of a Birmingham, Alabama church. While Martin Luther King, Jr. urged nonviolent demonstrations, there were thousands who were rioting in Harlem and Rochester, New York; Jersey City, New Jersey; Philadelphia, Pennsylvania; Macon and Albany, Georgia; Montgomery, Alabama; and Biloxi, Mississippi. In fact, the Southern Regional Council announced that the sit-in movement had affected twenty states and more than one hundred cities in Southern and border states in a period from February 1960 to September 1961. Approximately seventy thousand blacks and whites had participated in these demonstrations in the South alone. It was during the 1960s that Americans witnessed the assassinations of three great political leaders: President John F. Kennedy in 1963, Malcolm X in 1965, and Dr. Martin Luther King, Jr. in 1968. More disillusionment set in as black men, who did not feel free in the United States, were forced to fight in the Vietnam war of

the late 1960s and early 1970s. While many of America's men were overseas
fighting, black and white women joined forces to battle for equality in what
has since come to be known as the Feminist Movement. The turmoil of
the 1960s could not have gone unrecorded in the plays of so sighted a
playwright as Hansberry.

The tumultuous 1960s produced revolutionaries, as is reflected by the
characters Joseph Asagai in *A Raisin in the Sun* and Hannibal in *The Drinking
Gourd* (1960). The insecurity experienced by so many blacks of the 1950s
found expression in the explosive Black Power Movement. Having ex-
hausted themselves with waiting for an end to racial discrimination, the
blacks rebelled against white supremacy. In many plays of the 1960s, black
activists react violently to free themselves of the emotional chains of bondage. Speaking of the emotional shackles placed on black men, Michele
Wallace argues: "Black men have a tendency to react violently when they
realize that the chains are in their head and not on their arms. America has
always said that a black man is not a man, and it should not shock white
America when black men try to prove their manhood by using violence."[36]

Hansberry's activists are driven by despair, anger, frustration, and an
unyielding commitment to justice for blacks. Keenly aware of the inequit-
able sociopolitical system, they seek to make their existence a matter of
significance. Their assertiveness stems from self-pride and self-determination. Hansberry's militants desire and work unceasingly to be a part of the
machine that destroys the society that has for too long denied black men
their civil rights.

Asagai, a young, Nigerian activist studying in America, is the catalyst
for Beneatha's growing awareness of a need to fight for black people's rights
and women's rights. He is a proud young man who teaches Beneatha about
the beauty of blackness, a concept that gained momentum during Marcus
Garvey's turn of the century Back-to-Africa Movement, peaking during
the 1960s. Asagai teases Beneatha about mutilating her hair, trying to
straighten the beautiful curls made by Mother Africa. Though he brings
her traditional African attire, he tries to instruct Beneatha that she must not
focus on the trivial blackness as expressed through garments, but must
work toward making blacks free to choose their destiny. He teaches her
about striving for her own identity and independence as a woman and as
a black. Accepting the call, Beneatha grows into a low-level activist, one
of the few black females to be designated as such in the literature of the
period by black women dramatists.

Asagai views himself as a liberator, a militant. He is consumed with
thoughts of independence as Beneatha notes, "You with the dreams of the
future will patch up all Africa—you are going to cure the Great Sore of
colonialism with Independence" (p. 113). Asagai insists that he plans to
return to his country where he will lead a revolution against an oppressive
white government. This brilliant young embodiment of the Black Power

Movement in America and Africa poignantly reveals that he will go home to teach and work while activists plan and organize the revolution. Asagai argues that there must be a revolution to rid his country of illiteracy, disease, and ignorance, which by the way are the same ailments that plague blacks and poor people in America. It is in this fusion of the suffering of blacks in America and Africa that Hansberry shapes Asagai as the symbol of humanity's interconnectedness. Asagai becomes the instrument that facilitates change in society. With plans to overthrow his country's government, Asagai predicts the inevitable bloodshed: "Guns, murder, revolution. And I even will have moments when I wonder if the quiet was not better than all that death and hatred" (p. 115). Asagai aims to destroy the existing British power structure in Africa and to rebuild it in such a way that blacks may no longer suffer the indignities heaped upon them by their white brothers.

Hannibal, in Hansberry's *The Drinking Gourd*, is very much like Asagai in his aggressiveness and rebelliousness.[37] *The Drinking Gourd*, set during the pre–Civil War era, was written in 1960 and therefore reflects Hansberry's personal commitment to equal rights and embodies the spirit of the revolutionary 1960s. An activist, Hannibal tries to convince those around him that it is not normal for one group of people to enslave another. He attempts to motivate his girlfriend, Sarah, to become rebellious. Hannibal berates his mother for her contentedness in a slavocracy. At another point, he ridicules the black assistant to the overseer, Coffin, who takes great pride in helping to keep blacks suppressed. When Hannibal fails to draw those nearest him into the revolutionary spirit, he does not drift into passivity. Instead, he steps up his own retaliatory tactics. He reacts violently against his master's possessions, breaking tools every chance he gets to slow up production. Hannibal takes great pleasure in devising machinations to keep from working.

Refusing to accept his place as a slave, Hannibal tricks his master's young son into teaching him to read and write. Hannibal's plan is first to free himself of illiteracy in order that he might successfully extricate himself from the physical and emotional chains of slavery. When he shares with Sarah that he can read and is planning to escape, she tries to persuade him to abandon such thoughts. She cautions him about the difficulty he will encounter as a wandering fugitive. Imbued with the 1960s consciousness, Hannibal boldly tells her that he refuses to dwell on what freedom might bring and that he only knows he cannot tolerate remaining a slave. In short, Hannibal reminds Sarah that to be a slave means automatically and irrevocably to be denied recognition as a human being. His message to Sarah is that every slave ought to run off before he dies. Far removed from the docile, contented slave stereotype, Hannibal is bold and proud. He boasts that as long as he can make a half-step do for a whole, pretend sickness instead of health, act stupid instead of smart, move lazily instead of quickly,

he will do it. He shames and angers Coffin by telling him that the more
the master is pained by his rebelliousness, the more he will feel like a man.
Hannibal, though his eyes have been gouged out at the end of the play,
escapes with the assistance of his mother and Sarah and with his dignity
intact.

Two plays by Alice Childress, *Wedding Band* (1966) and *Wine in the Wilderness* (1969), yield to the spirit of the 1960s. Fanny in *Wedding Band* is a
humorously drawn character who embodies everything that the Civil Rights
Movement worked to eradicate.[38] Emphatically she is not a militant or
revolutionary, but thinks that she is an activist par excellence. She never
lets the black community forget that she is the only black woman who
owns a string of houses and a substantial amount of property, all of which
the whites across the tracks have sanctioned because she is the upholder of
racial pride.

Fanny sets herself above the black race. At one point, she confides to one
of her tenants, Julia, that "some people are ice cream and others just cow-
dung. I try to be ice cream" (p. 261). She weaves her way in and out of
practically every house in the small black community reminding them that
black is beautiful and that she is so terribly burdened with having to demonstrate to whites that black people are worthy, decent human beings. When
Julia's white boyfriend becomes ill in her home, the "activist/entrepreneur"
becomes infuriated. She tells Julia she will have to get rid of her white lover
because she does not want whites to change their high opinion of her. With
great pride she parrots that she has overheard whites whisper that she
represents her race in an approved manner. In the same breath, she quips,
"I can't afford to mess that up on account-a you or any-a the rest-a these
hard-luck, better-off-dead, triflin' niggers" (p. 298). In another instance
when Fanny is questioned about why she has no male companion, she
boasts, "Only reason I'm sleepin' in a double bed by myself is 'cause I got
to bear the standard for the race" (p. 300). Later when one of her tenants,
Nelson, rejects a proposition to serve as her business advisor and live-in
love technician, Fanny condescendingly retorts, "Roll on. Just trying to
help the race" (p. 301). Childress mirrors the concerns of blacks of the 1960s
by evoking laughter at the foibles of Fanny, a would-be activist.

Childress' *Wine in the Wilderness* deals with race consciousness less humorously.[39] The stage instructions indicate that noises, screaming, running
feet, bullets, explosions, and the authorities on loud speakers can be heard
in the distance. Using the rioting and looting mainly as a backdrop, Childress does not focus on the activists or revolutionaries or the violence
perpetrated on white America. In fact, the activists do not appear on stage
in this play. Unlike the leading Black Arts Movement playwright Amiri
Baraka, whose plays *Dutchman* (1963) and *The Slave* (1964) focus on the
ritualistic, brutal killing of whites, Childress concentrates on blacks as vic-

tims of white oppression. She places the violence of the 1960s in perspective by holding up for all to see the poverty and sense of helplessness that blacks experience in a society where there is rank racial discrimination.

The raging racial storm outside has been internalized by Oldtimer, an elderly grass-roots gentleman who provides insight into the nature and quality of the ongoing riot in *Wine in the Wilderness.* He describes the anger, violence, and frustration that has led blacks to smash windows of uptown department stores and to plunder bombed or burned out grocery stores. Feeling a little sorry for himself, Oldtimer tells Bill Jameson, a middle-class black artist, that Father Time is an oppressive, mean white cat who has stepped all over him, worn him down, and forced him to steal to survive. Oldtimer epitomizes poor blacks who are the consummate victims of across-the-board racial discrimination.

Tommy Marie, another riot victim whose apartment has been burned out, is depicted as a struggling grass-roots woman. Oppression has left her illiterate. She had to quit school as an adolescent to work to keep from starving. Childress treats the 1960s not so much as a decade of violence and irrational behavior, but as one in which the disenfranchised blacks of America struggled with great composure and nonviolent protestations to survive against the worst possible odds.

Another very popular image that dominates these plays in the late 1950s and 1960s is "the assimilationist," who is not sympathetically drawn by Childress or Hansberry. The assimilationist appears in plays of the 1950s as a heckler, eagerly warning fellow blacks that they should accept the status quo. During the 1960s, however, the assimilationist serves as a foil to the activist. These black dramatists deliberately pit the assimilationist against the activist to demonstrate the unacceptable behavior of the former. For the purpose of this study, the black assimilationist is a person who not only adopts the characteristics of presumably another culture but who shows no love or empathy for the less fortunate. Usually middle class, the black assimilationist is almost always a college-educated pseudointellectual. An assimilationist becomes an object of scorn for criticizing or blatantly chastising grass-roots blacks, and haughtily advertising economic and social security associated with the middle class. An assimilationist is portrayed as someone who has lost all sense of identification with the black race and is encumbered by the most meaningless values and idiosyncrasies of white middle class. Frequently, the assimilationist places a great deal of emphasis on gourmet cooking, wine sampling, and fashionable clothing. Characterized as insipid, artificial, arrogant, malicious, deceitful, manipulative, and empty, the assimilationist feigns blackness but wishes to cut all ties with poor, uneducated, unrefined blacks.

George Murchison in Hansberry's *A Raisin in the Sun* is a typical assimilationist for whom integration has not been an advantage. Murchison's counterpart, Walter Lee Younger, voices the opinions of such Black Arts dramatists as Baraka and Bullins who advocate separation of the races to minimize or prevent black exploitation or "blaxploitation." Walter Lee mouths this theory of blaxploitation when he tells George, whom he considers an exploited product of integration, that whites are not teaching him about blackness or manhood at the college he attends. Walter Lee sneers, "Filling up your heads . . . with the sociology and the psychology—but they teaching you how to be a man? How to take over and run the world, and how to run a rubber plantation or a steel mill?" (p. 71). Walter Lee denigrates George by telling him that whites are merely teaching him how to talk proper, read books, and wear white shoes.

Son of middle-class parents and a college student, George is described by Beneatha as shallow. When Mama asks Beneatha to explain why George would not make a good husband for her, she tells her that the Murchisons are affluent blacks and that "the only people in the world who are more snobbish than rich white people are rich colored people" (p. 37). George's behavior and remarks suggest that he considers himself better than poor blacks. During the scene in which Beneatha and Walter Lee imagine that they are on African soil, Walter Lee urges George to no avail to join in the ritual by calling George his spiritual black brother. When Beneatha, dressed in an African robe, indicates that she is ready to leave, George tells her to get dressed to go to the theater, not to be in it. Beneatha accuses George of assimilationism, which she emphatically defines for her sister-in-law, Ruth, as "someone who is willing to give up his own culture and submerge himself completely in the dominant, and in this case, oppressive culture" (p. 67). To Beneatha's comment that she hates assimilationist Negroes, George tells her that the African past is a myth and that he does not want to hear about the great Ashanti empires, the great Songhay civilizations, or the great sculpture of Benin. Commenting that he is particularly offended by the word heritage, George shouts, "Let's face it, baby, your heritage is nothing but a bunch of raggedy-assed spirituals and some grass huts" (p. 68).

While disdainful of talk of black heritage and culture, George insists that he is cultured. Hansberry characterizes George as a man who places emphasis on fashion by calling attention to his casual tweed sports jacket, over a cashmere V-neck sweater, over a soft eyelet shirt and tie, and soft slacks finished off with white buckskin shoes. He intimates he has a penchant for traveling and for the finer things in life when he complains that he hates to be late for the theater even if it is an 8:30 curtain. He ostentatiously announces that Chicago theaters do not follow the standard New York 8:40 show time. When Walter Lee quips that Chicago has everything that New York has, George condescendingly asks him when was the last time he had a chance to visit New York. An argument based upon class difference ensues only to end with George exiting and calling Walter Lee a Prometheus. Unfamiliar with the mythical figure, Walter Lee is infuriated that George is not courageous enough to insult him with words he can understand. George Murchison's haughtiness and disavowal of his African heritage epitomize the most negative qualities associated with black assimilationism.

Like George Murchison, Bill Jameson, Sonny-Man, and Cynthia in Childress' *Wine in the Wilderness* are black assimilationists. Hatch and Shine argue that Childress' elitist characters preach blackness, brotherhood and love simply because it is in vogue, but that they really wish to eradicate all ties with lower-class blacks. Commenting that these bourgeois characters are cold, cruel, and self-centered individuals, Hatch and Shine contend that they are residuals of the old slave masters.[40] Bill is especially narcissistic. He turns an unsympathetic ear to Tommy, a grass-roots black woman who has been burned out during a Harlem riot. Instead of empathizing with her, he deliberately tries to minimize her plight by babbling about his gourmet cooking. Though Bill lives in a black community and boasts of the revolution that is coming, he is repulsed by impoverished blacks, especially by those who complain of being oppressed. When confronted by Tommy about his lack of pride in his heritage and about his apathy toward the black struggle, Bill explains that black folk are not together and are without a plan. He points out that black folk are despoiling Harlem and getting their bodies beaten and broken without really effecting change. Tommy teaches Bill that he has abandoned the black masses because he does not love himself. Bill's attitude about the Black Power Movement was one held by many black assimilationists as the 1960s waned.

A new wave swept the country in the 1970s. The race rioting diminished considerably. According to educational consultant Joseph Pierre,

> Blacks experienced an appeasement period in the 1970s. The key leaders of the movement were given what they wanted, an entre into corporate America. Many of them were bought off and became assimilationists, leaving the masses or grass-roots folk without strong leadership. Other activists of the 1960s were diffused, short-circuited with threats of imprisonment. Still others continued to fight but were too splintered to sound any alarms.[41]

Several important major gains were made in the 1970s, however, including the appointment of Congressman Andrew Young of Georgia as ambassador to the United Nations, the election of a number of black mayors in major cities in the United States, and the awarding of a special Pulitzer Prize to Alex Haley for the landmark book *Roots*. The 1970s was a decade that saw the continued growth of the rebirth of the Feminist Movement of the 1960s. Black women, in particular, made significant gains as a result of the Black Power and women's movements. One case in point was activist/author Angela Davis, whose imprisonment incurred the wrath of women and blacks across the country. Angela Davis' 1974 book *Angela Davis* chronicles the black struggle. Other leading black women of the Civil Rights Movement turned to the pen, such as Alice Childress, Sonia Sanchez, Mari Evans, Nikki Giovanni, Toni Morrison, Audre Lorde, Alice Walker, June Jordan,

Ntozake Shange, and a host of others. The emergence of the voice of the black woman in the 1970s has resulted in a myriad of portraits of blacks that, when juxtaposed to the images created by black men, make for a richer, fuller, and more solidly based history of black men and women.

One of the dominant images of the 1970s is "the evolving black woman," a phrase that embodies the multiplicity of emotions of ordinary black women for whom the act of living is sheer heroism. This creature emphasizes understanding and taking care of herself. Not always a powerhouse of strength, the evolving black woman is quite fragile. Her resiliency, though, makes her a positive image of black womanhood. Self-respecting, self-sufficient, and assertive, these women force others around them to respect them.

With her special blend of poetry and drama, Ntozake Shange explores the nuances of the lives of black women of the 1970s. The evolving black women in Shange's works are preoccupied with themselves because they have been disappointed by the men who have come into their lives. These are women who have had their share of "deferred dreams" and are no longer willing to play the role of "woman-behind-her-man" to the men who do not appreciate their submissiveness or docility. These women rebel and claim that no man is ever going to oppress them again. They are not women who give up on men or feel that all men are insensitive beasts; instead, they are women who have become independent because of their fear of being abused physically and emotionally in subsequent relationships. The controlling image in these plays is that of a woman who has to "sing the blues" before she is able to make sense of the chaos in her life. Though black women who are abandoned in Shange's plays bewail their losses, emphasis is placed on their ability to survive in a world where they are forced to care for themselves. The evolving black women in these plays fight back after they have been bruised, and they work toward improving their lifestyles.

Ntozake Shange's *For Colored Girls Who Have Considered Suicide/When the Rainbow is Enuf* strongly advocates that women band together to shield themselves from the enemy: men.[42] The women have journeyed through one emotional minefield after another, bouncing back from the explosions that have left many of them fragmented and cautious about males. These women console each other as they tell of their struggle for integrity and autonomy. Though the evolving black women in this feminist choreopoem speak of the brutal treatment accorded them by their men, Shange emphasizes their determination to rise above this form of bondage, and their success at coping in a world where "Being alive, being a woman, and being colored is a metaphysical dilemma."[43] These women have been knocked down, but they pick themselves up and strut right along, searching for a way to hold on to their sanity and to improve their lifestyles. In her essay, "For Colored

Girls—And White Girls Too," Toni Cade Bambara gives credence to the resiliency of Shange's female characters:

> What is curious about the work is that though men appear exclusively as instruments of pain, there is no venom, no resorting to a Queen of Hearts Solution—off with his head! No god-like revenge, no god-like forgiving. Hell, some things are unforgivable. The women of the various pieces suck their teeth, storm, sass, get on with the miracle of living.[44]

One of the defense mechanisms that black women in the literature of the 1970s uses is that of contrariness. Barbara Christian's "The Contrary Women of Alice Walker: A Study of *In Love and Trouble*" treats contrariness as a vehicle of growth and points out that it is a positive step taken by women as they refuse to tolerate physical and emotional abuse by the men in their lives.[45] Following Christian's lead, Sandra L. Richards discusses contrariness of black women as a "public, political act, a sign of a woman's attempt to become whole."[46] Both Christian and Richards treat the act of contrariness as a deliberate strategy used by women whose pleas for decent treatment from their men have fallen upon deaf ears. These contrary women learn to say no to their men. Sometimes the contrariness comes in the form of violence directed either at themselves or at the object of pain, as Michael G. Cooke suggests in "Recent Novels: Women Bearing Violence."[47] At other times, the contrariness may take the form of the black woman killing with kindness the person who is mistreating her. Shange's evolving black women empower themselves by resorting to contrariness.

The women of this theater piece experience a communal yet intensely private discovery of their own worth and strength. These evolving black women come to realize that they will not suffer a nervous breakdown but can move on to as many positive, invigorating, and regenerative experiences as the many hues of the rainbow. One case in point is lady in red who speaks of the many ways she tried desperately to encourage a man to love her. Instead of reciprocating, he used her only to satisfy his sexual desires. When she refuses to continue in a relationship that debases her, one sees a woman who has grown:

> this waz an experiment
> to see how selfish i cd be
> if i wd really carry on to snare a possible lover
> if i was capable of debasin myself for the love of another
> if i cd stand not being wanted
> when i wanted to be wanted & i cannot
> so
> with no further assistance & guidance from you
> i am endin this affair

this note is attached to a plant
i've been waterin since the day i met you
you may water it
yr damn self (p. 14)

Lady in blue, like lady in red, is an evolving black woman who speaks
of the countless excuses given to black women by black men who are not
capable of providing love, closeness, and protection because of the crippling
effects of oppression in America. She speaks of those men who abuse their
women emotionally and physically and attempt to pacify them with apologies. Her speech suggests that battered black women must learn to love
themselves enough to protect themselves and, if necessary, to survive on
their own. Choosing contrariness over acquiescence, lady in blue emphatically expresses her newfound intolerance of ineffectual apologies from men:

one thing i dont need
is any more apologies
i got sorry greetin me at my front door
you can keep yrs
i dont know what to do wit em
they dont open doors
or bring the sun back
they dont make me happy
or get the mornin paper
didnt nobody stop usin my tears to wash cars
cuz a sorry
i am simply tired
of collectin
"i didnt know
i was so important to you"
i'm gonna haveta throw some away
i cant get to the clothes in my closet
for alla the sorries
i'm gonna tack a sign to my door
leave a message by the phone
"if you called
to say yr sorry
call somebody
else
i dont use em anymore"
i let sorry
didnt meanta
& how cd i know abt that
take a walk down a dark & musty street in brooklyn
i'm gonna do exactly what i want to (pp. 52–53)

Such determination, willfulness, and boldness in black female characters had not graced the American stage with such forcefulness prior to Shange's *For Colored Girls*. The evolving black women in Shange's play are survivors who take full responsibility for their own completeness.

Though a case can be made that a dominant image appears in each decade between the 1950s and the 1980s, there are several images that appear and evolve during the course of these several decades. One such image is the evolving black woman. Though this image matures in the 1970s, it can be seen in the literature as early as 1950 in Childress' *Florence* (1950).[48] Florence, a struggling actress, strives to survive in a hostile world. Placed in the position of supporting herself and her son because her husband was killed by whites in the South, Florence relocates to New York. This South to North movement, a motif that runs through much of African American literature from Colonial times to the present, changes very little for Florence. She does not meet with much success in the American theater, except for the several times that she has played the part of a maid in plays. She does not despair but continues to try to find a way to improve her lifestyle. Florence is portrayed as a gutsy woman who rejects prescriptive roles.

Beneatha Younger in Hansberry's *A Raisin in the Sun* (1959) typifies the evolving black woman. The daughter of one-time sharecropper, Beneatha aspires to become a physician. At several points in the play, Beneatha implies that becoming a doctor is far more important to her than securing a husband. She feels confident that she can take care of her own needs. Beneatha is a young, intelligent black woman who is aware of her capabilities and refuses to let anyone, including both of her suitors, George Murchison and Joseph Asagai, minimize her potential. When her sister-in-law, Ruth, chides her for not trying to entrap and marry the affluent George, Beneatha tells her that she would never consider such nonsense because he is shallow, snobbish, and unable to accept the fact that she wants to become a professional. Her sense of independence is particularly apparent in her interaction with Asagai. She boldly tells him that he is a manipulator. Whenever she tries to speak of her dreams and hopes, he confuses her with pretty words and soft kisses. Beneatha realizes that flattery can be used as either medicine or manipulation. She demands time to think about Asagai's marriage proposal because she fears that his flattery smacks too much of control. The play concludes without Beneatha making a serious commitment to anyone or anything except to her dream of becoming a doctor. Preoccupied with taking care of herself, Beneatha rejects the idea that her happiness or completeness depends upon the guidance or support of a man.

The evolving black woman in Childress's *Wine in the Wilderness* (1969) is assertive and dynamic. When Bill Jameson chooses to include Tommy in his triptych, she gets the impression that he is interested in starting a relationship with her. Cynthia, however, Bill's bourgeois friend, intimates to her that she is not good enough for Bill and that she must look elsewhere for a possible provider. Tommy immediately sets the record straight by telling Cynthia that she is not looking for a meal ticket and that she has been doing for herself her whole life. She does, however, admit that she wants "Somebody in my corner. Not to wake up by myself in the mornin' and face this world alone" (p. 744). A little later, Tommy comments, "I'm so lonesome ... I want somebody to love. Somebody to say ... 'That's alright' when the world treats me mean" (p. 744).

This evolving black woman is not afraid to show her vulnerability. She reaches out for love but is repaid with arrogance and hostility. When Tommy discovers that she is represent the "lost womanhood" in his painting, she defiantly tells him that she is equipped to take care of herself and to survive alone because men like him keep insulting her intelligence and taking advantage of her tenderness. Tommy Marie is a positive image of black womanhood because she is honest, and she is a survivor who refuses to despair. At the end of the play, Tommy is confident that if Bill Jameson does not see her worth and beauty, another male will. What is important is that Alice Childress has created an image of a woman whose inner strength will protect her as she searches for a stable relationship in which there is reciprocity.

The evolving black woman in the plays by Childress, Hansberry, and Shange toughen because of "The chauvinists," another image that seems to flourish between the 1950s and the 1980s. The chauvinists "sometimes callously and sometimes subtly oppress the women entangled in their lives."[49] A close examination of the literature reveals that the chauvinist often becomes the absent black father/spouse/lover when he is unable to cope with the pressure of not being able to provide for his family or significant others, a symbol of manhood. Tommy in *Wine in the Wilderness* recalls that her father ran off with a trifling woman and was never heard from again. Her father had been unable to provide for the basic needs of his family, and thus removed himself from the pain and frustration of the home environment.

Tommy is a repeat victim of chauvinism because it seems that the men she becomes interested in suffer from male supremacist tendencies. Bill Jameson, for all the reasons discussed earlier, is prejudiced against women. He wounds Tommy as he battles with his own insecurities. Similarly, Irene in Childress' *Mojo* reminisces about her father's leaving.[50] Her mother wanted her father to show affection, but he seemed incapable. During a heated argument, she tells him to get out and he does. Irene recalls her mother's words, "Ain't like no Teevee story with us. . . . Love is hard to live round when a woman is washin out her last raggy pair-a drawers . . . and her man ain't got a quarter to put in her hand" (p. 72). The black men in these two plays are portrayed as powerless.

The chauvinists, both those who eventually leave and those who choose to stay with their families, often become abusive, physically and emotionally. They shift blame for their inadequacy to black women by accusing them of emasculation. They often view their women's attempt to reach out to them as a sign of a need to dominate and to suppress their manhood. The chauvinists are sympathetically drawn because they are portrayed as men who struggle against a myriad of personal and social pressures and who often fail under the debilitating effects of racism.

Though it is evident that he loves the women in his family, Walter Lee in *A Raisin in the Sun* is a chauvinist. He openly acknowledges that his sister's notions about becoming a doctor are outlandish and masculine. Walter Lee's chauvinism is apparent when he blurts out, "If you so crazy 'bout messing 'round with sick people—then go be a nurse like other women—or just get married and be quiet" (p. 26). Walter Lee's notion is that women should not aspire to positions of authority and prestige. Throughout the play, Walter Lee badgers and tries to intimidate Beneatha into giving up her dreams of going to medical school, thereby increasing his chances of getting the insurance money for his goals. Walter Lee is also hostile toward his mother for refusing to give him money to invest in a liquor store business. Rising, shouting, and pounding on the table, Walter Lee asks his mother if she has done something crazy with the money. He does not trust his mother's judgment and finds her downpayment on a house in a white neighborhood utterly feminine and foolish. Walter Lee's opinion of his wife is in keeping with how he perceives most black women: as emasculators. He is particularly brutal to Ruth when she insists that she will not try to convince Mama to turn over the money to him. Walter Lee's prejudice against black women is most apparent when he comments, "That is just what is wrong with the colored woman in this world . . . Don't understand about building their men up and makin 'em feel like they somebody. Like they can do something" (p. 22). The implication is that black women have joined forces with white racists to destroy black men. Later, Walter Lee insults Ruth by telling her that black men are tied to a race of women with small minds.

Steven Carter maintains that as Walter Lee grows, he becomes less chauvinistic. Carter contends that when Walter Lee refuses the bribe from whites who do not wish for blacks to move into their neighborhood, "he learns that his pride in himself and his pride in his family are inseparable, that anything harming one also harms the other, and he further sees that the three women in his life have always helped him bear the burdens of living in a racist system and are now prepared to be powerful allies in the struggle against this new racist insult."[51] Carter suggests that Walter Lee not only gathers his own strength to fight the racist system, but also comes to recognize the strength and talents of the women in his life.[52]

Two other chauvinists in *A Raisin in the Sun* are Beneatha's two suitors, George Murchison and Joseph Asagai. George tells Beneatha that she annoys him with her moodiness. He insults her intelligence by telling her that he does not date her in order to discuss quiet desperation. He proceeds to tell her, while simultaneously groping at her, that he goes out with her because she has a beautiful body. Shallow and biased against women, George arrogantly says to Beneatha, "You're a nice looking girl . . . all over. That's all you need, honey" (p. 82). He reminds her that guys are stimulated by what they see, not by a woman's intelligence or any other characteristic. A true philistine, George tells her that he does not want to hear about her thoughts, which he says are worthless since they do not change the world. Beneatha later tells her mother that George is a fool and that she will not squander any more time with him.

Asagai, for all of his talk about oppression in his country, can not see that he is a male supremacist. He tries to pressure Beneatha into intimacy. She, on the other hand, tells him that there is more than one kind of feeling that can exist between a man and a woman. Asagai's response to Beneatha's distinction between "agape" and "eros," borders on the risque: "No. Between a man and a woman there need be only one kind of feeling. I have that for you . . . Now . . . even . . . right this moment" (p. 50). Escaping his clutches, Beneatha tells him that sexual love would never be enough for her. Asagai hastily remarks that for a woman, sexual love should be enough. When Beneatha tells him that she is not interested in becoming his little American episode, Asagai insults her by telling her that every American woman he has been drawn to has given him the same speech. Not only is he telling her that she has old-fashioned ideas about morality, but also that she is unoriginal and unimaginative as well.

Shange's *For Colored Girls* and *A Photograph: Lovers in Motion* are replete with chauvinists. Beau Willie Brown in Shange's choreopoem is the consummate male supremacist. He visits his mistress and their two children only when he has no money or place to go. A Vietnam War veteran, Beau Willie Brown is mentally inept. He violates Crystal as he struggles with his perception that white America is out to get him. He denies paternity of his first child and nearly beats Crystal to death when she becomes pregnant with a second child. Crystal determines to rid herself of Beau Willie Brown after what seems like a lifetime of chairs thrown at her head, only to discover that he finally wants to marry her. This lunatic's response is to take a chair to Crystal again, presumably to prove to her that he needs her and is ready to do right by her. When he could do no more damage with the table chair, Beau Willie Brown grabs the high chair with his son intact and commences to brutalize Crystal. After Crystal recovers, Beau Willie Brown breaks into her apartment to convince her to marry him so that he can get additional veterans benefits, give up cab driving, and be the man of his house. He snatches the children from her, runs to the window with one in each hand, and threatens to drop them if she does not agree to marry him. It is too powerful a moment to ever forget Crystal's silent scream and her ensuing whisper: "I stood by beau in the window/with naomi reachin for me/& kwame screamin mommy mommy from the fifth story/but I cd only whisper/& he dropped em" (p. 60).

Shange's middle-class chauvinists are no less brutal than the grass-roots black men who violate their women. Sean, in *A Photograph: Lovers in Motion* (1981), explains to Michael, his favorite lover, "there are a number of women in my life/who i plan to keep in my life/& i'll never let any of them come between us/between what we have in our world" (p. 61).[53] During an argument, however, over Sean's lack of confidence in himself and his work, Michael tries to tell him that she knows he is capable of great things. Viewing Michael's encouragement as an attempt at emasculation, Sean tells her that she does not know anything about him except that he takes care of her sexual needs. Becoming abusive when she dares to tell him not to confuse sex with genuine love, Sean raves, "yr really outta yr mind/stupid bitch/i know how to deal with you/or any other bitch comes in here" (p. 85).

Sean is equally disrespectful and vulgar to Claire and Nevada. To him, Claire is solely a mindless sex object. When Claire jokingly intimates that she may share with some other man some of her rhinestones and palm leaves and magnolia, Sean's ego is bruised. He retaliates by telling her that if he ever finds out that she has gone to bed with another man, he will take her to the 500 club and "give everybody some of that magnolia" (p. 65). That Sean could threaten to participate in the rape of his paramour illustrates his regard for womanhood. Nevada, a lawyer, also falls victim to Sean's verbal abuse. Since he is only interested in her money and connections, he has little patience with her when she exhibits jealous behavior. He allows her to make up for her little indiscretions by buying things for him. At one point when she tells him that she loves him, he responds apathetically and noncommittally and orders her to get out of his sight. Sean's chauvinism toward women is also expressed by his friend, Earl, who tells Nevada that she deserves someone better than Sean who only knows women and cruelty. The key thread that joins these three women is that Sean seems to feel that each one in her own way is trying to deprive him of his manhood.

The Black woman as emasculator stems from the black matriarchy myth. There is little doubt that the image of "the black mother" invariably has been influenced by the negative attention called to the black mother and her family in the famous Moynihan Report of the late 1960s.[54] Mae C. King argues that "the fact that the matriarchy myth was popularized and widely accepted in this country by all segments of society is a reflection of the depth of the cruelty that America from its inception has inflicted upon the black woman."[55] King notes that the matriarchy notion has been posited by whites who wish exemption from the responsibility for the oppression of blacks.[56] King notes that the matriarchy myth is absurd because "matriarchy in its historical usage denotes a position of power, which, of course, neither black women nor black men have secured in America."[57] Gerda Lerner, in *Black Women in White America*, concurs that "black women have been the most powerless group in our entire society."[58] Angela Davis argues that the myth of a black matriarchy is a cruel misnomer because "it implies stable kinship structures within which the mother exercises decisive authority."[59] Davis contends that there can be no matriarchy if the male is not present in the home because a matriarchy implies that the woman in a male/female home makes decisions that go against the male's wishes.[60]

As a result of the popularization of the matriarchy myth, unyielding, stalwart, religious women who rob their sons of manhood appear in much of the literature written by blacks and whites. Mapp suggests that "the thin line between black mammy and black matriarch may be distinguished largely by whether the old girl is presiding over a white or black household."[61] Regardless of her moral and physical strength, though, she traditionally has been "relegated to her place in the kitchen or pantry."[62] When no other job was open to the black mother, she could find work in the kitchens of white Americans. Alice Childress, once a maid herself, contends that the black mother's function has been to serve as maid of the world. In her article "The Negro Woman in American Literature," Childress asserts that "facing the world alone makes a woman strong. The emancipated Negro woman of America did the only thing she could do. She earned a pittance by washing, ironing, cooking and cleaning, and picking cotton."[63] In response to the myth that the black mother has unmanned black males, Childress says that the black woman has "helped her man, and if she often stood in the front line, it was to shield him from a mob of men organized and dedicated to bring about his total destruction."[64]

Many multidimensional images of the black mother appear in literature written by black women. Mary Helen Washington asserts that the black mother is depicted as "fiercely protective of her children, often sacrificing herself to prepare them to live in a violent and racist world."[65] In her essay "Black Women Playwrights: They Speak: Who Listens?" Barbara Molette contends that black women dramatists have traditionally written positive images of black motherhood and tried to promote mores that were humanistic.[66] In keeping with the traditional stereotypes, many of the mothers in plays by Childress, Hansberry, and Shange are selfless, determined, and saintly. They symbolize sincerity, depth, strength, and vitality. There are two black mother characters, however, that escape the narrow confines of stereotyping and that are especially new and different: Lorraine Hansberry's Rissa in *The Drinking Gourd* and the nameless mother in Shange's *Boogie Woogie Landscapes*.

Rissa moves from mammy to militant in *The Drinking Gourd*, placing her family's needs above all others. Rissa breaks the mold shaped by Southern attitudes and manages to bring new life to the worn portrayal of "the black mother." Her slave master, Hiram Sweet, respects and trusts the

docile Rissa who is like part of the family. He, however, deludes himself
into thinking that Rissa can be pacified when her family's well-being is at
stake. Rissa destroys the myth of the black mammy when she rebels against
the institution of slavery that has separated her from one son and inflicted
physical abuse upon the second son. Rissa blames Hiram when Hannibal,
her son, comes to her sightless. When Hiram comes to beg Rissa's forgiveness and to tell her that he had nothing to do with Hannibal's injury,
she furiously turns on him unlike any stereotypical mammy: "Why? Ain't
you Marster? How can a man be marster of some men and not at all of
others?" (p. 734). Surprised, disappointed, and angered by Rissa's brazen-
ness, Hiram cautions her to know her place. Rissa, however, has transformed into a rebellious black mother who says, "Oh—? What will you
have done to me? Will your overseer gouge out my eyes too? I don't spect
blindness would matter to me. I done seen all there was worth seein' in
this world—and it didn't 'mount to much" (p. 734). Shortly after Rissa's
victory over her master, he falls outside near her door with a heart attack.
Hearing Hiram's call for help, Rissa flagrantly turns her back and continues
ministering to her blind son. Robert Nemiroff, executor of the Hansberry
estate, contends that Hansberry reverses the sacred image and that she
intended Rissa to be the counterpart to Lena Younger in *A Raisin in the
Sun*.[67] Hansberry apparently believed that not all slaves were content and
chose to portray a black mother whose devotion to her family and whose
simple, human, motherly act of vengeance set her apart from the archetypal
black mother figure.

Another atypical mother appears in Shange's *Boogie Woogie Landscapes*.[68]
While there is not a great deal said about this mother, she deserves to be
examined because she is more vulnerable, confused, disorganized, and nervous than any other mother figure to appear in literature by blacks of the
period. The mother in Shange's theater piece is a professional woman who
cannot cope with the pressures of a career and a family. She is very intolerant
of her children's mischievousness and even less patient with the steady flow
of maids who come into her home to keep the family intact. In spite of
domestic help, "the house got crazy. mama tryin to feed nine people &
make lunches for five/put each one of us at a different bus stop. cuz a
integration/none of us went to the neighborhood school" (p. 131). The
mother gives in to her temptation to leave behind the madhouse of a home.
She turns over the responsibility of the family to her physician husband,
leaving the family without any assurance that she is ever coming back. By
the time the mother does return, the children, husband, and maid have
shaped up and agree to be supportive of the modern-day, high-powered,
high blood pressure and heart-attack-prone career mother.

Alice Childress, Lorraine Hansberry, and Ntozake Shange are contemporary black women playwrights whose visions or perspectives are uniquely
black and feminine. To exclude black women playwrights as a source for
examining black life is to omit a large piece of the human puzzle. These

three women dramatists are important because they supply America with plausible, and in some cases unique, images of black men and women. Some dare to ask, "Do black women playwrights really depict black life?" Unequivocally, they do, but these images must be viewed in conjunction with the images portrayed by black males in order to piece together an accurate picture of black life. Others may ask, "Do black women playwrights represent the majority of blacks?" These selected playwrights do not depict images that represent the majority of blacks. No two or three writers can, nor should have to try. These three dramatists do, however, present a vital slice of life, and it is up to many more black writers to capture the multitude of images of blacks.

Perhaps the most important question to be asked is "Will society be different after meeting the characters in the plays of these black women?" The answer is yes, significantly so. When blacks turn to the theater for better ways to live, Childress, Hansberry, and Shange offer them a multiplicity of options via black characters who come from the heart of the black community. Contemporary black women playwrights give to the American stage a view from the other half: the black and feminine perspective.

NOTES

1. Alvin Goldfarb and Edwin Wilson, *Living Theater: An Introduction to Theater History* (New York: McGraw-Hill Book Co., 1983), p. 427.

2. Jean Fagan Yellin, *The Intricate Knot: Black Figures in American Literature, 1776–1863* (New York: New York University Press, 1972), pp. 3–8.

3. Goldfarb and Wilson, p. 415.

4. Ibid., p. 420.

5. Jeanne-Marie A. Miller, "Black Women Playwrights from Grimke to Shange: Selected Synopses of their Works," in *All the Women Are White, All the Blacks Are Men, But Some of Us Are Brave* (Old Westbury, N.Y.: The Feminist Press, 1982), eds. Gloria T. Hull, Patricia Bell-Scott, and Barbara Smith, p. 280.

6. Sterling Brown, *Negro Poetry and Drama and the Negro in American Fiction* (New York: Atheneum, 1972), p. 139.

7. Donald Bogle, *Toms, Coons, Mulattoes, Mammies, and Bucks: An Interpretive History of Blacks in American Films*, (New York: The Viking Press, 1973).

8. Ibid., p. 230.

9. Michele Wallace, *Black Macho and the Myth of the Superwoman* (New York: The Dial Press, 1978), p. 22.

10. Jeanne-Marie A. Miller, "Images of Black Women in Plays by Blacks," *CLA Journal*, vol. 20 (June 1977), p. 494.

11. Robert Staples, *Black Masculinity: The Black Male's Role in American Society* (San Francisco, Cal.: The Black Scholar Press, 1982), p. 1.

12. Maya Angelou's comments about the existing stereotypes of black women are cited by Trudier Harris in *From Mammies to Militants in Black American Literature* (Philadelphia, Penn.: Temple University Press, 1982), p. 4.

13. Mary Helen Washington, "Black Women Image Makers," *Black World*, vol. 23 (August 1974), p. 10.

14. Ibid., p. 11.

15. Lynora Williams, "Violence Against Women," *The Black Scholar*, vol. 12 (January/February 1981), p. 18.

16. Barbara Smith, "Readers' Forum: Black Women in Film Symposium," *Freedomways*, vol. 21 (Third Quarter 1974), p. 267.

17. Mae C. King, "The Politics of Sexual Stereotyping," *The Black Scholar*, vol. 13 (Summer 1982), p. 2.

18. Edward Mapp, "Black Women in Films," *The Black Scholar*, vol. 13 (Summer 1982), p. 2.

19. Ibid, p. 39.

20. W.E.B. DuBois, *Darkwater: Voices From Within the Veil* (New York: AMS Press, 1969), p. 172.

21. Brown's *The Escape*, Anderson's *Appearances*, and Richardson's *The Idle Head* appear in *Black Theater U.S.A.: Forty-Five Plays by Black Americans, 1847–1974*, eds. James V. Hatch and Ted Shine (New York: The Free Press, 1974).

22. Sandra Hollins Flowers, "Colored Girls: Textbook for the Eighties," *Black American Literature Forum*, vol. 15 (Summer 1971), p. 51.

23. Branch's *In Splendid Error*, Baraka's *The Slave*, and Shine's *Herbert III* appear in *Black Theater U.S.A.: Forty-Five Plays by Black American, 1847–1974*, ed. James V. Hatch and Ted Shine (New York: The Free Press, 1974).

24. Lorraine Hansberry, quoted in Nan Robertson's *Dramatist Against Odds,"* *New York Times*, March 8, 1959 (NYPL, Schomburg Collection, "A Raisin in the Sun" Folder).

25. Lorraine Hansberry, "The Negro in the American Theatre," in *American Playwrights on Drama*, ed. Horst Frenz (New York: Hill and Wang, 1965), p. 166.

26. Miller, "Black Women Playwrights from Grimke to Shange," p. 289.

27. Ibid.

28. Ibid.

29. Mary Helen Washington, *Black-Eyed Susans: Classic Stories By and About Black Women* (New York: The Anchor Books, 1975), p. x.

30. Details about the emotional, political, social, and economic climate of the 1950s through the 1980s are based upon four sources: Lerone Bennett, Jr., *Before the Mayflower: A History of the Negro in America, 1619–1964* (Baltimore: Penguin Books, 1966); Robert L. Southgate, *Black Plots and Black Characters: A Handbook for Afro-American Literature* (New York: Gaylord Professional Publications, 1979); educational consultants Joseph and Ann Pierre of St. Louis, Missouri, and Lucius M. Guillory of New Orleans, Louisiana.

31. Darwin T. Turner, "Visions of Love and Manliness in a Blackening World: Drama of Black Life from 1953–1970, *Iowa Review*, vol. 6 (Spring 1975), p. 98.

32. Adam David Miller, "It's a Long Way to St. Louis," *The Drama Review*, vol. 12 (Summer 1968), p. 150.

33. Alice Childress, "Trouble in Mind," in *Black Theatre: A Twentieth Century Collection of the Work of its Best Playwrights*, ed. Lindsay Patterson (New York: Dodd, Mead, and Co., 1971), pp. 137–174. All quotes and references to the play are based on this source.

34. James Baldwin, "Notes for the *Amen Corner*," in *Black Theatre: A Twentieth*

Century Collection of the Work of its Best Playwrights, ed. Lindsay Patterson (New York: Dodd, Mead, and Co., 1971), p. 524.

35. Lorraine Hansberry, "A Raisin in the Sun," in *A Raisin in the Sun and The Sign in Sidney Brustein's Window*, (New York: New American Library, 1966), pp. 11–130. All quotes and references to the play are based upon this source.

36. These comments were made by Michele Wallace during a presentation regarding her book, *Black Macho and the Myth of the Superwoman*, at Florida Agricultural and Mechanical University (FAMU) in January of 1980.

37. Lorraine Hansberry, "The Drinking Gourd," in *Black Theater, U.S.A.: Forty-Five Plays by Black Americans, 1847–1974*, ed. James V. Hatch and Ted Shine (New York: The Free Press, 1974), pp. 714–736. All quotes and references to the play are based upon this source.

38. Alice Childress, "Wedding Band: A Love/Hate Story in Black and White," in *New Women's Theatre: Ten Plays by Contemporary American Women*, ed. Honor Moore (New York: Vintage Books, 1977), pp. 257–337. All quotes and references to the play are based upon this source.

39. Alice Childress, "Wine in the Wilderness", in *Black Theater U.S.A.: Forty-Five Plays by Black Americans 1847–1974*, eds. James V. Hatch and Ted Shine (New York: The Free Press, 1974), pp. 738–755. All quotes and references to the play are based upon this source.

40. James V. Hatch, in *Black Theater U.S.A.: Forty-Five Plays by Black Americans, 1847–1974*, (see note 21), p. 737.

41. Joseph Pierre, personal interview, September 12, 1987, New Orleans, Louisiana.

42. Ntozake Shange, *For Colored Girls Who Have Considered Suicide/When the Rainbow is Enuf* (New York: Macmillan Publishing Co., 1977). All quotes and references to the play are based upon this source.

43. Elizabeth Brown, "Ntozake Shange," in *Afro-American Writers After 1955: Dramatists and Prose Writers*, vol. 38 of *Dictionary of Literary Biography*, (Detroit, Mich.: Gale Research Co., 1985), p. 240.

44. Toni Cade Bambara, "For Colored Girls—And White Girls Too," *Ms.*, vol. 5 (September 1976), p. 38.

45. Barbara Christian, "The Contrary Women of Alice Walker: A Study of *In Love and Trouble*," *The Black Scholar*, vol. 12 (March/April 1981), pp. 21–30, 70–71.

46. Sandra L. Richards, "Conflicting Impulses in the Plays of Ntozake Shange," *Black American Literature Forum*, vol. 17 (Summer 1983), p. 74.

47. Michael G. Cooke, "Recent Novels: Women Bearing Violence," *The Yale Review*, vol. 66 (October 1976), pp. 146–155.

48. Alice Childress, "Florence," in *Masses and Mainstream*, vol. 3 (October 1950), pp. 34–47. All quotes and references to the play are based upon this source.

49. Steven R. Carter, "Images of Men in Lorraine Hansberry's Writing," *Black American Literature Forum*, 19 (Winter 1985), p. 161.

50. Alice Childress, "Mojo: A Black Love Story," in *Black World*, vol. 20 (April 1971), pp. 54–82. All quotes and references to the play are based upon this source.

51. Carter, p. 161.

52. Ibid., p. 161.

53. Ntozake Shange, "A Photograph: Lovers in Motion," in *Three Pieces* (New

York: St. Martin's Press, 1981), pp. 53–108. All quotes and references to the play are based upon this source.

54. See Daniel P. Moynihan, *The Negro Family: The Case for National Action* (Washington D.C.: U.S. Department of Labor, Office of Planning and Research, March 1965).

55. King., p. 6.

56. Ibid., p. 6.

57. Ibid., p. 6.

58. Gerda Lerner, *Black Women in White America: A Documentary History* (New York: Pantheon Books, 1972), p. xxiii.

59. Angela Davis, "Reflections on the Black Woman's Role in The Community of Slaves," *The Black Scholar*, vol. 12 (November/December, 1981), p. 5.

60. Ibid., p. 5.

61. Mapp, p. 37.

62. Ibid., p. 36.

63. Alice Childress, "The Negro Woman in American Literature," *Freedomways*, vol. 6 (First Quarter 1966), p. 19.

64. Ibid.

65. Washington, *Black-Eyed Susans*, pp. xx–xxi.

66. Barbara Molette, "Black Women Playwrights: They Speak: Who Listens?, *Black World*, Vol. 25 (April 1976), p. 28–34.

67. Robert Nemiroff, "Critical Background," *Lorraine Hansberry: The Collected Last Plays*, ed. Robert Nemiroff (New York: New American Library, 1983), p. 159.

68. Ntozake Shange, "Boogie Woogie Landscapes," in *Three Pieces*, pp. 109–142. All quotes and references to the play are based upon this source.

6

The African Continuum: The Progeny in the New World

One of the prime concerns of black women playwrights in America is the black family or the African continuum. Alice Childress, Lorraine Hansberry, and Ntozake Shange view the black family through very new and wide lenses that allow them to enlarge this social unit to include not only blood-related individuals, but also persons linked by race, culture, heritage, and shared ancestry. This interactional family, one that connects black peoples of the world, informs, reinforces, inspires, and empowers blacks to survive the worst possible odds. To approach the black family, in America and elsewhere, as the progeny of Africa is to give credence to its wholeness. A close examination of selected plays of these authors reveals that the portraits of the black family are varied, but the message remains constant: an indissoluble and intimate bond exists that fortifies and preserves the integrity of the black family.

Childress, Hansberry, and Shange insist that the black family is viable and stable, and does have a heritage beyond slavery. In fact their plays uniquely demonstrate that the black family in America is indestructible and regenerative almost solely because of the strong bonds that exist between African Americans and their immediate and distant past. In redefining and broadening the black family, these playwrights clearly point out that black people have a common history, a common set of reactions to the white world, and a common destiny.

The black families in the plays of Childress, Hansberry, and Shange, generally are headed by women, are transplants from the South to the North, are severely disadvantaged, and are active seekers of survival strategies. Some social scientists contend that black families of the type portrayed in these plays are disorganized, pathological, and disintegrating.[1] Eleanor Engram, in *Science, Myth, Reality: The Black Family in One-Half Century of Research*, concludes that "families headed by women with children are likely to be the poorest of all. Of all black families below the official poverty level, 75 percent are families of women with children."[2] In his famous report in 1965, *The Negro Family: The Case for National Action*, Daniel P. Moynihan presumptuously and erroneously contends that the black family is the fundamental source of weakness of the Negro community. Moynihan argues that "at the heart of the deterioration of the fabric of Negro society is the deterioration of the Negro family."[3]

Diametrically opposite of Moynihan's hasty and scientifically imprudent conclusions regarding the black family are the findings of Robert Hill in *The Strengths of Black Families*. Hill calls attention to the five basic strengths of the black family: adaptability of family roles, strong kinship bonds, strong work orientation, strong religious orientation, and strong achievement orientation. Hill's research indicates that the black family is the unit that has historically kept the black community intact.[4]

Like Hill, Dr. Martin Luther King, Jr. refutes the myth of the deteriorating black family: "The Negro family is scarred, it is submerged, but it struggles to survive. It is working against greater odds than perhaps any other family experienced in all civilized history ... No one in all history had to fight against so many physical and psychological horrors to have a family life."[5] Noted social scientist Andrew Billingsley, in *Black Families in White America*, poignantly comments that the black family is absorbing, adaptive, and amazingly resilient.[6]

The concept of the interactional black family is prominent in plays by black women. The blacks in these plays are bound by tradition and history. Engram boldly states that the black family is African in nature and American in nurture (training), meaning that there are many African Americans who find their support, sustenance, and survival in African traditions. She maintains that "black families brought their traditions, affiliations, mutual support, and extendedness with them to the New World. Their ability to see the ultimate interdependence of all humanity flows from the African philosophical influence on the black world view, and it has been manifest in black culture in Africa, in slavery, and in freedom."[7]

Engram suggests that among the African cultural continuities noted in modern black society was family networking, among consanguineal (blood-related), conjugal (marriage-related), and interactional or fictive families.[8] This networking is a coping mechanism that serves to unite blacks. John Scanzoni, in *The Black Family in Modern America*, argues that blacks increasingly have begun to form linkages nationally through such organizations as the National Association for the Advancement of Colored People (NAACP), The Urban League (UL), The Southern Christian Leadership

Conference (SCLC), and The National Council of Negro Women (NCNW).[9] Billingsley suggests that there is a strong movement in the direction of ethnic solidarity, and views it as a powerful force for change and as a potential for the development of a more viable, pluralistic, and democratic society.[10]

A study of the plays of Childress, Hansberry, and Shange reveals a preoccupation with blacks turning to Africa for identity and viewing blacks around the world as family. In nearly all of the plays there are numerous references to Africa as homeland and as wellspring of strength. There is little doubt that these playwrights see African Americans as part of the African continuum.

Alice Childress' portraits of the black family come closest to the images discussed by social scientists who claim that the black family is alive and well. Childress writes about the downtrodden who turn the absolute horror of living in poverty and in untenable emotional conditions into an extraordinary demonstration of dogged determination. In awe of those who survive and succeed in the face of discrimination, derogation, and prejudice, Childress feels compelled to tell their story: "I recall teachers urging me to write compositions about Blacks who were 'accomplishers'... I turned against the tide and to this day I continue to write about those who come in second, or not at all."[11] Some indomitable black families have sprung from Childress' keen awareness that a spirit is almost impossible to break.

The family in Childress' *Florence* is attenuated, with Mrs. Whitney as the head of the home in which she, her daughter, Marge, and the son of her second daughter, Florence, live.[12] Mrs. Whitney, rather than see her grandson reared in an urban ghetto, takes on the responsibility of rearing him while Florence goes North.

While Mrs. Whitney waits to board the train for New York to encourage Florence to come home, she urges Marge to go straight home to care for the boy. She reminds Marge that Florence's son misses his mother a great deal. Mrs. Whitney is not above humbling herself to ask her son, Rudley, for money to keep the family together. Her commitment to her family is evident in her talk with Mrs. Carter, the white actress heading for New York. She tells her that she has always lived as best she knew how and raised her children properly. She even boasts that she has a fine family. She is proud of the morals and values she has imparted to her children. She is especially pleased about the closeness she shares with Florence. The mother–daughter relationship in this play is built on mutual trust and support. Childress' family in *Florence* is poor but dignified, loving, supportive, and strong.

Alice Childress' *Wine in the Wilderness* contains several different images of the black family.[13] She seems particularly sympathetic to women who are forced to head homes. Perhaps this empathy stems from the fact that "in a fatherless home, the mother carries a multiple burden: as head of the family, as breadwinner, as homemaker, as mentor, comforter, and caretaker of children."[14] Childress' sensitivity is best seen when Tommy, the heroine in *Wine in the Wilderness*, reveals her family's impoverished background: "We didn't have nothin' to rule over, not a pot nor a window. And my papa picked hisself up an run off with some finger poppin' woman and we never hear another word 'til ten, twelve years later when a undertaker call up and ask if mama wanta claim his body." (p. 745) Tommy proceeds to tell how her mother, though the father had abandoned them, claims the body out of loyalty to a man who was once family, regardless of the circumstances of the estrangement.

Childress focuses on the fact that Tommy's mother, in spite of living in contemptible poverty, did her best to provide the bare essentials for her family. The struggle for survival is evident when Tommy recalls the pain of growing up as a black girl in Virginia. She reveals that when she was a girl, she despised coming home to hunger and anguish. The conditions were such that Tommy was forced to quit school to help provide for the family, a fact that social scientists have found to exacerbate the plight of the black family because all too often poverty breeds illiteracy. Childress, however, chooses the least educated character in the play to teach humanity to those holding college degrees.

Childress subtly links the concerns and the conditions of the black family in *Wine in the Wilderness* to those of the larger family. The play opens during a Harlem riot, characteristic of the turmoil surrounding the Black Consciousness Movement. *Wine in the Wilderness* depicts grass-roots blacks across the country who are looting, burning, and injuring innocent people. Childress suggests that when one black family in Harlem or anywhere else in America goes hungry, it is a personal affront to all blacks. Bill Jameson opens himself up to criticism when he says that black folks are not together. He claims that the masses have no plan or strategy and will continue to get their heads whipped and bodies broken. Tommy becomes the spokesperson for the black family in her response to Bill. She tells Bill that maybe what everybody needs is somebody like him, who knows how things should go. She goads him to get out there and start some action to lead the revolution. Tommy's urgings illustrate the political climate and views held in common by many blacks of the 1960s.

Numerous references are made to Mother Africa in Childress' plays. John O. Killens, in "The Literary Genius of Alice Childress," argues that she seems particularly concerned that blacks see themselves as an integral part of the larger African family and that blacks change the negative images that they have of themselves. Killens points out that blacks' low self-concept is a result of years of conditioning in a racist patriarchy. He suggests that Childress' "primary and special concern has been the African image. She knew that Black was beautiful when so many of us thought that Black Beauty was the name of a storybook horse, a figment of a writer's fantasy."[15]

In *Wine in the Wilderness*, Tommy dons an African robe and becomes engulfed in African music. Of particular interest is that Bill Jameson is working on a triptych that will, among other things, include a picture of what he considers regal, black, perfect womanhood: an African queen in all her grandeur. Tommy, however, the epitome of earthiness, proves to be the best representative of Mother Africa. She is a black woman who genuinely cares about people and who teaches Bill Jameson that Africa is spirit, customs, and continuity, not some imagined, painted, flawless, black queen. Tommy is the beauty and courage that Africa has given to the New World.

Mojo, like *Florence* and *Wine in the Wilderness*, is saturated with images of the struggling black family.[16] Once again Childress sympathetically writes about single-headed homes when Irene, the central character, comments on the sorrow and despair of her childhood:

My daddy once said to mama . . . 'Sheeeeet . . . what's love, what's that? Better git yourself some money.' Saying them things right in fronta me. I'm tryin to eat the little bitta grits and bacon and make out that I don't hear what I'm hearin'. She say . . . 'Nigger, get the hell out.' He slam the door and gone. She sit down and cry. (p. 72)

It is because Irene is scarred by the poverty of her past and present that she gives up her child for adoption to a family that can provide for the instrumental needs (provisions of food, clothing, shelter, and health care) and expressive needs (enhancing of socioemotional relationships among family members).[17] Irene fears that she could not offer her child emotional stability and confidence which is, according to Robert Wench, in *The Modern Family*, the mental health function of the family.[18] Always mindful of Teddy's growing up among the horrifying rats, she gives up her child to keep her safe.

With Irene and Teddy as representatives, Childress mirrors the deplorable conditions of blacks across the United States. Childress links Irene and Teddy to the interactional black family by having them discuss the brutality surrounding the Civil Rights Movement. When Irene hears an announcement on the radio, she enthusiastically and approvingly shouts, "They passed some kinda civil rights" (p. 58). Though Teddy acknowledges that blacks across the country are victims of racism and oppression, he sees their methodology for improvement as questionable when he says, "A lotta crap, all that prayin and crawlin all over the ground, kneelin whilst the police dog snappin at your ass. Singin while whitey throw tear gas" (p. 59). Childress' concept of the family works because she poignantly portrays shared or common black experiences.

As if piecing together an elaborate quilt, Childress very skillfully links Irene and Teddy not only to blacks in other parts of the country, but also to their ancestral home: Africa. When Irene confesses to Teddy that she has cancer and must undergo surgery, she tells him that she must have something black in the hospital room. She has been reading a book about Africa, one that tells of African traditions, customs, achievements, garments, etc., and she decides that she will take with her this book, a piece of Africa, in the operating room. She tells Teddy that this book has taught her of a blackness she never knew and says that it will be her mojo, a good luck charm. While Irene and Teddy dance to African music, dressed in sweeping African robes, African spirits fill her soul and Irene finds courage, hope, and pride. Childress' message of the interconnectedness of blacks is apparent when Irene, inebriated with a sense that black is beautiful, clean, and sustaining and that black is unequivocally African, reaches out to claim her ancestral past:

You are Africa [she says to Teddy] . . . If I go in that white room without a little Black in my soul . . . I won't make it . . . I got to take Africa in there with me . . . When they knock me out with gas or ether or whatever the hell . . . I got to be hearin that drum in one corner of my mind . . . so my heart can beat. (p. 81)

Alice Childress, in linking Irene and Teddy to Africa refutes any claim that the black family is fragmented and falling apart. She seems to be saying in her plays that hardship in America has only made blacks strong and resilient, and that it is only when black families see themselves as connected to blacks throughout the diaspora that ethnic solidarity will force a noticeable change in the world.

Lorraine Hansberry's plays, like those of Alice Childress, center around the black family. Hansberry's family in *A Raisin in the Sun* is atypical because it transforms from an attenuated nuclear family, with Mama Younger as the head of a household, into a simple extended family, with Walter Lee and Ruth as joint heads of the household and Mama stepping down to assume the role of relative residing with her family.[19]

Hansberry's *A Raisin in the Sun* has been the subject of a great deal of controversy over the years. Mance Williams, in *Black Theater in the 1960s and 1970s*, comments that "Lorraine Hansberry's *A Raisin in the Sun* has been described as the quintessential integrationist play."[20] Another case in point is the indictment against Hansberry's treatment of the Younger family leveled by Paul Carter Harrison in *The Drama of Nommo*:

> It is highly improbable that a woman of her intelligence could have construed the inappropriate happy ending of the play as being meaningful unless it was in response to her deep-seated desire to accomplish what reality could not achieve. Even Hansberry could not have been so naive as to think that the modality of white oppression could be broken because of a black family's integration into a white neighborhood.[21]

Harrison contends that Hansberry neglects to deal adequately with the fact that she is sending the Younger family into combat, amidst possible physical and emotional stoning. Carter suggests that Hansberry, by omission, insinuates that the family will live happily ever after in the neighborhood where its welcoming committee chairperson has stridently warned of violence.[22]

Hansberry may not have chosen to conclude with Mama moving to the new neighborhood with a shotgun to blast her way into the hearts of her neighbors, but based on what Hansberry does show of this willful, consistent, and fearless woman, there is no doubt that Mama will fight whatever battles she has to in order to protect her family.

Early in the play, Hansberry sets up Mama Younger as a powerful and unyielding mother whose preoccupation is with keeping her family together while fending off the meanness of the ghetto. Mama Younger's family, however, does not always appreciate her assertiveness. Mama and her daughter, Beneatha, do not have an ideal relationship. Often flighty and arrogant, Beneatha is kept in check by Mama who constantly reminds her daughter of what will not be tolerated in the home. One example of Mama's firmness is when she slaps Beneatha hard across the face for saying that she does not believe in God. Mama, blinded by so sacrilegious a statement, forces Beneatha to repeat after her, "In my mother's house, there is still God" (p. 39). Driving home the point that she is head of the house, Mama with quiet dignity says, "There are some ideas we ain't going to have in this house. Not long as I am at the head of this family" (p. 39). When Ruth tries to soften Mama's blow by telling Beneatha that her childishness provoked Mama, Beneatha angrily tells her that Mama is a tyrant.

Beneatha, who has inherited her mother's willfulness and independence, is not easily slapped into submission. There is a constant tug-of-war between the two. When Beneatha calls Walter Lee a toothless rat for gullibly losing the family's inheritance, Mama again orchestrates what can be said or even felt in her house. Though she is commanding and overbearing, she gently teaches Beneatha that a person needs love the most when "he's at his lowest and can't believe in hisself 'cause the world done whipped him so" (p. 125).

Beneatha is not always without fault in her relationship with her mother. She is quick tempered, flippant, and sometimes condescending, as is the case when she cautions her mother about asking ignorant questions of her African friend, Asagai. Though this mother–daughter pair banter back and forth, they are very close and do confide in each other. As much as Mama has reprimanded Beneatha, she has pampered her as well. When Beneatha tells Mama that she will be late coming from school because she is starting guitar lessons, Mama gently chides her for the myriad of short-term hobbies she has abandoned: acting classes, horseback riding, photography, etc.

One main trait that mama and Beneatha share is their propensity for degrading Walter Lee. Despite Mama's harsh hand, Beneatha and Walter

Lee seem only to know how to insult each other. Perhaps their inability to be civil to each other, in part, is a reaction against the oppressive conditions that keep them in the ghetto. Walter Lee thinks that Beneatha is a spoiled little brat who is trying to manipulate their mother into turning over to her the bulk of the insurance money for medical school. Beneatha, on the other hand, sees Walter Lee as weak and worthless. There is a great deal of bickering between this brother and sister. Walter Lee antagonizes Beneatha the minute she walks into the room by saying, "You a horrible looking chick at this hour" (p. 23). A while later, Beneatha snidely remarks, "I dissected something that looked just like you yesterday" (p. 24). When Walter Lee tells Ruth that no one understands his dreams, Beneatha quips, "Because you're a nut... Thee is mad, boy" (p. 26). At another point, Beneatha levels the ultimate insult at her brother: "I look at you and I see the final triumph of stupidity in the world" (p. 118). Clearly, Hansberry is making the point that when people are drowning in their own unfulfilled dreams, due to psychological and economic impoverishment, it is difficult to express love.

Mama unintentionally reinforces Beneatha's poor treatment of Walter Lee. Mama treats her thirty-five-year-old son like a child, especially when she insists that she does not allow any yelling in her house. She emphatically tells him that there is not going to be investing in a liquor store and that she does not plan to speak on it again. Enraged by his mother's emphatic resolution not to endorse his business deal, Walter Lee attempts to go for air but is circumvented by his mother, who tells him that as long as he is under her roof, he will speak civilly to his wife. She orders him to sit down. Throughout much of the play, Mama either ignores or invalidates Walter Lee's dreams.

When Mama learns that Walter Lee has not gone to work in several days but has been riding around aimlessly during the day and spending evenings in bars, she comes to realize that she has helped demean and cripple the male of her family. According to Harrison—and this aptly applies to Walter Lee—"When a man loses his sense of malehood, the entire community is castrated... When a man is not able to designate his own goals, he cannot be considered a determining force in the lifestyle of his community."[23] Hoping to free her son to chart his own course and to lead his family, Mama spiritually cements the family when she says to Walter:

Listen to me, now. I say I been wrong, son. That I been doing to you what the rest of the world been doing to you... There ain't nothing worth holding onto, money, dreams, nothing else—if it means it's going to destroy my boy... [She gives him the money.] It ain't much but it's all I got in the world and I'm putting it in your hands. I'm telling you to be the head of this family from now on like you supposed to be. (pp. 86–87)

Walter Lee, like a baby struggling to walk, stumbles when the protective hand is removed.

Relinquishing power is no easy task for Mama. She forgets momentarily her resolution when Walter naively squanders the insurance money she entrusted to him. When news comes that Walter Lee has been duped, Mama conjures up the spirit of Walter Lee's father:

I seen . . . him . . . night after night . . . come in . . . and look at that rug . . . and then look at me . . . the red showing in his eyes . . . the veins moving in his head . . . I seen him grow thin and old before he was forty . . . working and working like somebody's old horse . . . killing himself . . . and you give it all away in a day . . . Oh, God . . . Look down here and show me the strength. (p. 109)

Mama initiates Walter Lee into the manhood that she acknowledges having inadvertently taken from him. It is ultimately the memory of his father that serves as a catalyst for Walter Lee's growth. The Younger family is strengthened or made whole only when the son becomes whole. Filled with the spirit of his father, Walter Lee finds the strength to chase off the representative from the Clybourne Park Improvement Association, an act that earns him respect, possibly for the first time, from his family.

Lorraine Hansberry was acutely aware of the importance of memories and looking back in order to move forward. Not only does Hansberry resurrect the spirit of Walter Lee's father, but she summons African ancestral spirits to serve as a dim light of hope and strength to help the black family survive in America. Hansberry was an eager pupil of her uncle, William Leo Hansberry, one of the world's foremost scholars of African antiquity, and Dr. W.E.B. DuBois, whose seminar on African history she completed. Robert Nemiroff contends that Hansberry was on fire with black liberation not only here but in Africa. Nemiroff recalls a Hansberry speech in which her vision embraces two continents:

The foremost enemy of the Negro intelligentsia of the past has been and in a large sense remains—isolation . . . The unmistakable roots of the universal solidarity of the colored peoples of the world are no longer "predictable" as they were in my father's time . . . And I for one, as a black woman in the United States in the mid-Twentieth Century feel . . . that the ultimate destiny and aspirations of the African peoples and twenty million American Negroes are inextricably and magnificently bound up together forever.[24]

An insurgent with a vision for solidarity, Hansberry wrote with a sense of immediacy and power.

The African presence in *A Raisin in the Sun* is pervasive. As the play opens, Mama is described as carrying herself with "the noble bearing of the women of the Hereros of Southwest Africa—rather as if she imagines that as she walks she still bears a basket or a vessel upon her head" (p. 27).

Mama's daughter looks like an "assimilationist" with her straightened hair and middle-American attire, but she too is touched by Africa as the play unfolds. Beneatha apprentices herself to the Nigerian intellectual and political activist, Asagai, who serves to link the black family in America to its African counterpart.

Asagai tenderly recalls his first encounter with Beneatha who sought him out to tell him that she wanted to know more about Africa and that she was looking for her identity. Asagai, serving as a cultural conduit, baptizes Beneatha in African history and mores, including teaching her about Africa's struggle for freedom in the ongoing battle with the French and British colonizers, about African dress, customs, songs, dance, and spirit of survival. Harold Isaacs, in "Five Writers and Their Ancestors," suggests that Asagai is "the most literate, the most self-possessed, the most sophisticated, most purposive, I-know-where-I'm going character in the play. He offers the girl [Beneatha] a life of dedication, work, and self-realization in emergent Africa."[25]

Beneatha's personal odyssey toward wholeness culminates in an African folk dance into which she draws Walter Lee. She tells Walter Lee that the dance is from Nigeria and that it is a dance of welcome. This magical, therapeutic dance allows her momentarily to reach out to a brother she apparently despises. Together Beneatha and Walter Lee embrace their African heritage. Like Irene in Childress' *Mojo*, Walter Lee dances feverishly when he hears the African drums, the heart beat of Africa in America. It is this dance that urges Walter Lee to fight to make life better for his family. Transformed, Walter Lee shouts, "YEAH... AND ETHIOPIA STRETCH FORTH HER HANDS AGAIN... Do you hear the singing of the women, singing the war songs of our fathers to the babies in the great houses... singing the sweet war song? OH, DO YOU HEAR, MY BLACK BROTHERS! " (pp. 64–66). Walter Lee's plea is to black brothers around the world to recognize their connectedness, to band together in the war against worldwide oppression.

In an effort to dispel the myth that Africa does not claim her black children in America, Hansberry has Asagai deliver one of the most potent lines in the play to Beneatha: "Nigeria. Home. I will... teach you the old songs and ways of our people—and, in time, we will pretend that you have only been away for a day" (p. 116). Hansberry's belief in the African continuum is never more apparent than when Asagai says to Beneatha, "How often I have looked at you and said, 'Ah—so this is what the New World hath finally wrought' " (p. 117). Asagai seems very proud of this African American woman, his kindred spirit.

Billingsley argues that "while Negroes have always been aware of this historical connection with each other and with Negroes in other parts of the world, we have not always been free to recognize it, make it explicit, define it, and build on it."[26] Hansberry, like Childress, seems to be intimating that it is only when blacks in America recognize their connection to the larger family that substantial political and social gains will be made.

Like the works of Childress and Hansberry, Ntozake Shange's writings reveal a preoccupation with blacks as an integral part of the African continuum. Shange's own connectedness to Africa is evident in her name change from Paulette Williams to Ntozake Shange, which was a deliberate act of protest against her Western roots.[27] Shange insists that her background shaped her view of the interconnectedness of African Americans and other people of color:

> My parents have always been especially involved in all kinds of Third World culture... I was always aware that there were different kinds of black people all over the world because my father had friends from virtually all of the colonized French-, Spanish-, and English-speaking countries. So I knew I wasn't on this planet by myself. I had some connection with other people.[28]

Shange's sketches of the family are comprised of feeling and thinking people. In Claudia Tate's *Black Women Writers at Work*, Shange explains that a dramatic piece "should bring a new person into your life, somebody to whom you can refer, even have a conversation with, because you ought to get to know them well."[29] These feeling persons, however, are not always sensitive to each other.

One of the poems in Shange's *For Colored Girls* makes a poignant statement about the African continuum.[30] One sees a sense of ancestral pride when lady in brown speaks of Toussaint L'Ouverture: "he was dead and livin to me/cuz Toussaint and them/they held the citadel gainst the french/ wid the spirits of ol dead africans from outta the/ground" (p. 27). In the "Toussaint" poem, Shange describes this folk hero as one who fought to free blacks in Haiti, a man whose source of emotional and physical strength was drawn from his distant African past. Armed with the knowledge of Toussaint's great struggles for the freedom of blacks and wishing to emulate this legendary figure, the persona attempts to free herself from her "integrated home, integrated street, integrated school," (p. 27) and to travel to Haiti to meet Toussaint L'Ouverture who "dont take no stuff from no white folks & they gotta country all they own & there aint no slaves" (p. 30). The persona eventually joins with Toussaint Jones, a scruffy little black boy, who symbolizes strength and courage in black America. Shange's uniting of these two suggests that together they will stand firm against racism in America.

One sees Shange's connection to Africa in the poem "sechita," where the dancer is linked to Nefertiti, "hence to Africa and the Olduvai Gorge, the cradle of civilization."[31] Similarly, Shange merges the two cultures in "a nite with beau willie brown," wherein the children of beau willie and crystal are named naomi kenya and kwame beau willie.[32]

Shange's *Three Pieces*, which includes *Spell # 7, A Photograph: Lovers in Motion*, and *Boogie Woogie Landscapes*, has as its central thread the black family.[33] Quite an evocative mother–son relationship appears in the Sue-Jean story in *Spell # 7*. Sue-Jean, the daughter of a woman who (during a storm and flood) "died/drownin/holdin me up over the mud crawlin in her mouth," (p. 30) grows up to be "the town's no one" (p. 30). This young woman's dream in life was to give birth to a baby that she could shower with love. Warped by her desperation for love, she names her child Myself, nurses and nurtures him, and slits his wrist when "myself wanted to crawl and discover a world of his own" (p. 31). The plot becomes increasingly violent and perverted as the persona sucks the baby's blood back into herself, watches him shrivel up in his crib, and spends the rest of her life pining for a new Myself.

Shange, like early black women playwrights Angelina Grimke and Myrtle Smith Livingston, apparently feels that black and brown babies must be protected from those forces that would torture them. Sue-Jean's protectiveness is apparent when she says, "i gotta prayer cloth for the boy/myself waz gonna be safe from all that his mama/waz prey to" (p. 29). Mentally deranged, Sue-Jean prefers to murder her child rather than see him victimized in an oppressive American society. This abnormal treatment of a son is highly symbolic and suggests that black women are instrumental in emotionally crippling their sons inadvertently as they try to teach them how to be proud black men in a racist world.

On another level, Shange presents flashes of the larger black family, one which shares the humiliation of slavery and continued degradation and inequity in America. Alex, a frustrated black actor, speaks for the masses when he comments:

none of us ever got no apology from no white folks abt not bein considered human beings/ . . . the success of 'roots' is the way white folks assuaged their consciences . . . someone shd make a day where a few minutes of the pain of our lives is acknowledged . . . just three minutes for our lives/just three minutes of silence & a gong in st. Louis/oakland/in los angeles. (p. 46)

Black people across the United States, not just in the three cities listed, share as brothers and sisters in the struggle for freedom to live and prosper. They are bound together because of their common history: children of slaves and generations of trying to recover from mental and emotional shackles. Shange links African Americans to Africa when the persona refers to the black people in South Africa who are "humiliated and oppressed like in slavery" (p. 51).

There are two potent sketches of the family in Shange's *A Photograph: Lovers In Motion*. The first is a portrait of a father and son. Sean finds it impossible to tell Michael that he loves her because of the emotional scars left on him by his alcoholic and sadistic father. Sean recalls hearing his father having sex, beating, and laughing at the countless women in his bedroom. He painfully shares how as a boy he often forced himself into silence and made no trouble when he was abused by his father in order to prove that he was a man. He desperately wanted his father's approval and affection. The father's emotional whippings are apparent when Sean says, "my daddy didnt like me/daddy didnt like me he used ta say/mamma neither but it dont matter cuz im not theirs no how" (p. 89).

This attenuated nuclear family, in which the mother is absent, is atypical in black literature. Rarely are black men shown rearing their children. In this portrait, Shange does not deal with the whys, only the pain of a young black boy searching for the love that his father cannot give. The result is that Sean can only physically and emotionally abuse the women in his life as he had learned from his psychotic father. As the plot thickens, Michael helps Sean to grow and to cope with the negativism of his past family life, a primary function of the interactional or fictive family.

The family in Shange's *Boogie Woogie Landscapes* is one not frequently seen in literature. First, it is an augmented middle-class black family as opposed to the grass-roots black family that graces the stage so often. Second, the images of middle-class blacks in this family are positive, including the image of the black father. The husband, a physician, and his wife, a career woman, earn enough money to afford a luxurious two-story home and to provide for a series of live-in domestics who are perpetually plagued and provoked by the children and then terminated. These maids/nannies may be considered as part of the family because they do exert a great deal of influence over the children, including teaching them manners, values, and practical skills such as how to manage a home.

Though primarily an augmented one, the family for an undetermined amount of time shifts to an augmented, extended, attenuated family because the mother, anxiety- and stress-ridden, abandons the husband and children. The mother, depicted as puritanical, hypersensitive, and color-and class-conscious, does not like her "common" children. The young girl recalls her mother saying "that I always pick the most niggerish people in the world to make my friends & then she would list mavis & freddie & charlenetta & linda susan (who waz really po white trash) so I didnt say nothin" (p. 134). Overwhelmed and unhappy, the mother abandons her family. In the absence of the mother, the father, who is gentle, patient, and loving, cares for his children with the help of the grandmother and a housekeeper. The persona says of her father, "daddy brushed our braids to a point like a dunce's cap & patted them down. he gave us way too much money for lunch & tol grandma she waz overworkin her heart so he wd have to get someone to come in til mama figured out whether she waz comin back"

(p. 132). Shange chips away at the myth that black fathers do not take responsibility for their children. Billingsley's findings lend credibility to Shange's portrait of this middle-class black father:

> Social workers have known for a long time that there is nothing like a good steady job with adequate and dependable income to make a man get married, stay married, remain with his family, and support it, while the absence of such economic viability is highly correlated with the refusal of men to ensure the stability of their families.[34]

On another level, Shange connects this middle-class black family to its larger family, one that is not as fortunate and does include the masses of disadvantaged blacks. One of the characters, who serves as a voice of African Americans, criticizes the *New York Times* for its shallowness and ineffectuality at treating the concerns of colored peoples of the world. She speaks of other papers that serve as a forum and a medium in the linking of all black people. She says she will not read the *New York Times* again until it acknowledges the existence of blacks and begins to print news of merit, such as the following:

> EXTRA EXTRA READ ALL ABOUT IT:
> ZIMBABWE CELEBRATES FIFTY YEARS OF INDEPENDENCE...
> EXTRA EXTRA READ ALL ABOUT IT:
> WHITE SOUTH AFRICANS DENIED ENTRY TO THE UNITED
> STATES AS WAR CRIMINALS
> EXTRA EXTRA READ ALL ABOUT IT:
> NOT ONE AFRO-AMERICAN CHILD WHO CANT READ &
> WRITE/CELEBRATION OF CAMPAIGN AGAINST NATIONAL
> ILLITERACY (pp. 125–126)

Shange's images of the black family are powerful and diverse.

Childress, Hansberry, and Shange cannot be accused of writing only about domestic, narrow issues. Their scope, instead, is at once local, national, and global. Their writings reveal a preoccupation with Africa, which shapes the content, conflicts, and tone of the bulk of their works. The family is the vehicle that allows these three women to express their feelings about the joys and sorrows facing the progeny of Africa.

All three of the playwrights have written about black families that, regardless of the many problems or obstacles, have survived and sometimes succeeded. One of the most important reasons why black families have been able to withstand slavery, reconstruction, urbanization, unemployment, and poverty is because of their adaptability of family roles. Where blood-related members of the black family create voids, the interactional or fictive members of the family provide the spirit, the history, and the courage that blacks need to sustain themselves in American society.

There is a strong kinship bond that exists among blacks, one that links the blood-related family to other African Americans and to their African ancestors. Jim Haskins, in "Some African Influences on the Afro-American Theater," contends that "as acquaintance with things African grows, as the essential and difficult work of tracing Africanism in America continues, we will come to know how really vast and invisible the African influence on all American theater has been."[35] The black women playwrights of this study have drawn, both consciously and intuitively, upon African traditions to solidify the African American family. Childress, Hansberry, and Shange speak of the drums that beckon and prompt them to write of the heartbeat and the rhythms of a people whose single most important forte is its sense of family.

NOTES

1. Robert B. Hill, *The Strengths of Black Families* (New York: Emerson Hall Publishers, 1977), p. 37.

2. Eleanor Engram, *Science, Myth, Reality: The Black Family in One-Half Century of Research* (Westport, Conn.: Greenwood Press, 1982), p. 37.

3. Daniel P. Moynihan, *The Negro Family: The Case for National Action* (Washington D.C.: U.S. Department of Labor, Office of Planning and Research, March 1965), p. 1.

4. Hill, p. 37.

5. Martin Luther King, "An Address by Martin Luther King" in *The Moynihan Report and the Politics of Controversy*, eds. Lee Rainwater and William Yancey (Cambridge, Mass.: M.I.T. Press, 1967), p. 408.

6. Andrew Billingsley, *Black Families in White America* (Englewood Cliffs, N.J.: Prentice Hall, Inc. 1968), p. 24. Information on the various types of black family structures is based upon this source.

7. Engram, p. 123.

8. Ibid., p. 26.

9. John H. Scanzoni, *The Black Family in Modern Society* (Boston, Mass.: Allyn and Bacon, Inc. 1971), p. 12.

10. Billingsley, p. 13.

11. Alice Childress, "A Candle in a Gale Wind," in *Black Women Writers (1950–1980)*, ed. Mari Evans (New York: Anchor Press/Doubleday, 1984), p. 112.

12. Alice Childress, "Florence," in *Masses and Mainstream*, vol. 3 (October 1950), pp. 34–47. All quotes and references to the play are based upon this source.

13. Alice Childress, "Wine in the Wilderness," in *Black Theater U.S.A.: Forty-Five Plays by Black Americans 1847–1974*, eds. James V. Hatch and Ted Shine (New York: The Free Press, 1974), pp. 738–755. All quotes and references to the play are based upon this source.

14. Lee Rainwater and William Yancey, eds. *The Moynihan Report and the Politics of Controversy* (Cambridge, Mass.: M.I.T. Press, 1967), p. 32.

15. John O. Killens, "The Literary Genius of Alice Childress," in *Black Women*

Writers (1950–1980), ed. Mari Evans (New York: Anchor Press/Doubleday, 1984), p. 132.

16. Alice Childress, "Mojo," in *Black World*, vol. 20 (April 1971), pp. 54–82. All quotes and references to the play are based upon this source.

17. Billingsley, p. 21.

18. Robert Wench, *The Modern Family* (New York: Holt, Rinehart, and Winston, 1962), p. 295.

19. Lorraine Hansberry, "A Raisin in the Sun," in *A Raisin in the Sun and The Sign in Sidney Brustein's Window* (New York: New American Library, 1958). All quotes and references to the play are based upon this source.

20. Mance Williams, *Black Theater in the 1960s and 1970s* (Westport, Conn.: Greenwood Press, 1985), p. 112.

21. Paul Carter Harrison, *The Drama of Nommo* (New York: Grove Press, 1972), p. 202.

22. Ibid.

23. Ibid., p. 200.

24. Robert Nemiroff, ed. *Lorraine Hansberry: The Collected Last Plays* (New York: New American Library, 1983), p. 31.

25. Harold Isaacs, "Five Writers and Their African Ancestors," *Phylon* vol. 21 (Fourth Quarter 1960), p. 330.

26. Billingsley, p. 10.

27. Claudia Tate, *Black Women Writers at Work* (New York: Continuum, 1982), p. 149.

28. Ibid., p. 157.

29. Ibid., p. 160.

30. Ntozake Shange, *For Colored Girls Who Have Considered Suicide/When The Rainbow Is Enuf* (New York: Macmillan Pub. Co., 1976). All quotes and references to the play are based upon this source.

31. Sandra Hollins Flowers, "Colored Girls: Textbook for the Eighties," *Black American Literature Forum* vol. 15 (Summer 1981), p. 52.

32. Ibid., p. 53.

33. Ntozake Shange, *Three Pieces* (New York: St. Martin's Press, 1981). All quotes and references to the play are based upon this source.

34. Billingsley, p. 24.

35. James Haskins, "Some African Influences on the Afro-American Theatre," in *The Theater of Black Americans*, ed. Errol Hill (Englewood Cliffs, N.J.: Prentice-Hall, Inc. 1980), pp. 28–29.

Afterword

Gloria T. Hull

Sometime around the 1920s, the multitalented black woman writer Alice Dunbar-Nelson scripted a three-act play called *Gone White*.[1] The hero is Allan Franklin Cordell, a fair-skinned, light-haired young black man who graduated at the head of his civil engineering class but is not employed because of his race. The heroine is Anna Martin, his beautiful brown-complexioned sweetheart, who has sacrificed her life to caring for a cranky old grandmother and a crippled orphan nephew. At great pain to herself, Anna cruelly spurns Allan and sends him off to success passing as a white man in the white world. When they chance to meet one night years later—after her wearing life of poverty and his of ease as a Rotarian businessman—their old love flares and they decide to finally be together, leaving behind her husband and responsibilities, his wife, wealth, and standing. In the sobering next day's lights, however, Allan instead proposes that they should simply ignore "conventions, man-made laws" and "love" each other. Anna snaps to fury in the longest speech of the play:

You are offering me the position of your mistress. You are giving me the wonderful opportunity of having a secret liaison with you. You love me, but you love your position in the world of white men more. . . . You would keep your white wife, and all that that means, for respectability's sake—but you would have a romance, a liaison with the brown woman whom you love, after dark. No Negro could stoop so low as to take on such degraded ideals of so-called racial purity. And this is the moral deterioration to which you have brought your whole race. White Man! Go on back to your white gods! Lowest and vilest of scum. White Man! Go Back!

Anna is only one of a long line of black female dramatic characters who transform their broken bodies and mangled spirits into something that can serve them better. (When ntozake shange's colored girls found the healing goddess within themselves, they not only struck tender nerves but also sensitive chords whose vibrations had already been sounded.) Here, in this book Elizabeth Brown-Guillory has walked us down this line, acting as worthy guide and faithful interpreter. From her research and her thoughts, she has presented a history of Afro-American women playwrights that is intensely interesting.

We see Marita Bonner's 1928 fantasy *The Purple Flower* and find tradition for Lorraine Hansberry's *What Use Are Flowers?*, written three decades later. We hear the impassioned words of Alice Childress (whose full life is a study in itself) as they echo the way that shange's private furies counterpoint what she projects on stage. There is an excellent discussion of Childress' skillful use of restroom signs and of the low, dividing rail in *Florence*. The remarks about "initiation and survival rituals" broaden into suggestiveness about black women's fiction, and indeed, the whole of diasporic black literature. We see the originality of the household in *Boogie Woogie Landscapes* as a possible inspiration for moving beyond the platitudes—both positive and negative—about the weaknesses and strengths of black families. And there is the tangled thread of racism–sexism.

At every turn, something in Brown-Guillory's book sets us to remembering and thinking. She has begun an exploration that leads to additional exciting places. What about black women playwrights as actresses and poets (as many of them were)? What about their history in community theater and the way that overworked English teachers kept drama alive in our segregated schools and churches? Looking even more closely at these writers' texts, what more subtle Afrocentric strategies of presentations do they utilize and what new categories and theories do we need to formulate— from the inside out—for analyzing their work? Finally, the forerunners in chapter one and the three main figures of this study make a space for considering all the other black women dramatists who could not be treated here (for example, Sonia Sanchez, Alexis DeVeaux). What do they bring to the dialogue, and contribute to the conversation?

Taking up these questions would constitute further mining of the riches of black women's drama, a richness that Elizabeth Brown-Guillory has clearly opened up to us in *Their Place on the Stage*.

NOTE

1. This play is now available in *The Works of Alice Dunbar-Nelson*, Gloria T. Hull, ed., 3 vols., (New York: Oxford University Press, 1988).

Selected Bibliography

PRIMARY SOURCES

Childress, Alice. "Florence." *Masses and Mainstream*, Vol. 3 (October 1950).

———. "Mojo: A Black Love Story." *Black World*, vol. 2, (April 1971).

———. "Trouble in Mind." In *Black Theater: A Twentieth Century Collection of the Work of its Best Playwrights*, edited by Lindsay Patterson. New York: Dodd, Mead, and Co., 1971.

———. "Wedding Band: A Love/Hate Story in Black and White." In *New Women's Theatre: Ten Plays by Contemporary American Women*, edited by Honor Moore. New York: Vintage Books, 1977.

———. "Wine in the Wilderness." In *Black Theater U.S.A.: Forty-Five Plays by Black Americans, 1847–1974*. Edited by James V. Hatch and Ted Shine. New York: The Free Press, 1974.

Hansberry, Lorraine. "A Raisin in the Sun." In *A Raisin in the Sun and The Sign in Sidney Brustein's Window*. New York: New American Library, 1966.

———. "The Drinking Gourd." In *Black Theater U.S.A.: Forty-Five Plays by Black Americans, 1847–1974*. New York: The Free Press, 1974.

Shange, Ntozake. *For Colored Girls Who Have Considered Suicide/When the Rainbow is Enuf*. New York: Macmillan Pub. Co., 1977.

———. "Spell # 7." In *Three Pieces*. New York: St. Martin's Press, 1981.

———. "A Photograph: Lovers in Motion." In *Three Pieces*. New York: St. Martin's Press, 1981.

———. "Boogie Woogie Landscapes." In *Three Pieces*. New York: St. Martin's Press, 1981.

SECONDARY SOURCES

Books

Abramson, Doris E. *Negro Playwrights in the American Theatre, 1925–1959*. New York: Columbia University Press, 1969.

Aptheker, Bettina. *Woman's Legacy: Essays on Race, Sex, and Class in American History*. Amherst, Mass.: The University of Massachusetts Press, 1982.

Bennett, Lerone Jr. *Before the Mayflower: A History of the Negro in America 1619–1964*. Baltimore, Md.: Penguin Books, 1966.

Benston, Kimberly W. "The Aesthetics of Modern Black Drama: From Mimesis to Methexis." In *The Theatre of Black Americans*, Vol. I. Edited by Errol Hill. Englewood Cliffs, N.J.: Prentice Hall, Inc., 1980.

Bentley, Gerald Eades. *The Art of the Drama*. New York: D. Appleton-Century, Co., 1935.

Beckerman, Bernard and Howard Siegman. *On Stage: Selected Theater Reviews from the New York Times 1920–1970*. New York: An Arno Press Book, 1970.

Bigsby, C.W.E. *A Critical Introduction to Twentieth-Century American Drama: Beyond Broadway*. New York: Cambridge University Press, 1985.

Billingsley, Andrew. *Black Families in White America*. Englewood Cliffs, N.J.: Prentice Hall, Inc. 1968.

Bladel, Roderick. *Walter Kerr: An Analysis of His Criticism*. Metuchen, N.J.: The Scarecrow Press, 1976.

Bogle, Donald. *Toms, Coons, Mulattoes, Mammies, and Bucks: An Interpretive History of Blacks in American Films*. New York: The Viking Press, 1973.

Brawley, Benjamin. *The Negro Genuis*. New York: Biblo and Tannen, 1969.

Brockett, Oscar G. *Historical Edition: The Theatre*. New York: Holt, Rinehart and Winston, 1979.

Brown, Janet. *Feminist Drama: Definition and Critical Analysis*. Englewood Cliffs, N.J.: The Scarecrow Press, Inc., 1979.

Brown, Sterling A. *Negro Poetry and Drama*. Washington D.C.: The Associates in Negro Folk Education, 1937.

———. *Negro Poetry and Drama and The Negro in American Fiction*. New York: Atheneum, 1972.

Burke, Kenneth. *Counter Statement*, 2nd edition. Los Altos, Cal.: Hermes Publications, 1953.

Cameron, Kenneth M. and Theodore J.C. Hoffman. *The Theatrical Response*. New York: The Macmillan Pub. Co., 1969.

Campbell, Paul Newell. *Form and the Art of Theatre*. Bowling Green, Ohio: Bowling Green State University Popular Press, 1984.

Childress, Alice. *Black Scenes: Collection of Scenes from Plays Written by Black People About Black Experience*. New York: Doubleday, 1971.

———. "A Candle in a Gale Wind." In *Black Women Writers 1950–1980*. Edited by Mari Evans. New York: Anchor Press/Doubleday, 1984.

———. "Knowing the Human Condition." In *Black American Literature and Humanism*. Edited by R. Baxter Miller. Lexington, Ky.: The University Press of Kentucky, 1981.

Cruse, Harold. *The Crisis of the Negro Intellectual.* New York: William Morrow and Co., Inc., 1967.

Davis, Arthur P. and Michael W. Peplow. *The New Negro Renaissance.* New York: Holt, Rinehart and Winston, 1975.

Davidson, Clifford, C.J. Gianakaris, and John H. Stroupe, eds. *Drama in the Twentieth Century.* New York: AMS Press, 1984.

DuBois, W.E.B. *Darkwater: Voices from Within the Veil.* New York: AMS Press, 1969.

Engram, Eleanor. *Science, Myth, Reality: The Black Family in One-Half Century of Research.* Westport, Conn.: Greenwood Press, 1982.

Evans, Mari, ed. *Black Women Writers, 1950–1980.* New York: Anchor Press/Doubleday, 1984.

Fabre, Genevieve E. Afro-American Poetry and Drama, 1760–1975. Detroit, Mich.: Book Tower, 1979.

———. *Drumbeats, Masks, and Metaphor: Contemporary Afro-American Theatre.* Mass.: Harvard University Press, 1983.

France, Rachel. *A Century of Plays by American Women.* New York: Richards Rosen Press, Inc., 1979.

Frye, Northrop. *Anatomy of Criticism.* New York: Atheneum, 1967.

Gayle, Jr., Addison, ed. *The Black Aesthetic.* New York: Doubleday and Company, Inc., 1971.

George, Kathleen. *Rhythm in Drama,* Pittsburgh, Penn.: University of Pittsburgh Press, 1980.

Goldfarb, Alvin and Edwin Wilson. *Living Theater: An Introduction to Theater History.* New York: McGraw-Hill Book Co., 1983.

Hansberry, Lorraine. *To Be Young, Gifted and Black.* Englewood Cliffs, N.J.: Prentice Hall, 1969.

———. "The Negro in the American Theatre." In *American Playwrights on Drama.* Edited by Horst Frenz. New York: Hill and Wang, 1965.

Harris, Trudier. *From Mammies to Militants: Domestics in Black American Literature.* Philadelphia, Penn.: Temple University Press, 1982.

Harrison, Paul Carter. *The Drama of Nommo.* New York: Grove Press, 1972.

———, ed. *Kuntu Drama: Plays of the African Continuum.* New York: Grove Press, Inc., 1974.

Hartigan, Karelisa V. *The Many Forms of Drama.* New York: University Press of America, 1985.

Haskins, James. "Some African Influences on the Afro-American Theatre." In *The Theater of Black Americans.* Edited by Errol Hill. Englewood Cliffs, N.J.: Prentice Hall, Inc., 1980.

———. *Black Theater in America.* New York: Thomas Y. Crowell, 1982.

Hay, Samuel. "Alice Childress' Dramatic Structure." In *Black Women Writers (1950–1980).* Edited by Mari Evans. New York: Anchor Press/Doubleday, 1984.

Hill, Errol, ed. *The Theatre of Black Americans,* vol. 1 and 2. Englewood Cliffs, N.J.: Prentice-Hall, Inc., 1980.

Hill, Robert B. *The Strengths of Black Families.* New York: Emerson Hall Publishers, 1977.

Hornby, Richard. *Drama, Metadrama and Perception.* Lewisburg, Pa.: Bucknell University Press, 1986.

Hughes, Langston. "The Negro Artist and the Racial Mountain." In *Black Expres-sion*. Edited by Addison Gayle, Jr. New York: Weybright and Talley, 1969.

Hull, Gloria T. *Color, Sex, and Poetry: Three Women Writers of the Harlem Renaissance.* Bloomington, Ill.: Indiana University Press, 1987.

———, ed. *Give Us Each Day: The Diary of Alice Dunbar-Nelson.* New York: Norton, 1984.

———, ed. *The Works of Alice Dunbar-Nelson*, 3 vols. New York: Oxford University Press, 1988.

Hunter, Frederick F. *The Power of Dramatic Form.* New York: Exposition Press, 1974.

Kerr, Walter. *Tragedy and Comedy.* New York: Simon and Schuster, 1967.

Keyssar, Helene. *Feminist Theatre.* New York: Grove Press, 1985.

Killens, John O. "The Literary Genius of Alice Childress." In *Black Women Writers, (1950–1980).* Edited by Mari Evans. New York: Anchor Press/Doubleday, 1974.

King, Woodie and Ron Milner, eds. *Black Drama Anthology.* New York: New American Library, 1986.

Ladner, Joyce A. *Tomorrow's Tomorrow: The Black Woman.* Garden City, New York: Doubleday and Co., 1971.

Langer, Susanne K. *Feeling and Form.* New York: Scribner's Son, 1953.

Lerner, Gerda. *Black Women in White America: A Documentary History.* New York: Pantheon Books, 1972.

Longman, Stanley Vincent. *Composing Drama for Stage and Screen.* Boston, Mass.: Allyn and Bacon, Inc., 1986.

Mersand, Joseph. "When Ladies Write Plays." In *The American Drama Since 1930.* New York: Kennikat Press, Inc., 1949.

Miller, Jeanne-Marie A. "Black Women In Plays by Black Playwrights." In *Women in American Theatre: Careers, Images, Movements.* Edited by Helen Krich Chinoy and Linda Walsh Jenkins. New York: Crown Publishers, Inc., 1981.

———. "Black Women Playwrights from Grimke to Shange: Selected Synopses of their Works." In *All The Women Are White, All The Blacks are Men, But Some Of Us Are Brave.* Edited by Gloria T. Hull, Patricia Bell-Scott, and Barbara Smith. Old Westbury, N.Y.: The Feminist Press, 1982.

Miller, May and Willis Richardson, eds. *Negro History in Thirteen Plays.* Washington D.C.: The Associated Publishers, 1935.

Mitchell, Loftin. *Black Drama: The Story of the American Negro in the Theatre.* New York: Hawthorn Books, 1967.

Nemiroff, Robert, ed. *Lorraine Hansberry, The Collected Last Plays.* New York: New American Library, 1972, 1983.

Pearson, Carol and Katherine Pope. "The Female Hero." In *The Female Hero in American and British Literature.* New York: R. R. Bowker, Co., 1981.

Perry, Margaret. *Silence to the Drums: A Survey of the Literature of the Harlem Renaissance.* Westport, Conn.: Greenwood Press, 1976.

Phillips, Elizabeth C. *The Works of Lorraine Hansberry: A Critical Documentary.* New York: Simon and Schuster, Inc., 1973.

Richardson, Willis, ed. *Plays and Pageants from the Life of the Negro.* Washington D.C.: The Associated Publishers, 1930.

Reiter, Seymour. *World Theater: The Structure and Meaning of Drama*. New York: Well Publishing Co., 1973.

Southgate, Robert L. *Black Plots and Black Characters: A Handbook for Afro-American Literature*. New York: Gaylord Professional Publications, 1979.

Staples, Robert. *Black Masculinity: The Black Male's Role in American Society*. San Francisco, Cal.: The Black Scholar Press, 1982.

Tate, Claudia, ed. *Black Women Writers At Work*. New York: Continuum, 1983.

Turner, Darwin T. *Images of the Negro in America*. Mass.: D.C. Heath and Co., 1965.

Wallace, Michele. *Black Macho and the Myth of the Superwoman*. New York: The Dial Press, 1978.

Washington, Mary Helen. *Black-Eyed Susans: Classic Stories by and about Black Women*. New York: The Anchor Books, 1975.

Wilkerson, Margaret B., ed. *9 Plays by Black Women*. New York: A Mentor Book, 1986.

Williams, Mance. *Black Theatre in the 1960s and 1970s: A Historical-Critical Analysis of the Movement*. Westport, Conn.: Greenwood Press, 1985.

Woll, Allen. *Dictionary of Black Theatre*. Westport, Conn.: Greenwood Press, 1983.

Yellin, Jean Fagan. *The Intricate Knot: Black Figures in American Literature, 1776–1863*. New York: New York University Press, 1972.

Periodicals

Allen, Walter R. "The Social and Economic Statuses of Black Women in the United States." *Phylon*, vol. 42 (March 1981).

Anderson, Mary Louise. "Black Matriarchy: Portrayals of Women in Three Plays." *Black American Literature Forum*, vol. 10 (Spring 1976).

Beal, Frances M. "Slave of a Slave No More: Black Women in Struggle." *The Black Scholar*, vol. 12 (November/December 1981).

Bond, Jean Carey. "Lorraine Hansberry: To Reclaim Her Legacy." *Freedomways*, Vol. 19 (Fourth Quarter 1979).

———. "For Colored Girls Who Have Considered Suicide." *Freedomways*, vol. 16 (Third Quarter 1976).

Brown, Floyd W. "Lorraine Hansberry as Ironist: A Reappraisal of 'A Raisin in the Sun.' " *Journal of Black Studies*, vol. 4 (March 1974).

Brown-Guillory, Elizabeth. "Contemporary Black Women Playwrights: A View From the Other Half." *Helicon Nine: The Journal of Women's Arts and Letters*, no. 14 & 15 (1986).

———. "Alice Childress: A Pioneering Spirit." *SAGE: A Scholarly Journal on Black Women*, Vol. 4 (Spring 1987), pp. 66–68.

Carter, Steven. "Images of Men in Lorraine Hansberry's Writing." *Black American Literature Forum* vol. 19 (Winter 1985).

Childress, Alice. "Black Writers' Views on Literary Lions and Values." *Negro Digest*, vol. 17 (January 1968).

———. "The Negro Woman in American Literature." *Freedomways*, vol. 6 (First Quarter 1966).

Christian, Barbara. "The Contrary Women of Alice Walker: A Study of 'In Love and Trouble.' " *The Black Scholar*, vol. 12 (March/April 1981).

Cooke, Michael G. "Recent Novels: Women Bearing Violence." *The Yale Review*, vol. 66 (October 1976).

Edwards, Sister Ann. "Three Views on Blacks: The Black Woman in American Literature." *The CEA Critic*, vol. 37 (May 1975).

Farrison, W. Edward. "Lorraine Hansberry's Last Dramas." *CLA Journal*, vol. 16 (December 1972).

Flowers, Sandra Hollins. "Colored Girls: Textbook for the Eighties." *Black American Literature Forum*, vol. 15 (Summer 1981).

Hansberry, Lorraine. "A Challenge to Artists." *Freedomways*, vol. 3 (Winter 1963).

———. "The Negro Writer and His Roots: Toward a New Romanticism." *The Black Scholar*, vol. 12 (March/April 1981).

Hay, Samuel. "African-American Drama, 1950–1970." *Negro History Bulletin*, vol. 36 (January 1973).

Isaacs, Harold. "Five Writers and Their African Ancestors." *Phylon*, vol. 21 (Fourth Quarter 1960).

Johnson, Helen Armstead. "Playwrights, Audiences, Critics." *Negro Digest*, vol. 19 (April 1970).

King, Mae. C. "The Politics of Sexual Stereotyping." *The Black Scholar*, vol. 13 (Summer 1982).

Mapp, Edward. "Black Women in Films." *The Black Scholar*, vol. 13 (Summer 1982).

Miller, Adam David. "It's a Long Way to St. Louis: Notes on the Audience for Black Drama." *Tulane Drama Review* (Summer 1968).

Molette, Barbara. "Black Women Playwrights: They Speak: Who Listens?" *Black World*, vol. 25 (April 1976).

Molette, Carlton. "Afro-American Ritual Drama." *Black World*, vol. 22 (April 1973).

Nemiroff, Robert. "From These Roots: Lorraine Hansberry and the South." *Southern Exposure*, vol. 12 (September/October 1984).

Pawley, Thomas D. "The First Black Playwrights." *Black World*, vol. 14 (April 1972).

Rahman, Aishah. "To Be Black, Female, and a Playwright." *Freedomways*, vol. 19 (Fourth Quarter 1979).

Richards, Sandra L. "Conflicting Impulses in the Plays of Ntozake Shange." *Black American Literature Forum*, vol. 17 (Summer 1983).

Washington, Mary Helen. "Black Women Image Makers." *Black World*, vol. 23 (August 1974).

Wilkerson, Margaret B. "The Sighted Eyes and Feeling Heart of Lorraine Hansberry." *Black American Literature Forum*, vol. 17 (Spring 1983).

———. "Lorraine Hansberry: The Complete Feminist." *Freedomways*, vol. 19 (Fourth Quarter 1979).

Index

About the Author

ELIZABETH BROWN-GUILLORY is an Associate Professor of English at the University of Houston. Her award-winning plays *Bayou Relics* and *Snapshots Of Broken Dolls*, which was produced at Lincoln Center in New York City in 1986, have been published by Contemporary Drama Service. Currently, she is editing an anthology, *Wines in the Wilderness: Plays by Black Women from the Harlem Renaissance to the Present* (Greenwood Press, forthcoming).